CLYDE CRUISING CLUB

Firth of Clyde including North Channel, Solway Firth and The Isle of Man

Contents

Preface 2

Introduction
- Sailing in The Firth of Clyde and Approaches 3
- Notes on Sailing Directions. 5
- Charts and Publications. 7

Firth of Clyde
- The Upper Firth 10
- The Kyles of Bute. 29
- Loch Fyne. 34
- Crinan Canal. 42
- Upper Loch Fyne 44
- Kintyre 48
- Isle of Arran. 54
- Ayrshire Coast. 58
- Loch Ryan. 68

North Channel
- The Clyde to Northern Ireland. 71
- Antrim - North Coast. 73
- Antrim - East Coast. 75
- Belfast Lough. 78
- The Rhinns of Galloway 80

Solway Firth
- Dumfries and Galloway Coast. 82
- Cumbrian Coast. 92

Isle of Man
- Approach from the North. 94
- East Coast. 95
- West Coast. 98

Appendices 100

Index. 103

Edward Mason, Editor, Clyde Cruising Club Sailing Directions

Published by Clyde Cruising Club Publications Ltd.
Suite 101, The Pentagon Centre, 36 Washington St. Glasgow, G3 8AZ
Tel: 0141 2212774, Fax: 0141 2212775, Email: hazel@clyde.org, http://www.clyde.org
Printed by Centric Print Solutions Ltd. Milnthorpe, Cumbria, LA7 7LR Tel: 015395 64592

Cover photograph: CCC Muster at Wreck Bay, Kyles of Bute by Mike Balmforth

5/10

Preface

The Clyde Cruising Club has published Sailing Directions for the West Coast of Scotland for over 90 years. In 1912 they formed part of the Club's journal, and from 1923 to 1981 were published as a separate volume. In 1981 a decision was taken to print the Club's West Coast Sailing Directions in 4 volumes. These are the Firth of Clyde, Mull of Kintyre to Ardnamurchan, Ardnamurchan to Cape Wrath and the Outer Hebrides.

This 2004 fully revised, altered and extended edition, published by Clyde Cruising Club Publications Limited, for the Firth of Clyde and Approaches updates with additions and amendments all the information given in earlier editions, the latest of which was published in 1998. A section formerly included in the Club's Sailing Directions for passage making across the North Channel and covering the North East Irish Coast has been reinstated with updated pilotage information.

Users of these Sailing Directions are asked to send to the publishers any information that they consider will add to or amend these Directions, including date and time and prevailing weather conditions experienced. Of particular value are conditions in anchorages under certain winds and tides, the sea bed composition, newly discovered hazards, transits and clearing marks and facilities, or lack of them as may be the case. Photographs are always very useful and welcome.

Our thanks are due to all past and present members of the Club and very many others who over the years have contributed to the information contained in this volume, and I warmly acknowledge the support given by the Irish Cruising Club.

The Clyde Cruising Club is very appreciative of the financial support given by British Waterways towards the publication of these Sailing Directions.

Edward Mason March 2009
Editor

Caution These Sailing Directions are based on observations made over many years, together with a study of original surveys and aerial photographs, and consultation with locals and people with specialist knowledge. However, some places are rarely visited, and a complete knowledge cannot be claimed for all anchorages and passages under all conditions. The information contained in these Directions and all amendments which are made to them, is selective and does not include all known information for each and every location described. This applies to both the text and the plans in particular, which should not be used for navigation. The Sailing Directions are written for yachts of moderate draft, and are not intended for larger craft. They should only be used as an aid-to-navigation in conjunction with current Admiralty charts, pilots and official hydrographic data. A yacht's skipper must be personally satisfied that it is safe to approach any anchorage or passage before doing so. Skippers should not place reliance on these Sailing Directions in preference to exercising their own judgement.

Disclaimer **Clyde Cruising Club Publications Ltd. and the Clyde Cruising Club (including its individual Members and specifically but not limited to those Members acting as editors and as authors) entirely exclude any and all responsibility or liability for any loss, injury, damage, expenses or costs incurred by any person whether directly or indirectly from any error in or omission from these Sailing Directions or any subsequent amendments.**

Note **The cut off date for the pilotage information in this edition is 1st May 2010.** Future additions and amendments may be obtained from the Sailing Directions page, which is maintained by Clyde Cruising Club Publications Ltd, within the Club's website (http://www.clyde.org) or by writing to Clyde Cruising Club Publications Ltd. c/o the Club office.

Introduction

Sailing in the Firth of Clyde and Approaches

General

The navigation of the Firth of Clyde from its exposed approaches between the Mull of Kintyre and the Mull of Galloway, Ailsa Craig and Arran north to the comparatively sheltered waters of the Upper Firth presents few dangers which are not well marked. The Upper Firth N of the Cumbraes including the Holy Loch, the Gareloch, Loch Long and Loch Goil and, to the west, the Sound of Rothesay leading to the Kyles of Bute, the beautiful area around the Burnt Isles and Caladh Harbour, offer interesting and safe sailing areas with adequate shelter for most conditions. Ardlamont Point at the west entrance to the Kerry Kyle marks the beginning of more exposed waters leading to Inchmarnock Sound, Kilbrannan Sound and the dangerous Mull of Kintyre just south of Campbeltown. Although beautiful Loch Fyne is well worth exploring with its often quiet, even remote anchorages, it should be visited with due regard to the weather.

South of the Cumbraes, the Ayrshire Coast and the east side of Arran to Loch Ryan is increasingly exposed and offers little shelter easily obtainable in the prevailing winds. Visits to Loch Ryan, Portpatrick, the Solway Firth or the Isle of Man and passage making across the North Channel should be left to those with considerable experience.

Sailing in the Clyde in small boats has been enjoyed since at least the 1860's though the passage of time has seen the square lug of the small rowing boat and the great white wings of the hundred ton Cutter replaced in recent times by 'birds' of more exotic hue with their colourful sails and spinnakers. The area remains a wonderfully varied and safe cruising ground if all its moods are respected. Although we do not suggest you put to the test the advice given in the earliest CCC Sailing Directions that "you could round the Mull of Cantyre in a rowing boat in suitable weather", it does highlight however the importance of ascertaining weather and sea conditions before undertaking a passage.

Tides

In general the tidal streams in the Firth of Clyde are weak and rarely exceed 1.5 knots except at the Kyles of Bute, Otter Spit and the Rhu Narrows. The tidal rates given are as for mid-channel areas and will be greater in extreme conditions of wind and rain and at salient points.

In certain parts of the North Channel and at the Mull of Kintyre, also W and S of the Rhinns of Galloway, in the Solway Firth and around the Isle of Man, the tides frequently are in excess of 4 knots and should be treated with great care especially in strong winds.

The tidal rise in the Firth of Clyde does not significantly exceed 3.4m springs and 2.9m neaps. South of Corsewall Point, in the Solway Firth and the Isle of Man it averages 5.5m springs and 3.1m neaps and rises to 7.4m springs, 3.9m neaps in the E side of the Solway.

Weather

On the West Coast of Scotland it is very variable at any time, being influenced by the passage of depressions from the Atlantic. The prevailing wind is between South and West, with a higher proportion of Northerly and Easterly winds in May and June, when an anticyclone is more likely to become established to the North of Scotland. Except in September and the winter months, gales are not common, although they may occur at any time. Fog as such, is rare, and visibility of less than 2 miles is unlikely on more than 3 days per month in summer. Low cloud however may more often obscure the tops of hills, and heavy rain may reduce visibility for a time. On the whole the best weather may be expected during May and June. October is quite often found to have better weather than August.

Forecasts

Inshore Waters Forecast
BBC Radio 3 1215 kHz (247m) and VHF frequencies.
BBC Radio 4 198 kHz (1500m) and VHF frequencies.

Shipping Forecast
BBC Radio 4 198 kHz (1500m) - Sea areas Malin and Irish Sea

Landward forecasts
BBC Radio Scotland 810 kHz (370m) and VHF frequencies.

Coastguard forecasts
In addition to BBC Shipping and Inshore Waters forecasts, local weather forecasts for the Firth of Clyde including the North Channel are broadcast by Clyde Coastguard. Initial announcements are made on VHF channel 16 and at the same time guidance is given as to the appropriate channel to switch to depending on the area in which you are situated. As from 1 February 2007 forecasts by Coastguards are being made at local time, ie. the 'clock time' that the broadcast is made remains the same throughout the year. The forecasts by **Clyde Coastguard** are now made every three hours commencing at 0210 and thereafter at 0510, 0810, 1110, 1410, 1710, 2010, and 2310. **Belfast Coastguard** broadcast times are also every three hours commencing at 0110 and thereafter at 0410, 0710, 1010, 1310, 1610, 1910, and 2210. **Liverpool Coastguard** broadcast at three hourly intervals commencing at 0130. The times given are not precise as forecasts may be delayed or omitted during casualty working.

Introduction

Anchors It is essential to have at least two anchors of not less than the weight recommended by the anchor manufacturers for the size of boat,with appropriate sizes of cable. These weights are likely to be greater than those supplied by manufacturers of stock boats. At least 60m of chain should be available so as to be able to let out three times as much chain as the depth at high water. An "angel" or weight to let down the cable to reduce snubbing in heavy conditions is always worth carrying. In view of the variety of conditions two different types of anchor should be carried. The choice is very much a matter of individual preference, but the Bruce and CQR types seem less likely to pick up weed than the Danforth or Meon type.

Anchorages In this well populated area, space in many anchorages is becoming increasingly restricted by boat moorings and by fish farming equipment, of which the Club may not have up to date information. Some of the most popular anchorages become full to overflowing. Moorings may be available for visitors at some yachting centres.

In an area increasingly populated with moorings and the ground tackle of old moorings, it is often difficult to find a spot to anchor without fouling such moorings. This problem can be helped by ensuring that an anchor tripping line is used.

Nothing causes more annoyance to the owners of moorings than to have them used by visiting yachts who have not bothered to obtain permission. Do not use a mooring unless you have checked its suitability and its availability. Ensure it is adequate to hold your vessel for prevailing wind conditions. Common courtesy suggests that if you borrow a vacant mooring, be sure to stay aboard ready to move should the owner return.

Piers and Jetties, may be used by fishing boats, ferries or other boats, and yachts should never be left unattended alongside without it being made absolutely certain that access will not be needed.

Swinging room must be left for any vessel already anchored, including allowing for changes in wind direction.

Under suitable conditions adventurous yachtsmen will find with the help of charts and sketch plans, anchorages other than those described.

Chartering About 50% of all charter yachts in Britain are based on the West Coast of Scotland; both motor and sailing yachts are available, either "bareboat" or with a skipper. Details may be had from the Scottish Tourist Board, 23 Ravelston Terrace, Edinburgh (tel 0131 332 2433) or found from advertisements in sailing periodicals.

Launching The Upper Firth of Clyde provides many opportunities for day sailing and an attempt has been made to indicate possible slips for launching small craft. In settled conditions the coast from Dunure Harbour to Maidens Harbour is suitable for small boat expeditions. The N shores of Wigtown Bay, the Dee and Urr Estuaries are also suitable for this type of sailing.

Cables Submarine power and telephone cables have been laid across many lochs and channels and their presence is indicated by shore marker boards, with a yellow diamond on a yellow post. Avoid anchoring near cables and note that the cables do not necessarily lie in a straight line between markers. Damage to cables can result in very large claims. If a cable is inadvertently fouled, one should note the position, slip and buoy the anchor, and report either to British Telecom if it is thought to be a telephone cable, or if a power cable within the Gareloch, report to Scottish Power 0845 2727 999, or to Scottish Hydro Electric 0800 300 999 if elsewhere. Depending on circumstances, in the interests of safety, the authorities will assist in the recovery of anchors.
Yachtsmen who launch and haul out their own yachts and sailing dinghies are further warned to take extreme care in the vicinity of overhead cables, and masts should be lowered. There have been a number of serious accidents involving injury to yachtsmen and damage to yachts.

Water Water from burns should only be taken above any houses. It may be affected by toxic chemicals, but these are only likely where the water runs off arable land. A brown colour and sediment in the water are usually due to the presence of peat, and the water may have more flavour than city dwellers are accustomed to.

Emergencies

Coastguard In the Clyde area, North Channel, Solway Firth and Isle of Man HM Coastguard Service is responsible for initiating and coordinating all civil maritime search and rescue measures for vessels or persons in need of assistance in the United Kingdom Search and Rescue Region. The Service maintains a continuous listening watch on VHF distress frequency (Channel 16) and operates a safety service on Channel 67 when necessary. The Clyde Maritime Rescue Coordination Centre (MRCC) at Greenock (tel: 01475 729 988) with the Maritime Rescue Sub-centres (MRSC) (Belfast Coastguard) at Bangor (tel: 02890 358 250) and Liverpool (tel: 0151 931 3341) are responsible for rescue measures in the areas covered by these Sailing Directions.

Introduction

Lifeboats

Clyde, North Channel and Solway area
All-weather lifeboats are stationed at Campbeltown, Troon, Girvan, Portpatrick, Donaghadee and Larne Inshore Lifeboats (ILB) are stationed at Lamlash, Tighnabruaich, Helensburgh, Largs, Stranraer, Kippford, Kirkcudbright, Bangor and Larne.

Isle of Man
All-weather lifeboats are stationed at Ramsey, Douglas, Port St. Mary and Peel.
Inshore Lifeboats (ILB) are stationed at Port St. Mary, Port Erin and Douglas.

Notes on Sailing Directions and Plans

Bearings

The bearings given in these Sailing Directions both in text and on the plans are always from seaward and always refer to True North. All plans are orientated with True North at the top as the plan is read.

Depths & heights

All Depths and Heights in the text are in Metres. Depths are in metres below Lowest Astronomical Tide (LAT). This datum (Chart Datum) is the lowest level to which the surface of the sea will fall due to astronomical causes. High barometric pressure or strong offshore winds combined with a low spring tide can cause the level to fall lower. Drying heights of rocks are related to Chart Datum (LAT). Heights on land and above-water rocks and bridges and cable clearances are related to MHWS.
These directions are primarily written for yachts of moderate draft, of 2 metres or less, but hazards at greater depths are generally mentioned. Shoal draft yachts will find many more anchorages and passages available to them, but current charts tend to be lacking in detail inside the 2 metre contour.
Some anchorages and passages are only suitable for very manoeuvrable yachts in the hands of crews familiar with local conditions. All information available should be carefully consulted, and the scale of charts and plans must be appreciated before making an approach. Some anchorages are more easily approached near low water when some of the hazards may be visible. The advantages of a rising tide are obvious. Some places are remote from habitation, and assistance may be hard to come by.
It is assumed that most yachts are equipped with a reliable echo-sounder. Some dangers project so abruptly from the bottom as to give no warning by observing the depth, but usually the depth will be a valuable guide, as may be found from a study of charts and plans.

Place names

In some cases the popular name for a place, or its spelling, differs from that on Admiralty Charts. The latter is usually given, and both where appropriate.

Marks

Only those used in identifying and approaching the entrance to an anchorage, or for coastal passage-making, are listed separately. Inner marks are referred to in the approach directions to anchorages and harbours.

Lights

Light characteristics are as used on Admiralty Charts.

F	fixed
Fl	flashing
Gp Fl or Fl( )	Group flashing
Occ or Oc	Occulting at regular intervals
Iso	Isophase - equal duration of light and eclipse
Q or Qk Fl	Quick Flashing - about 60 flashes per minute
VQ or V Qk Fl	Very Quick Flashing - about 120 flashes per minute
s or sec	time in seconds to exhibit one complete sequence
M	maximum distance in sea miles at which a light can be seen when visibility is 10 miles (taking account of the earth's curvature)
m	elevation of light source above HW in metres

Colours of lights, buoys and beacons (lights are White if not stated) are:- B: black Bu: blue G: green R: red V: violet W: white Y: yellow. Sectors and arcs of visibility, and the alignment of direction lights and leading lights, are given in the text and on the plans as seen by **an observer from seaward.** All bearings are true.

Introduction

Charts & plans

The Plans in these Sailing Directions are drawn at a suitable scale to illustrate the text. **All plans are orientated with True North at the top as the plan is read.** It is emphasised that sufficient Admiralty Charts must be carried. Below is a full list of charts for the area covered by this book, grouped according to their scale, and listed as such in the Sailing Directions. - viz (i), (ii), (iii) & (iv) ALF (Admiralty Leisure Folio, see (iv) below).

Group (i) charts are at a scale of 1:75,000 or smaller. Complete coverage at this scale should be carried, including waters beyond those which it is intended to visit. Note that some of this group of charts omit any detail within inshore waters. Charts should be obtained in good time to ensure that those purchased give sufficient coverage.

Group (ii) charts are at a scale of 1:50,000 or greater. Some of these are essential to the extent that it would be hazardous for a stranger to enter the waters covered without the appropriate chart. Those which are considered essential for safe navigation in certain areas are marked with an asterisk (*). Even in other areas it may be found that a yacht is confined to a main fairway by not having charts at this scale.

Group (iii) charts are principally large scale plans.

Group (iv) This group comprises the Admiralty Leisure Folio (ALF) for the Firth of Clyde which was published in January 2005 and contains twelve charts (size A2). The Folio covers the Firth of Clyde from the Mull of Kintyre and Ayrshire coast northwards, including Loch Fyne, Kyles of Bute, Largs Channel, Loch Long, Loch Goil, The Gareloch and River Clyde to Bowling. It is similar in design to the popular Leisure Chart Folios for the South Coast of England and should prove invaluable for those wishing to navigate in safety without the necessity of acquiring a full complement of the charts detailed in Groups (i), (ii) & (iii).

Chart Index

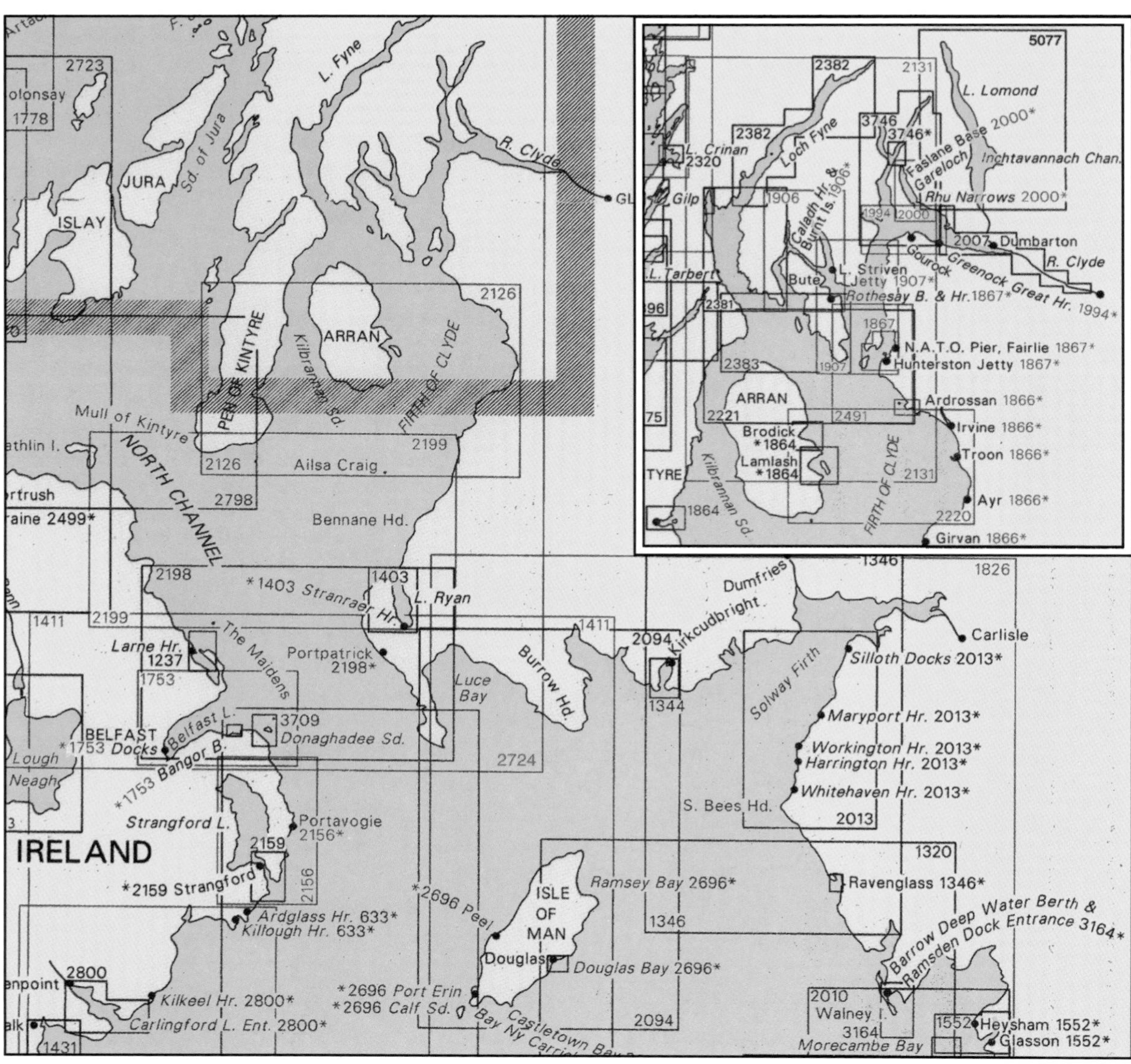

Introduction

Charts & Publications

The division of the Admiralty charts into groups (i), (ii) and (iii) for this book is as given below and shown opposite on the Chart Index

Firth of Clyde and Approaches

Group	Chart	Title	Scale
Group (i)	1411	Irish Sea — Western Part	200,000
	2724	North Channel to the Firth of Lorne	200,000
	2798	Loch Foyle to Sanda Island inc. Rathlin Island	75,000
	2126	Approaches to the Firth of Clyde	75,000
	2131	Firth of Clyde and Loch Fyne	75,000
	2198	North Channel — Southern Part	75,000
	2199	North Channel — Northern Part	75,000
Group (ii)	1906	*Kyles of Bute	25,000; 5,000; 10,000
	1907	*Little Cumbrae Island to Cloch Point	25,000; 10,000
	2220	Firth of Clyde - Pladda to Inchmarnock - S Sheet	36,000
	2221	Firth of Clyde - Pladda to Inchmarnock - N Sheet	36,000
	2381	*Lower Loch Fyne	25,000; 6,250; 10,000
	2382	*Upper Loch Fyne	25,000
	2383	Inchmarnock Water	25,000
	2491	Ardrossan to Largs	25,000
	3746	*Loch Long and Loch Goil	25,000; 12,500
Group (iii)	1403	Loch Ryan	25,000; 10,000
	1864	Harbours and Anchorages in the Firth of Clyde: Campbeltown, Lamlash, Brodick	25,000; 5,000
	1866	Harbours in the Firth of Clyde: Troon, Ardrossan, Ayr, Irvine	10,000; 6,250
	1867	Plans of the Firth of Clyde: Rothesay, Hunterston Jetty, Fairlie pier	12,500; 2,500
	1994	Approaches to the River Clyde	15,000; 5,000
	2000	Gareloch	12,500; 6,250
	2007	River Clyde	15,000

North Channel

Group	Chart	Title	Scale
Group (i)	2198	North Channel - Southern Part	75,000
	2199	North Channel - Northern Part	75,000
	2093	Southern Approach to North Channel	100,000
	2798	Loch Foyle to Sanda Island inc. Rathlin Island	75,000
Group (ii)	2156	Strangford Lough and Portavogie	37,500; 5,000
	1753	Belfast Lough	37,500
Group (iii)	2159	Strangford Narrows	12,500
	3709	Cope Islands and Donaghadee Sound	12,500
	1237	Larne Lough and Approaches	10,000

Solway Firth

Group	Chart	Title	Scale
Group (i)	1411	Irish Sea — Western Part	200,000
	1826	Irish Sea — Eastern Part	200,000
	1346	Solway Firth and Approaches	100,000
	2094	Kirkcudbright to Mull of Galloway and Isle of Man	100,000
Group (ii)	2013	St. Bees Head to Silloth	50,000
Group (iii)	1344	Kirkcudbright Bay	15,000

Isle of Man

Group	Chart	Title	Scale
Group (i)	1411	Irish Sea — Western Part	200,000
	1826	Irish Sea — Eastern Part	200,000
	2094	Kirkcudbright to Mull of Galloway and Isle of Man	100,000
Group (iii)	2696	Plans in the Isle of Man	7,500; 10,000; 20,000

Introduction

Publications (continued)

References

Admiralty publications

Admiralty Pilot, West Coast of Scotland 1995 12th Edition (NP 66), with supplements to date.
Admiralty Pilot for the Irish Coast 2000 15th Edition
Tidal Atlas for the Firth of Clyde and Approaches (NP 222)
Admiralty Pilot for West Coasts of England and Wales 1996 13th Edition (NP 37) with supplements to date.
Tidal Atlas N Coast of Ireland and W Coast of Scotland (NP 218).
Irish Sea Tidal Atlas (NP 256).
Admiralty Tide Tables Vol 1 (NP 200).
Admiralty Lists of Lights Vol A (NP 74).

Sailing Directions

Irish Cruising Club Sailing Directions for East and North Coasts of Ireland (2002)
Sailing Directions, Tidal Streams and Anchorages of The Isle of Man. Manx Sailing & Cruising Club.

Almanacs

Reeds OKI Nautical Almanac (Western Edition)
Reeds PBO Small Craft Almanac

Maps

Ordnance Survey Maps (1:50,000) and Bartholomew's 1:100,000 maps provide the topographical detail lacking from modern Admiralty charts.

Admiralty Chart Agents/Distributors in Scotland

Aberdeen	Thomas Gunn Navigational Services	Tel. 01224 595045
Glasgow	Kelvin Hughes	Tel. 0141 221 5452

Clydeport

General

The area north of the Cumbraes including Holy Loch, Loch Long, Loch Goil and Gareloch, is subject to some restrictions. Tankers in excess of 200,000 tons now ply regularly to the BP terminal at Finnart on Loch Long, fast container ships to the Clydeport Container Terminal at Greenock and submarines to the Royal Navy base at Faslane and Coulport. The following channels have been defined and buoyed to facilitate the safe passage of shipping within Clydeport.

Channels

Firth of Clyde channel

The main traffic lane from the Cumbraes to the Tail of the Bank is a two way channel divided by mid-channel pillar buoys with Mountstuart buoy, red and white vertical stripes, the most southerly mark and at its eastern extremity the green conical light buoy No.1 near the Container Terminal at Greenock.

Skelmorlie channel

This channel separates from the main traffic lane at the green conical light buoy 'A' and the yellow spherical light buoy 'B' at the W side of Great Cumbrae Island and terminates at its northern end at the green conical Warden Bank Light buoy. This is a one way channel for inbound vessels drawing more than 15m.

Hunterston channel

Leads through the Largs channel from the Skelmorlie Channel and then between Little Cumbrae Island and the mainland. It serves Hunterston Ore and Coal Terminal.

Loch Long channel

A branch of the Firth of Clyde Channel for vessels proceeding to and from Loch Long marked by the Loch Long mid channel pillar light buoy, with red and white vertical stripes, situated at the entrance to Loch Long.

Ardmore channel

Used by traffic bound to and from the Gareloch, it branches from the Firth of Clyde Channel off Gourock and leads north of Rosneath Patch to the Gareloch entrance. It is marked from E of Portkil Point by two light buoys close to shore.

Kilcreggan channel

A branch of the Ardmore Channel and is for traffic between the Gareloch and Loch Long. it is marked by three light buoys close to the Kilcreggan shore.

A degaussing range is established SW of Barons Point marked by two yellow conical buoys.

Designated large vessel anchorages

These are situated between Bute and the mainland and at the Tail of the Bank between Greenock and Helensburgh and sometimes in Loch Striven.

Introduction

Clydeport (continued)

Caution

Warning for yachts moving within the Recommended Channels and Designated anchorages:

Yachts and small craft may not moor or anchor within the channels and designated anchorages. When crossing the Recommended Channels yachts and small craft should do so as quickly as possible, crossing at an angle between 80° and 90° to the direction of the channel.

At all times within Recommended Channels and designated anchorages, yachts and small craft must keep clear of commercial and naval vessels. Within the meaning of the International Regulations for Preventing Collisions at Sea, 1972, all the Recommended Channels are considered to be 'narrow channels'. Rule 9(b) reads; "A vessel of less than 20 metres in length or a sailing vessel shall not impede the passage of a vessel which can safely navigate only within a narrow channel or fairway".

Naval vessels using these channels will normally be seen displaying the appropriate pennants.

Information on ships using the channels can be obtained on VHF from Estuary Control on Channel 12.

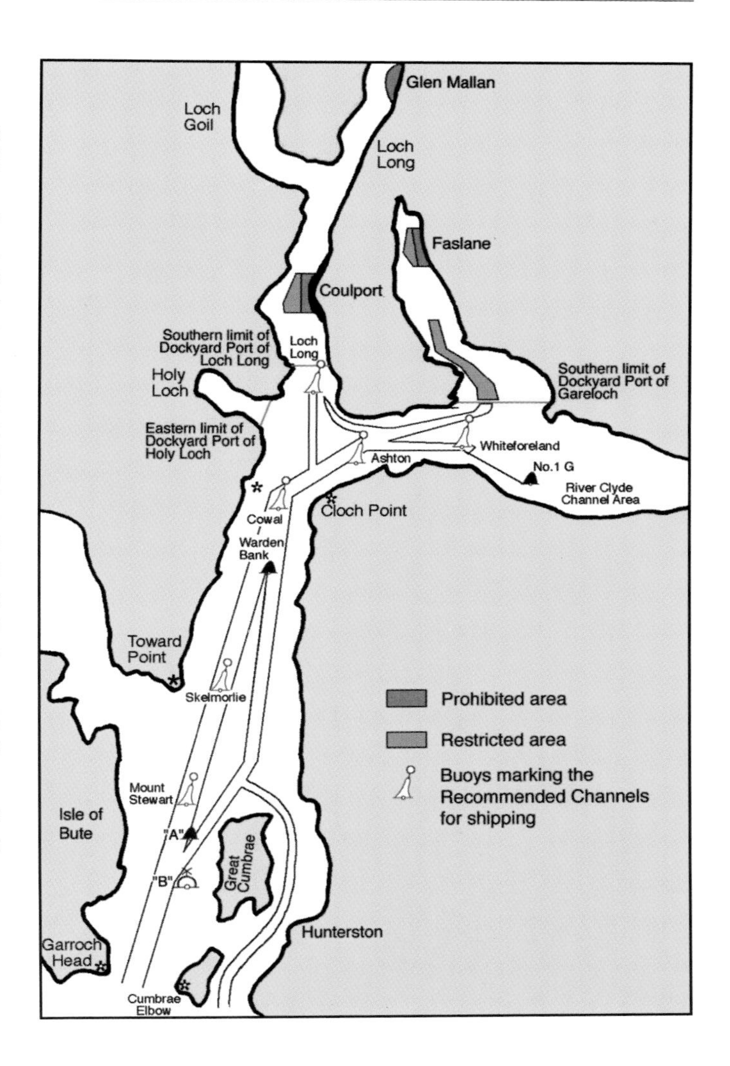

Naval Dockyard Ports

General

Parts of the **Gareloch, Loch Long,** including also part of **Loch Goil,** and the **Holy Loch** are designated as Naval dockyard ports. The limits of these Dockyard Ports, together with the limits of restricted areas and prohibited areas within them, are indicated on the above plan and shown on the relevant charts.

There are **Prohibited Areas** at Faslane, Coulport and Glen Mallan and no yacht or small craft should moor, anchor or come within 150m of any of Her Majesty's Establishments at these locations.

The Gareloch approaches and Rhu Narrows are a **Restricted Channel**. To safeguard the passage of submarines and large naval vessels, the movements of other craft within this area may be restricted temporarily. On these occasions appropriate signals will be displayed in the vicinity and particularly by all escorting tugs and patrol craft. During the period these signals are displayed, no yacht or small craft shall enter or remain in the restricted area. The signals are described in the appropriate places in these directions. For Rhu Narrows p.13, for Faslane p.17 and for Coulport p.18.

Greenock to Bowling

Charts (iii) 1994—Approaches to the River Clyde, 2007—River Clyde.
(iv) ALF 5610·2 & 5610·3 OS 63,64

Tides

Greenock Const.	+0115 Dover, (Rise 3.4m Sp, 2.9m Np.)
Port Glasgow	+0010HW Greenock
Dumbarton	+0020HW Greenock
Bowling	+0025HW Greenock (Rise 3.9m Sp, 3.1m Np)
Renfrew	+0030HW Greenock

The streams are not strong in the dredged channel but with heavy rain or melting snow and strong N to E winds the rate and duration of the out going stream are much increased and the ingoing stream correspondingly reduced.

At the entrance to the dredged channel the tidal streams run as follows:

Time	Direction
–0550 Greenock (–0430 Dover)	In-going stream begins
+0010 Greenock (+0130 Dover)	Out-going stream begins

Lights

Greenock		
Clydeport Container Terminal, NW corner	Qk Fl G 8m 8M	
Leading Lights to dredged channel	Front FG	Clydeport Control Tower, Floodlit on pylon
	Rear FG	Lts in line 194° 30'
Entrance to dredged channel to Upper River		
No.1 Green Con Lt buoy,	Fl G 5s	
No 2 Red Can Lt buoy	Fl R 2s	
S side of dredged channel (principal lights)		
Greenock (Victoria Harbour entrance W side)	2FG (Vert)	
Port Glasgow (Steamboat Quay) W end	FG 12m 12M	B&W chequered column
Beacon	FG 7m 9M	B&W chequered tower and cupola
Garrison Lt	Fl G 5s l0m 6M	Green pedestal, (opposite Dumbarton Rk)
No.45 Green Con Lt buoy	Fl G 2s	Opposite Bowling Harbour
N side of dredged channel (principal lights)		
Opposite entrance to River Leven :-		
No.70 Red can Lt buoy (Rock)	Fl R 2s	
Bowling Harbour W breakwater	Fl R 4s 10m 6M	

Beacon lights including John Brown's slipway opposite River Cart, to Renfrew Ferry slip and Kingston Bridge.

Approach The entrance to the dredged channel of the River Clyde is at the Tail of the Bank just off the Clydeport Container Terminal, Greenock. Entry is gained between the green con Lt buoy No.1 (Fl G 5s) at the W side of the entrance and a red can Lt buoy No.2 (Fl R 2s) on the E side.
Approaching from the direction of Gareloch, in order to avoid the Greenock Bank, which almost dries at LWS keep to the W of the Sugar Ship wreck buoy and a number of large moorings which extend about 1 mile NE of the channel entrance. Keep within the channel as it is soon shoal outwith it. Keep to the starboard hand side (the side with the green beacons and buoys).
It is forbidden to navigate the channel in the dark but if unavoidable take care to follow consecutive lights. A confusion of what is the 'next' light could lead you out of the channel.

Caution In order to navigate a yacht or small vessel up river E of No 1 buoy at the entrance to the dredged channel contact Estuary Control VHF Ch 16, 12 or Tel 01475 726221

Emergency If your vessel is in distress or has had a breakdown and is still within the River, you must contact the Estuary Control VHF Ch 16, 12 or tel 01475 726221.

Anchorage **Greenock:** Victoria Harbour lies one mile E from the entrance to the channel. There are no alongside pontoon facilities. Boats should not be left unattended. **Port Glasgow:** There are now no facilities for yachts.

Interest **Greenock** is the birthplace of James Watt. A dock, lecture hall and a scientific library are named after him.Early 19th Century Customs House is now partly a museum. At **Port Glasgow** there is Newark Castle which has a 15th Century tower and a full size replica of the 'Comet' designed by Henry Bell of Helensburgh. The 'Comet' which was the first ocean going steamship in Europe, was built here in 1812 by John Wood.

Dumbarton

Approach It is about 7 miles from the River Clyde Channel entrance to the entrance channel of the River Leven. Keep to the starboard side of the Clyde channel until the River Leven opens out SW of Dumbarton Rock at a prominent yellow and black beacon with a S Cardinal top mark. This is the Leven Perch and when entering the River Leven it must be left on the starboard hand in order to enter safely the buoyed channel leading up river. Keep to the starboard side of this channel. Leaving its N end, remain at the Dumbarton Rock side until the outer end of the pontoon at McAlister's Yard is abeam. Turn to port and now keep to mid-channel until level with McAlister's Boatyard. The river here is liable to siltation and there is a danger of running aground near LW. Keep clear of Sandpoint, the NE corner of McAlister's Yard, as it is very shoal. In certain conditions there may be a fast river current particularly on the ebb near LW.

Berthing & Facilities Moor on fore and aft moorings at distillery side of channel if over 2 metres draught. Under 2 metres berth at Pontoon at McAlister's Yard. These can be approached 2 hours either side of HW. Tie up and contact office. VHF Channel M(37) Call sign 'Dumbarton Marina'. Yard provides laying up and all repair facilities, chandlery, Calor gas, diesel and water.

Interest Dumbarton Rock is a volcanic plug of basalt. The Castle on the rock has a longer recorded history as a stronghold than any other place in Britain. From the 5th to 11th century—Capital of Kingdom of Strathclyde. Shipbuilding centre from 15th century. Windjammer 'Cutty Sark' completed in the shadow of the Rock at Denny's Yard in 1869.

Bowling and Canal Basin

Approach Lying about 3 miles E of Dumbarton the now disused old harbour is badly silted up and heavily obstructed with wrecks. In order to gain safe access to the sealock entrance to the canal the leading lines on the plan must be closely followed.

A depth of 1.5m in the access channel can be expected at half tide, but silting does occur and a check with the sealock keeper may be advisable. Call VHF ch.16, 74 'Bowling Basin' during sealock opening times 2 hrs either side of HW, or Tel. 01389 877969. Locking should be booked in advance.

Berthing There is no anchoring or berthing in the harbour. The canal basin is suitable for short or long term berthing of vessels up to 20m and drawing 2.5m.

Facilities The facilities in the canal basin have recently been upgraded. Finger pontoons with water and electricity, a new toilet and shower block, parking and hardstanding, improved craneage and a slip were installed in 2006.

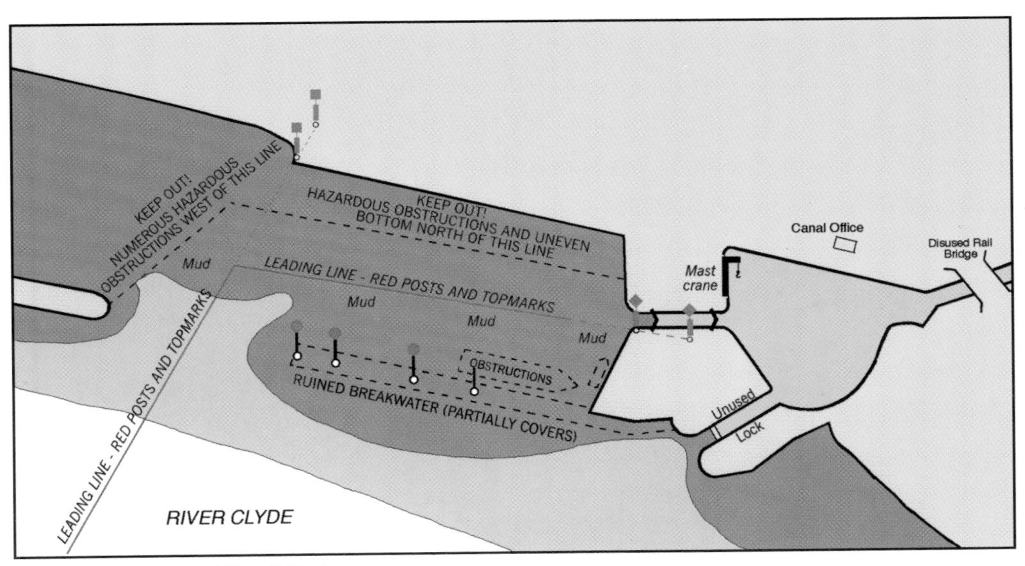

Bowling Harbour and Canal Basin

Forth and Clyde Canal

General In 2002 this canal, originally constructed in 1790, was re-opened for the passage of vessels between Bowling on the River Clyde and Grangemouth on the Firth of Forth. Although available for vessels up to 20m in length and 6m beam there are severe limitations in channel depth, 1.83m (6ft), and headroom below bridges, 3.0m (9ft) measured from the water surface. Vessels drawing more than 1.5m (5ft) are presently (2004) not advised to to attempt a passage through the canal. Full details for using this magnificent facility for suitable craft are available from British Waterways, Main Street, Camelon, Falkirk FK1 4DS, tel: 01324 671217, fax: 01324 671225, www.scottishcanals.co.uk. For Canal safety regulations see Appendix 1 (p.100).

It is a little over 4 miles from Bowling to Renfrew Ferry and the nearby yacht storage yards.

Cloch Point to Helensburgh

Charts

(ii) 3746—Loch Long and Loch Goil
(iii) 1994—Approaches to the River Clyde & 2000—Gareloch (Rhu Narrows)
(iv) ALF 5610·2 & 5610·4 OS 63,56

General

This region of the Upper Firth of Clyde is well protected and generally free from extreme weather conditions and is very suitable for the less experienced. It is easily navigated and is free from unmarked dangers. It is a busy yachting centre and commercial and Naval traffic activities require that a good look out be kept at all times.

Tides

Const. 0000 HW Greenock (+0115 HW Dover)
Gareloch (Shandon) –0005 HW Greenock (+0110 HW Dover)
Rise 3.4m Springs, 2.9m Neaps.

In the approaches to Gareloch between Castle Point and Cairndhu Point the spring rate is barely above 1 knot, about the same rate as occurs between Rosneath Pt. and Ardmore Head. In the Rhu narrows the maximum tidal flow is little over 1.5 knots in either direction. The ingoing stream reaches its peak 6 hours before HW Greenock and for some time thereafter. There is a back eddy in Rosneath Bay and in Rhu Bay from 2 to 5 hours after HW Greenock.

Lights

From Cloch Pt to Rosneath Pt

The Ashton or Southern shore:-		
Cloch Pt Lt	Fl 3 24m 8M	White tower, black band
Outflow mark near McInroys Pt	Oc (2) 10s 3M	Yellow buoy
McInroys Pt Ro-Ro Ferry Terminal	2 FG (vert) and QG	
Kempock Pt	Fl.G 6s 11m 3M	
Gourock Ro-Ro Terminal	2 FG (vert) 9m 5M	
Yellow Lt buoy (Gourock Bay)	Fl (4) Y 10s	
Clydeport Control tower	QG 8m 8M	
Mid-Channel:-		
Rosneath Patch	Fl (2) 10s 5m 10M	Concrete structure
The Kilcreggan or Northern shore:-		
Baron's Pt Green con. Lt buoy (Kil. No 3)	Fl G 5s	
Yellow buoy	Oc (2)Y 10s 3M	
Red can Lt buoy (Kil. No.2)	Fl R 2s	
Perch Rock Red can Lt buoy (Ard. No.24)	Fl R 5s	

From Rosneath Pt to Rhu Narrows (Entrance to Gareloch)

Rosneath shore:-		
Perch Rock Red can Lt buoy (Ard. No.24)	Fl R 5s	Culwatty Bay (S end)
Yellow beacon, 1M NW of Ardmore Head	VQ(4) Y 5s and DIR Q WRG 7M	
Castle Pt Lt	Fl (2) R 10s 8m 6M	
Rosneath DG Jetty	2FR (Vert)	
Yellow mooring buoy, Rosneath DG Jetty	Fl Y 3s	
Helensburgh shore:-		
Ldg. Lts Ardencaple Castle	Front 2FG (Vert) 12M	Beacon, Lts. in line 356°
	Rear FG 10M	Castle tower, NW of Helensburgh
Cairndhu Point Green Con Lt buoy	Fl G 2.5s	
Yellow Lt buoy off Helensburgh S.C.	Fl Y 3s	
Rhu Marina:-		
W Floating breakwater S end	Fl.R 5s	
S Floating breakwater W end	Fl.G 5s	
G con. buoy off S breakwater	Fl.G 4s	
Gareloch Entrance, Rhu Narrows:-		
Rhu Spit,	Fl.3s 6m 6M	White tower, green band
SE side Rhu Spit, Green con Lt buoy	Fl.G 3s	
N of entrance, Green con Lt buoy	Q.G	
S of entrance, Red can Lt buoy	Q.R	
N of entrance, red can Lt buoy	Fl.R 5s	

Directional Lights for entry to and exit from Gareloch.
See plans, pp.14 and 16.
Lights within Gareloch
Faslane Base: Numerous Jetty lights
Garelochhead: N and S Fuel jetties Lights
Mambeg Direction Light 391°

Caution Sailing in the area of Clydeport it is necessary to keep a careful watch at all times for other vessels, including Ferries, commercial traffic and Naval ships, particularly in the designated channels. For 'Restricted Areas and Channel' see pp.8 & 9.

Signals When restrictions are in force at **Rhu Narrows** and approach channels a red light above two green lights disposed vertically, supplemented by a red rectangular flag with a white diagonal bar, are shown at Rosneath Point inshore of buoy No. 24 and at the Naval Building E of Rhu Marina, and also on naval patrol craft. When these signals are shown no vessel may enter the restricted area.

At night it is difficult to discriminate, even in good visibility, between navigation lights and the general lights in this heavily built up area. The navigation lights of nearby ferries and other commercial traffic may be more easily seen.

Approach From the S the Upper Firth of Clyde turns eastwards from Cloch Point on the Ashton shore opposite Dunoon, and leads NE to the approaches to the Gareloch, indicated by a conspicuous radio mast on Rosneath Peninsula; or eastwards from Gourock to the entrance, off Greenock at the Tail of the Bank, to the dredged channel leading up river to Dumbarton (see p.10).

From Loch Long, the shore from Baron's Point to Kilcreggan has many rocks lying up to a cable offshore, some of which dry. Accordingly the shore should be given a wide berth.

Rosneath patch in mid-firth, marked by a concrete structure, can be passed quite close on either side.

Anchorage **On the Ashton shore:**
Ashton lies about 1.5 miles NE from Cloch Point and about half a mile beyond McInroys Pt Ferry Terminal. Given a reasonable offing this shore Is free from dangers. **Anchoring is not advised** as it is very steep to and the seabed is littered with old and new moorings. Nearby is the clubhouse of the Royal Gourock Yacht Club, with slipways and all necessary facilities. Visiting yachtsmen may be accommodated on spare moorings, some notice being preferable.

Gourock

Anchorage **Gourock Bay** The best anchorage in an emergency is on the SW side of the bay well clear of the Ro-Ro Ferry Piers. The E side is shoal but there are moorings opposite Cardwell Bay Sailing Club. **Anchoring cannot be recommended** in the bay as the sea bed is covered with old and new moorings. The N and S ends of the Ferry Terminal show two green lights (vert). Exposed to NW and NE winds.

Facilities Shops, PO, Tel. hotels, EC Wednesday. Slip, in Cardwell Bay for launching small craft. Train connections. Ro-Ro Ferry to Dunoon.

Interest On the Lyle Road, Greenock overlooking the area is the Cross of Lorraine Memorial in memory of the Free French Forces based here from 1940 to 1945.

Cloch Point Light *Mike Balmforth*

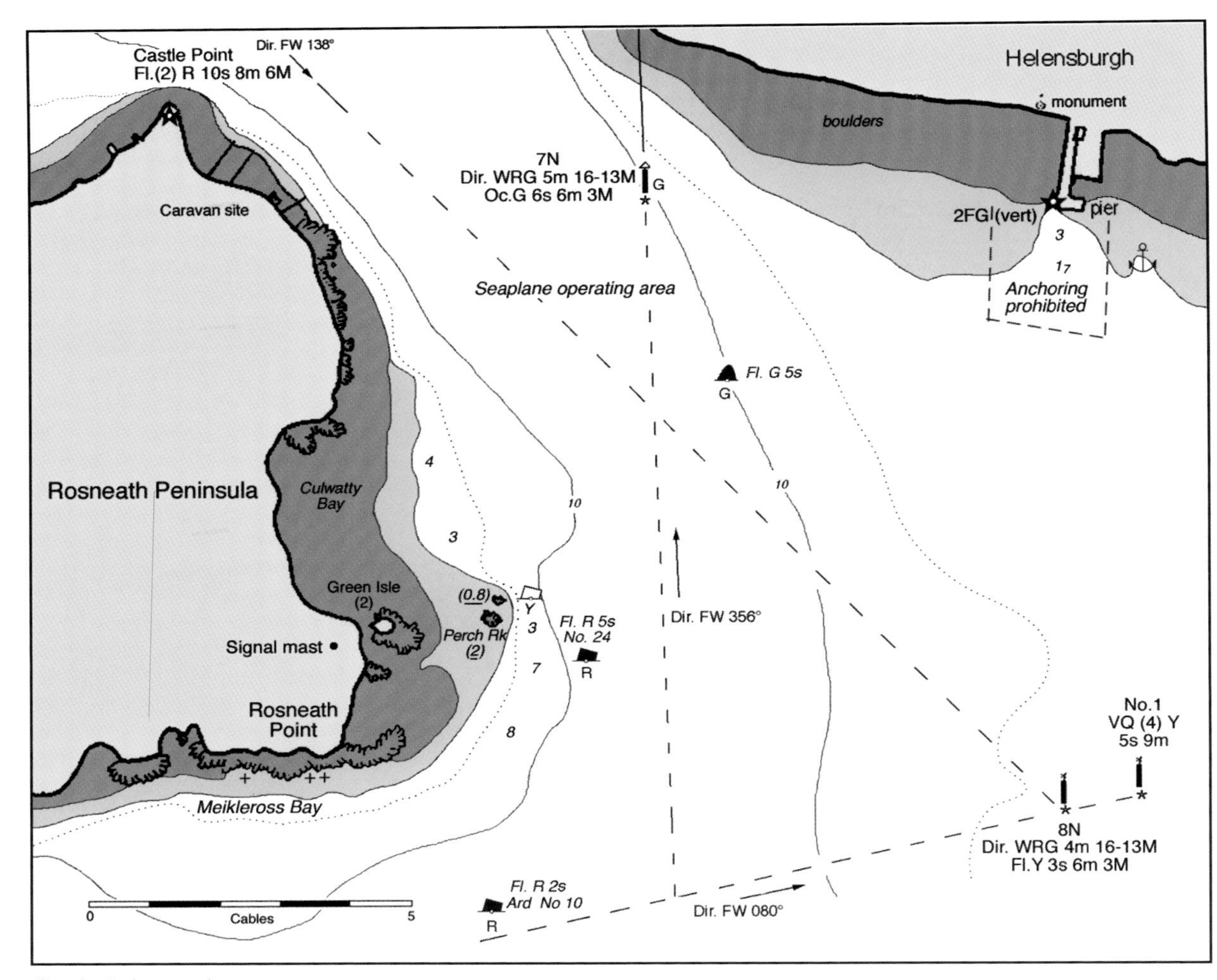

Gareloch Approach

Helensburgh

General The pier is used a great deal by fishermen and ferries and is lit, 2FG (vert), at its head. Anchoring is prohibited within the defined area shown on the plan and Chart 1994. Anchorage can be found to the E of this area although the shore is shoal and boulder strewn for more than 2 cables and care is needed to obtain suitable depth. The pier steps may be approached at most states of the tide. Exposed from S to W winds.

Anchorage **Ardmore Head** 2 miles SE of the pier at Helensburgh and about 1 mile E of the Sugar Ship wreck which is marked by a W cardinal (YBY) Lt buoy Qk Fl.(9) 15s. Anchor in 2m a cable offshore. The Cockle Bank is a mile to the S with the dredged channel leading up river on its S side. The bottom shoals just a little to the S of Ardmore Head. The Ardmore peninsular is an area of much interest to ornithologists.

Facilities Shops, PO, Tel, hotels, Calor gas, petrol. Water at the pier. Indoor swimming pool. EC Wednesday. Slip at pier for launching small craft. Yachts may dry out at W side of pier for inspection.

Interest Obelisk to Henry Bell designer of the `Comet', the first passenger steamboat in Europe. John Logie Baird, pioneer of television, born here. Hill House, a fine example of Charles Rennie Mackintosh's early 20th Century architecture and furnishing, is open to the public.

Rhu Marina *Stuart Cook (courtesy of Rhu Marina Ltd.)*

Gareloch Approach

Charts

(ii) 3746—Loch Long and Loch Goil (includes Gareloch)
(iii) 1994—Approaches to the River Clyde
(iv) ALF 5610·3 OS maps 63 & 56

General

It is about 1.5m from Rosneath Patch to the red can Lt buoy No.24 (Fl R 5s) at the E of Rosneath Pt. This buoy should be left to port to avoid Perch Rock. Between Perch Rock and the shore is Green Island which dries at LW and with local knowledge there is a passage between Perch Rock and Green island. Follow the Rosneath shore to Castle Point giving the shore and the moorings off the caravan site a reasonable berth. Castle Point, opposite Rhu Marina, has a spit to the N and should be given a fair berth. The entrance to the Gareloch is between Limekiln Point and Rhu Spit which is marked by a white tower beacon with a green band (Fl.3s 6m 6M). Entering, leave this beacon on the starboard hand. (see plan p.16)

At night it is not at first easy to locate the Rhu Spit beacon light against background lights. It is best to enter Gareloch through the buoyed channel. As the N shores on either side are shoal, do not leave the channel before reaching the appropriate channel buoys.

Lights

See pp.12 & 16

Caution

Sailing in the **Naval Dockyard Ports of Gareloch, Loch Long and Loch Goil** is subject to certain temporary restrictions. At such times certain signals will be displayed. Keep clear of Naval vessels, restricted channels and shore based establishments. (See Naval Dockyard Ports p.9 and Signals p.13 and p.17)

Gareloch has many unlit Admiralty moorings particularly along the W shore. Do not pass between them as some are connected by cables.

There are high intensity leading lights with R and G sectors either side of the W sector indicating the channel for deep draught submarines. It should not be necessary for small vessels to observe these sectors.

The channel between Rhu Point and Rosneath Point has been designated as a seaplane operating area.

Anchorage

Kilcreggan: About 1 mile E of the entrance to Loch Long. Anchor in 3m clear of moorings to the E of the pier. Exposed to winds from S to W but particularly SW. Visitors may pick up a mooring temporarily if available. The beach between the pier and the stone quay is suitable for landing. The shore from Kilcreggan to Baron's Point, at the entrance to Loch Long has many rocks, some which dry, extending at least a cable. The red can lit buoy (Kil No.2) Fl R 2s, midway between Kilcreggan Bay and Baron's Pt. indicates the most hazardous area. **Facilities:** Shops, PO, Tel, hotels, Calor gas, petrol, water at garage. EC Thursday. Ferry to Gourock.

Portkil Bay: About 0.5m N of Rosneath Patch. Anchor in 3 to 5m well off shore. Exposed to SW wind.

Meikleross Bay: 2 or 3 cables W of Rosneath Point. Anchor in 3 to 5m. Exposed to SW winds.

Culwatty Bay: N of Rosneath Point. Perch Rock, which dries 2m must be guarded against and given a wide berth. Anchor in 2 or 3m in the middle of the bay, well off shore, the bay dries out for 2 cables at LW.

Rhu Bay W of the marina, is full of moorings and is very shoal 2 cables off. Anchor in 2 to 5m well off shore and clear of the moorings in a position with the church tower to the N and Rhu Spit beacon to the W.
The moorings to the E of the Marina, near Cairndhu Pt are in the vicinity of Helensburgh Sailing Club.

Rosneath Bay Good well sheltered anchorage can be had on the E side of Rosneath Bay in 2 to 5m near but clear of a yellow spherical diving target buoy. Keep clear of a shoal patch of rocky sea bed. Shops, Calor gas, petrol and water at caravan site. Slip for launching trailer sailers nearby.

Alternative anchorage exists just to the N of the jetty and slip at the Boat sheds formerly operated by McGruers. Anchor in 2 to 5m clear of moorings.

Facilities

Camsail Bay: DRB Marine Services operate yacht facilities at Rosneath Jetty, the former NATO jetty S of the Boat sheds. Berthing at pier, depth 8m, and swinging moorings. For full details tel. 01436 831233.

Rhu Marina

Approach

This Marina lies E of the Rhu Narrows about 1/2 mile N of Castle Pt. The entrance is on the W side of the Marina between two sections of floating breakwater as indicated on the plan. Leave the G conical buoy Fl.G.4s to starboard and the Fl.R.5s light on the W section of the floating breakwater to port. Do not pass between the end of the solid breakwater and the G buoy.
VHF radio—Marina Ch 80/37 Call sign 'Rhu Marina'. Tel. 01436 820238

Facilities

Pontoon berths and swinging moorings, water and electricity, Chandlery, toilets and showers hoist, yacht and engine repairs, Sailmaker. Helensburgh Inshore Lifeboat nearby. Shops, PO, Tel, hotels

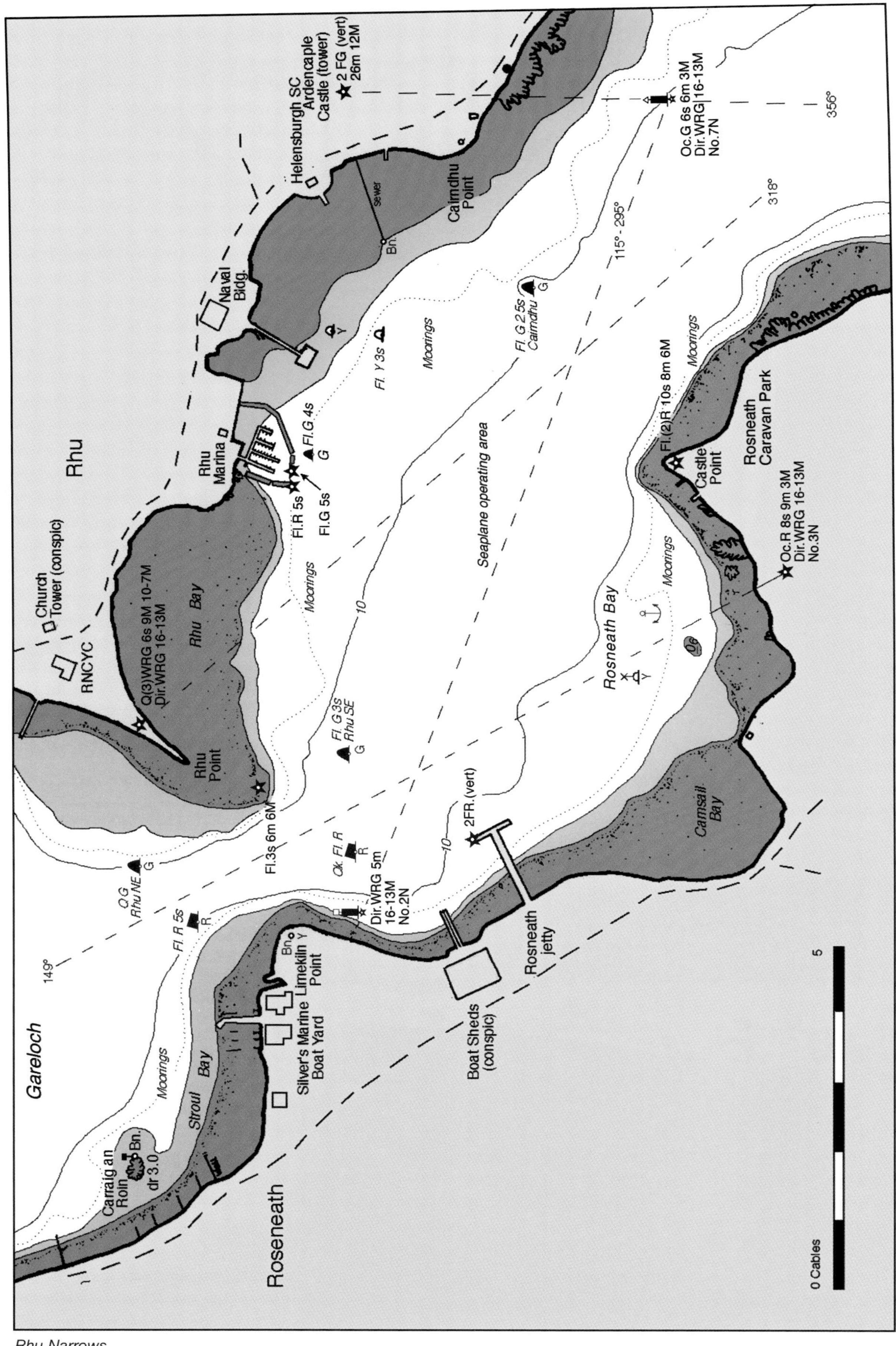
Helensburgh SC
Ardencaple Castle (tower)
2 FG (vert) 26m 12M
Oc.G 6s 6m 3M
Dir.WRG 16-13M
No.7N
356°
Cairndhu Point
sewer
Bn.
Naval Bldg.
Y
Fl. Y 3s
Moorings
Fl. G 2.5s
Cairndhu
G
115° - 295°
318°
Rhu
Rhu Marina
Fl.G 4s
G
Fl.R 5s
Fl.G 5s
Seaplane operating area
Moorings
Fl.(2)R 10s 8m 6M
Castle Point
Rosneath Caravan Park
Church Tower (conspic)
RNCYC
Q(3)WRG 6s 9M 10-7M
Dir.WRG 16-13M
Rhu Bay
Moorings
10
Oc.R 8s 9m 3M
Dir.WRG 16-13M
No.3N
Rosneath Bay
Moorings
Rhu Point
Fl.G 3s
Rhu SE
G
Fl.3s 6m 6M
2FR.(vert)
Camsail Bay
Qk.Fl.R
R
10
Q.G
Rhu NE
G
Dir.WRG 5m
16-13M
No.2N
Fl.R 5s
R
149°
Gareloch
Moorings
Stroul Bay
Bn.
Y
Limekiln Point
Silver's Marine Boat Yard
Rosneath jetty
Boat Sheds (conspic)
Carraig an Roin
Bn.
dr 3.0
Roseneath
0 Cables
5

Rhu Narrows

Rhu Narrows and The Gareloch *John Guthrie (courtesy of Rhu Marina Ltd.)*

Gareloch

Charts

(ii) 3746—Loch Long and Loch Goil (includes Gareloch)
(iii) 2000—Gareloch
(iv) ALF 5610·3(A) No coverage above Rhu narrows OS map 56

Signals

When restrictions are in force at **Faslane** three green lights disposed vertically and Pendant Nine are shown on naval patrol craft in the area and ashore. When these signals are shown no vessel may enter the restricted area.

Anchorage

Stroul Bay On the W side of the loch near the entrance. Entering the Gareloch, give the shore near Limekiln Point a wide berth as it is shoal more than a cable off. A red beacon marking Carraig an Roin, which dries 3m, marks the N end of Stroul Bay. Anchor well off shore in 2 to 5m clear of nearby moorings. Exposed to N and strong NW winds.

Clynder On the W side of the loch about a mile from the entrance. **Caution** When approaching, do not pass between the Admiralty mooring buoys nearby, between which cables are strung. Anchor in 5 to 10m in the vicinity of the terraced houses at the N end of the village. Exposed to N through to E. Anchorage may be had anywhere on the W shore from Clynder north for about a mile and beyond although the shore is steep to. Not recommended in E or strong NW winds. Visitors moorings.

Garelochhead About 4 miles from the loch entrance. Anchor in 4 to 8m either N or S of the old pier clear of moorings. The NW corner of the loch offers better protection from strong NW winds. Anchor well off the N shore as the head of the loch dries out for more than 1 cable at LW. Shops, PO, Tel, hotels, Calor gas, petrol. Slip for launching small craft. **Caution**: A dangerous wreck (LD 3.0m) has been reported (2009) approximately 1cable NW of the MOD jetty. (56° 04'.443N 4° 49'.890W)

Bay N of Rhu Point The moorings belong to the Royal Northern and Clyde Yacht Club (RNCYC) and may be available for visitors on request (tel. 01436 820322). This bay is shoal for more than a cable off to the N of Rhu Pt and must be given a wide berth. From the loch entrance to Shandon it may be possible to find temporary anchorage but the shore is steep to, exposed to the prevailing winds and the presence of small boat moorings may make anchoring impractical. From Shandon to the north of the Naval Oil Terminal near Garelochhead anchoring is prohibited. (See Naval Dockyard Ports p.9).

Facilities

Silver's Yard: A half-tide pier at Silver's Yard, hoist, yacht and engine repairs, diesel and water. Moorings available on request. Sailmaker.

Clynder: Shops, PO, Tel, hotel, Calor gas. Slips nearby for launching small craft.

East shore: There are slips for launching small craft close by Blairvadach Sailing and Outdoor Centre on the E side of the loch 1/2M N of the jetty at the Royal Northern and Clyde Yacht Club (RNCYC).

Interest

St. Modan's Well, a spot where a church was founded by St. Modan in the 7th Century.

Loch Long

Charts (ii) 3746—Loch Long and Loch Goil
(iv) ALF 5610·4 & 5610·15 OS map 56

General Loch Long and Loch Goil provide, in suitable wind and weather conditions, interesting sailing in beautiful surroundings.

Tides Arrochar const. –0005 Greenock (+0110 Dover)
Lochgoilhead const. +0015 Greenock (+0130 Dover)
Tidal Streams: Spring rate 3/4 knot at entrance. Imperceptible in Upper Loch Long and Loch Goil.

Lights

Lower Loch Long

At entrance: Strone Pt Pillar buoy (YB)	Qk Fl (6) + L.Fl 15s	
Loch Long Pillar buoy (RW)	Occ. 6s	(Safe Water Mark)
Baron's Pt green con light buoy	Fl G 5s	
Position 56° 04.03'N 4° 52.28'W light	2 F.G. (Vert)	9m marking SW corner of jetty.

On W side:

Ravenrock Pt	Fl 4s 12m 10M Dir. F WRG & Alt. WRG 9m
Portdornaige	Fl 6s 8m 11M
Blairmore Pier	Fl R 5s 5m 2M

On E side:

Coulport Jetty S end	2FG (vert.)
Coulport Jetty N end	2FG (vert.)

Caution (a) The effects of the slopes of the mountains and glens in these narrow lochs in fresh to strong winds creates such turbulence that the squalls are very fierce and erratic.
(b) Keep a look out for large tankers manoeuvring in the narrow confines of the loch.
(c) Loch Long and Loch Goil comprise a Naval Dockyard Port and are subject to certain restrictions. (see p.9 and below)

Signals When restrictions are in force at **Coulport** three green lights disposed vertically and Pendant Nine, are shown at Coulport Jetty and on naval patrol craft in the area. When these signals are shown no vessel may enter the restricted area.

Approach Loch Long is entered between Baron's Pt on the E side and Strone Pt on the W side which has a church with a conspicuous tower, about 1.5M to the west. There is no difficulty in the navigation of this loch, the shores being steep to quite close in.

Anchorage **Cove** On the E side just past Baron's Pt. Temporary anchorage in 4 to 6m off Cove Sailing Club. Exposed to S and N. There is an unlit Admiralty mooring buoy in Cove Bay. Shops, PO, tel, hotel, EC-Thursday. Water at public toilet.

Blairmore On the W side about 1 mile N of Strone Pt. Anchor in 3 to 5m just N of the pier. Sheltered from W winds. Exposed to S. Shop, tel, hotel.

Ardentinny On the W side almost 4 miles N of the loch entrance. Anchor just to the SE of the point with the conspicuous hotel on it. Good anchorage can be had in 3 to 5m inshore of the moorings. Shop, tel, crafts, Hotel specially caters for yachtsmen and provides moorings for patrons and pontoon for dinghies. Forest walks. Pony trekking. **Caution** The W edge of the moorings bounds a shoal area and an uncharted rock. To avoid these hazards, do not go W of a line joining the Lt on Ravenrock Pt and the seaward side of the point near the hotel. Exposed to SW winds.

Shepherd's Point About 3/4 mile from Ardentinny at the opposite end of Finnart Bay. There are in the bay numerous Admiralty unlit buoys which are usually occupied by lighters. Anchor in 3 to 5m off the beach about 1 cable W of the yellow beacon marking the point. Anchor well inshore of the Admiralty buoys and well away from the shoal bank at the burn. Exposed to the S and SW.

Knap Bay On the W side about 1 mile N of Shepherd's Pt. A small bay which affords temporary anchorage. Knap Rock is easily visible and is always above water. Exposed to S.

Toll a Bhuic (Bute Hole) About 2 miles N of Shepherd's Pt on the W side. A seemingly well protected anchorage except from the S. Once past Knap Rock the entrance is indicated by a nearby pylon near the W shore. Anchor in a suitable depth towards the head of the bay.

Portincaple On the E side at the entrance to Upper Loch Long, about 3.5 miles N of Coulport. Anchor In 3 to 5m well off the centre of the bay which dries out for about cable at LW. Shop, tel, hotel at Whistlefield above the bay.

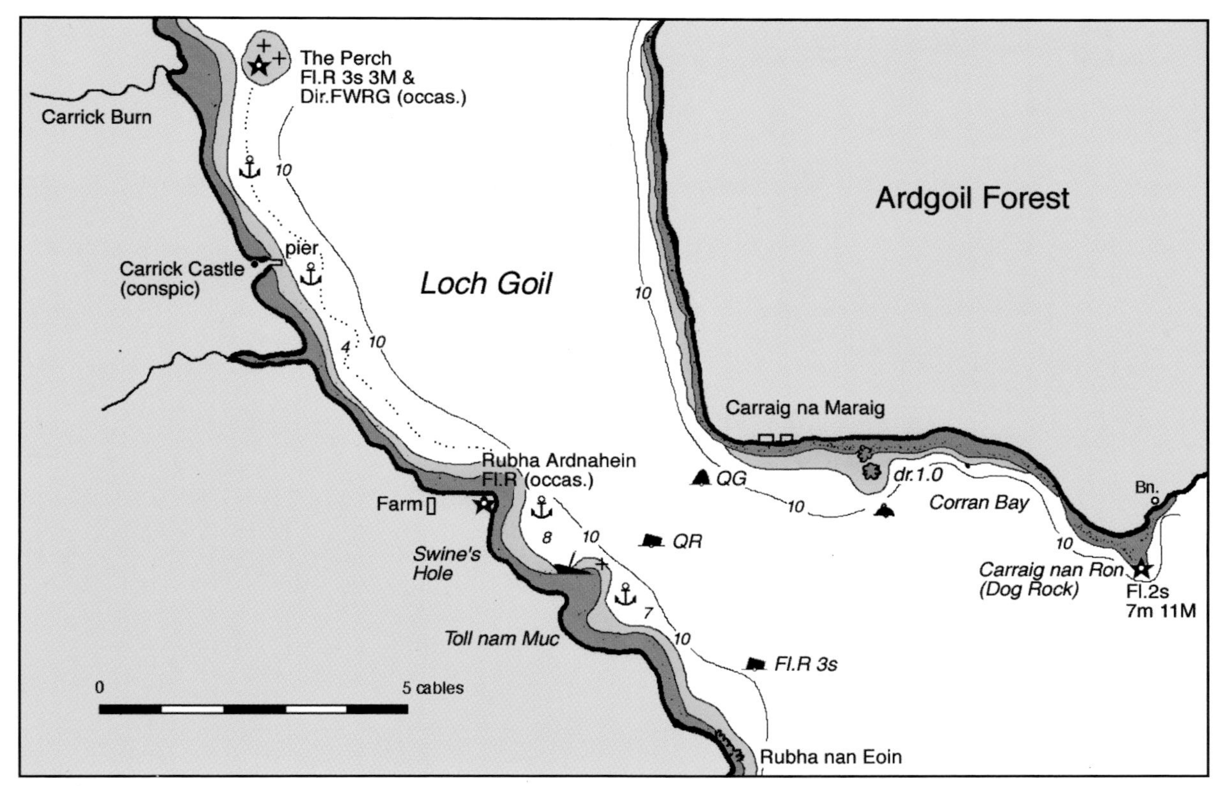

Loch Goil

Loch Goil

Charts (ii) 3746—Loch Long and Loch Goil
(iv) ALF 5610·15 OS map 56

General A narrow loch branching N from the W side of Loch Long. The shores are steep and sometimes precipitous.

Lights NE entrance Carraig nan Ron (or Dog Rock) Fl 2s 7m 11M and as shown on plan above.

Tides Spring rise 3.2m, Neap rise 2.7m

Caution There are 4 rafts and an experimental area (unlit) and Douglas Pier within the loch. Dangers at night due to unlit objects. The cautions (a) and (c) on p.18 should be noted.

Approach The loch is entered between Rubha nan Eoin at the SW and Carraig nan Ron (or Dog Rock) about 6 cables to the NE. 1/2 mile W of this conspicuous rock lies an unlit Admiralty buoy and 2 rocks In Corran Bay which dry at LW. Continuing on this side, the loch is free from dangers to its head.

On the SW side of the loch 5 cables from the entrance there is a spit which extends 1 cable off the shore at Toll nan Muc. The Perch, 4 cables to the N of Carrick Castle, marks a spit which extends for more than 2 cables off the W shore. The beacon on the spit does not mark the outer end. Almost a mile N a drying rock, about a cable N of Cormonachan Burn is well in shore. The head of the loch dries out for about 1.5 cables at LW.

Anchorage **Toll nam Muc** Less than mile from Rubha nan Eoin on the SW side. This small bay has NW shelter at LW by the point and mussel bank which dries and extends to divide it from the next bay off Ardnahein. Good holding can be had in 3 to 4m.

Ardnahein Bay (Swine's Hole) The second bay on the SW side about 1/2 mile from Rubha nan Eoin which should be given a fair berth. Keep well off shore until clear of the spit which forms the SE side of the bay and which extends offshore for a cable. Anchor in the W side of the bay in 4 to 7m.

Carrick Castle On the W side about 2 miles from Rubha nan Eoin. Anchor in 6 to 10m on either side of the pier, close inshore clear of moorings. A blue **Visitor's mooring,** approximately 1 cable N of the pier, is provided by the Carrick Castle Boat Club, charge £10. Good anchorage can be had anywhere in suitable depth between the N side of the pier and the perch about 1/2 mile to the N. Shop, tel, and guest houses. 15th Century Castle. In N'ly winds shelter may be obtained off the houses and clear of moorings at Gob a Chalmain, 1 mile N of the perch. Avoid the drying rock well in shore.

Carrow Bay Good anchorage in 4 to 8m clear of moorings at the head of the bay and N of the mouth of the Lettermay Burn. Avoid the shoal patch extending S from the burn, half way to Douglas Pier, about a cable offshore. Water and diesel are available at Cruiser Charters just S of Douglas Pier. Trekking Centre.

Loch Goil *Dennis Hardley*

Lochgoilhead

Anchorage Anchor in deep water close in-shore on the E side just S of the jetty and sheds. Do not go as far as a yellow beacon as the water there is shallow. Available space is restricted as many boats have moorings in the area. A dinghy landing pontoon is in place. There are **5 visitors moorings** marked 15 tons with pick-up buoys amongst the moorings in the NE part the loch. The head of the loch dries out for about 1.5 cables at LW. Anchorage also available in vicinity of **Douglas Pier** on W side. This is the area where Loch Goil Charters are based.

Facilities Shops, PO, tel, hotel, petrol, water at old pier sheds, Calor gas, Cruiser Charters. EC–Wednesday.

Interest Forest walks, Lochgoilhead and Kilmorich Parish Church is of historic interest. Tourist Centre.

Upper Loch Long

General Upper Loch Long extends from Carraig nan Ron (or Dog Rock) to Arrochar, a village at its head, a distance of about 7 miles. The loch is narrow, subject to heavy squalls and lies between generally steep mountainous shores. The navigation of this part of Loch Long presents no hazards which cannot be easily seen except for Ardgarten Point and the head of the loch (see Anchorages below).

Lights

Main navigation lights from SW to NE		
Carraig nan Ron (or Dog Rock)	Fl 2s 7m11M	At entrance on W side.
Leading lights on Cnap Point	Front Q 8m 10 M	
	Rear FW 13m	
Other navigation lights from SW to NE		
Channel to Finnart Oil Terminal-2 red buoys	Fl R.	On W side
Finnart Oil Terminal, series of dolphins & piers:		
South Jetty Lts	2FG (Vert.)+ 2FG (Vert.) and Qk Fl G	
North Jetty	Lts 2FG (Vert.)+ 2FG (Vert.) and Qk Fl G	
Glen Mallan	Fl.G 3s (vert)	At each end of jetty
Disused pier 1/2 mile N of Ardgarten Pt	Qk Fl.R	
Jetty 1 mile NE Ardgarten Pt.	2FR (Vert.)	

Caution For restrictions which apply to the Naval jetty at Glen Mallan on E shore N of the Finnart oil terminal see Naval Dockyard Ports p.9. Signals as for Coulport p.18.

Anchorage **Coilessan** On the W side 5 miles N of Carraig nan Ron (or Dog Rock). Anchor in 7 to 10m off the house on shore.

Ardgarten On the W side 1 mile N of Coilessan. Anchor in 6 to 8m, off the yellow beacons 2 cables W of the Croe Water. The mouth of the Croe forms a delta which dries out for a cable at LW. The E side of this extensive bank is marked by a red beacon. Nearby large caravan site and Youth Hostel. Slip for launching small craft.

Arrochar At the E corner at the head of the loch. Anchor in 4 to 8m to the N of the pier. The head of the loch dries out for 2 cables at LW. The shore on the W side gives good anchorage in 6 to 10m and may offer better protection in some winds.

Facilities Shops, PO, tel, hotels and petrol at Arrochar

Interest Spectacular views of `The Cobbler', a conspicuous crag of Beinn Arthur, and the Brack. Pony Trekking in the Argyll Forest Park.

Holy Loch

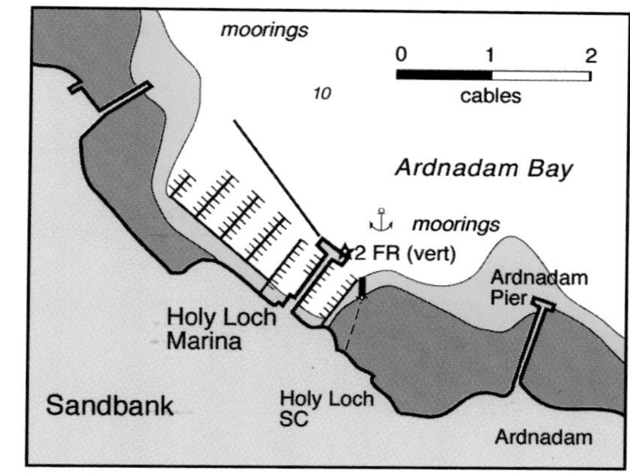

Holy Loch Marina

Charts

(ii) 3746—Loch Long and Loch Goil
(iii) 1994—Approaches to the River Clyde.
(iv) ALF 5610·4 OS map 63

General

Holy Loch extends about 2 miles W from the entrance to Loch Long. It is entered between Hunter's Quay and Strone Pt marked by a church spire (conspic.). Apart from the spit which runs out for about 2 cables from Strone Pt, marked by a S. Cardinal yellow Lt. buoy, the loch is free from dangers. The loch dries out for about 4 cables at its head. In fresh to strong winds from the NW the winds in the loch are extremely fierce and the effects may be alarming. The Dockyard Port of the Holy Loch comprises the whole of Holy Loch. The E limit is a line drawn from Strone Pt. to Hunter's Quay and remains under the jurisdiction of QHM Clyde following the withdrawal of the US Navy base.

Tides

Const. –0005 Greenock (+0110 Dover)

Lights

Entrance to Holy Loch, off Strone Point	Qk.Fl(6) + L.Fl(15s)	S Cardinal Pillar buoy
Off Hunters Quay Ro-Ro Terminal	2 FR (vert) and QR	Grey metal columns
Holy Loch Marina	2 FR (vert)	Grey metal pole

Marina

Holy Loch Marina has been established at the old MOD base and pier at **Sandbank,** to the NW of the Holy Loch Sailing Club**.** It presently (2008) offers 220 fully serviced pontoon berths and is steadily being extended. Onshore facilities include toilets, showers and laundrette, a coffee shop and nearby bar and restaurant. Diesel, petrol, gas and chandlery. Engineering repairs and winter storage outside and undercover. The pontoons are protected by a floating breakwater which should be left to port on entering. Contact on VHF ch80 or 37. Tel.01369 701800. Anchoring is possible well offshore NE of the marina pier and clear of moorings. Use a tripping line

Anchorage

Hunter's Quay At the S entrance to the Holy Loch. Anchor nearby but clear of a few moorings, well away from the Ro-Ro Ferry Terminal. Anchor in 4 to 8m. This anchorage is well sheltered from most winds. In E'lies shelter may be had at the anchorage to the W of Gibb's Pt on N side of the loch. The Ro-Ro Terminal has two fixed R lights (Vert). Shops, PO, tel, hotel, petrol, water near slip. Car ferry connections to Gourock (McInroy's Pt).

Ardnadam About 3/4 mile W of Hunter's Quay, and 3 cables W of Lazaretto Pt. (marked by a memorial tower). Good anchorage may be found about 1 cable SW of the Point, clear of moorings. Hotel and shops at Sandbank about 1/2 mile away. Temporary anchorage in settled conditions may also be had off Hafton House E of Lazaretto Pt. The hotel caters for yachtsmen and provides moorings for its patrons. If anchoring keep well off shore as it is shoal.

Kilmun On the N shore opposite Ardnadam. The anchorage provides excellent shelter in all conditions. Anchor in 6 to 8m about 1.5 cables NW of the pier. The loch shallows at its head. Alternatively anchor to the W and close by Graham's Pt on the N shore, marked by a monument. Shop, hotel, PO, tel. Water available at pier. Slipway nearby. **Interest;** Kilmun church (tower 15thC.) Nearby arboretum contains trees from all over the world.

Gibb's Point Anchoring just W of Gibb's Point, close to the shore, gives good shelter from E'ly winds.

Strone At the N entrance to the loch and rather exposed. Anchor to the NW of the pier in 4 to 6m fairly well off shore. There are steps at the pier. Shops, PO, tel, water at pier.

Holy Loch Marina *Mike Balmforth*

Cloch Point to Little Cumbrae

Charts

(ii) 1907—Little Cumbrae Island to Cloch Point
(iv) ALF 5610·4, 5610·5, 5610·6 & 5610·7 OS map 63

General

The main section of the Upper Firth of Clyde leads to Rothesay and the Kyles of Bute to the W and the Cumbrae Islands to the S. This is a generally well sheltered sailing area though increasingly exposed to SW winds nearer to the Cumbraes. All dangers to navigation are clearly marked. Attention is drawn to the Caution on p.9 warning that all yachts and small craft must not impede the passage of large vessels within the Recommended Channels in the Upper Firth which are considered to be Narrow Channels.

Tides

Millport const. –0015 HW Greenock (+0100 HW Dover) Rise: 3.4m Sp 2.9m Np

Tidal streams are weak between Cloch Point and Toward Point and do not exceed a spring rate of 1 knot in each direction though may be more over Skelmorlie Bank and similar banks.

It should be noted by those proceeding beyond the Cumbraes on passage to N Arran or Loch Fyne that the outgoing streams from the channels either side of Cumbrae Islands meet the stream W of the Island of Bute off Garroch Head where a tidal race is formed. This race can be very uncomfortable in strong winds and should be avoided.

Lights

Cloch Pt Lt	Fl 3s 24m 8M
Dunoon Pier	N end 2FR (Vert.) 5m 6M
Dunoon Breakwater	2FR (vert.) 5m 6M
The Gantock Beacon	Fl R 6s 12m 18M
Inverkip Oil Jetty	N end 2FG (Vert.) 11m 2M
	S end 2FG (Vert.) 11m 2M
Wemyss Bay Pier	2FG (Vert.) 7m 5M
Toward Pt Lt	Fl 10s 21m 22M
Cumbrae Elbow Lt, on Little Cumbrae	Fl 3s 31m 23M Horn (3)40s
Rubh'an Eun (Runnaneun Pt) Lt, SE corner of Bute	Fl R 8s 8m 12M

Firth of Clyde Designated Channel buoys (South to North) comprise:

Off Bute, Mount Stuart Lt buoy	L Fl 10s	R & W Vert. stripes.
Off Skelmorlie, Skelmorlie Lt buoy	Iso 5s	R & W Vert. stripes
SE of Dunoon, Cowal Lt buoy	L Fl 10s	R & W Vert. stripes
Off Gourock, Ashton Lt buoy	Iso 5s	R & W Vert. stripes
Off Greenock, Whiteforeland Lt buoy	L Fl 10s	R & W Vert. stripes

The positions of port, starboard and channel junction buoys can be seen for all the designated channels on the chart.

Measured distance

There is a measured distance 1/2 mile S of Wemyss Bay Pier. Two pairs of similar beacons at either end mark a distance of 1,853.8m (6082 ft). The S pair of beacons are close S of Skelmorlie Castle. The running courses are 000°/180°.

Anchorage

On the W side of the Upper Firth of Clyde

Kirn About 1/2 mile S of Hunter's Quay. Anchor in 3 to 5m anywhere along this shore, but the best place is N of the disused pier. Exposed to S. Shops, PO, tel, hotels, EC Wednesdays.

Dunoon On the Cowal shore about 2 miles W of Cloch Point. The E bay is shoal and boulder strewn. There is also a Ro-Ro Ferry Terminal Pier and a pier which dries out at LW. The best anchorage, although it is exposed to the S, is the W bay in 2 to 5m. The W shore is shoal about 1 cable off. Visitors moorings in both bays.

The Gantocks are SE of Dunoon Point and are marked by a beacon (Fl R 6s) on its S end and a N cardinal black and yellow buoy on its N end. Approaching the W bay give these rocks a reasonable berth.

An E cardinal buoy (Qk Fl (3) 10s) and a W Cardinal buoy mark the area of a wreck on the Dunoon Bank. Each buoy can be passed on either hand. The Bank is also marked by a N cardinal buoy (Fl (5)Y.20s) and data collection buoy with a cross topmark (Fl.Y 5s). These also can be passed on either hand.

Shops, PO, tel, hotels, Calor gas, diesel, petrol. Indoor swimming pool. Ro-Ro Ferry to Gourock.

Innellan 4 miles S of Dunoon. The anchorage is near the disused pier in 3 to 5m. There is a shoal patch, which extends 1 cable off shore for some distance N of the pier, to be guarded against. If approaching from the S give Innellan beacon, marking the Bridges, a fair berth. Do not pass inside the beacon. Exposed from NE through S to SW. Shops, PO, tel, hotels, EC - Wednesday. Bus connections to Dunoon. Moorings for hotel patrons.

Interest

Dunoon Castle and gardens are worth visiting also Knockarmillie Castle near the pier at Innellan.

Cloch Point to Little Cumbrae (continued)

Anchorage **On the W side of the Upper Firth of Clyde (continued)**

Toward In the bay just to the N of the Point. Anchor in 3m. The shore S from the Bridges is shoal 2 cables off for 3/4 miles. Exposed from NE through E to SW winds. Shop, PO, tel. Bus connections to Dunoon.

The Toward Bank green con Lt buoy No.35 (Barnhilt) Fl G 3s is 1 mile SW of Toward Pt and marks the entrance to Rothesay Sound leading to the Kyles of Bute. It can be passed on either hand. The E cardinal buoy 2 cables SSW of Toward Point is unlit. Pass S of this buoy.

Kilchattan Bay Near the SE end of Bute 3.5 miles W of Millport. Anchor to the NW of the disused pier in 4 to 6m but not beyond the hotel or stone quay. The head of the bay dries out for about 4 cables at this side. Exposed from SE to NE.

Shops, PO, tel, hotel. Water near old stone quay. Bus connections to Rothesay. Moorings available for hotel patrons.

Glencallum Bay (Callum's Hole) A small bay at the SE end of Bute. The NE entrance to the bay is marked by the white beacon on Rubh'an Eun (Runnaneun Point). Once inside the entrance, take care to avoid the rocks (dr. 2.1m) which lie towards the centre of the bay, rather to the NE side. Anchorage in over 2m can be had near the head of the bay or in 4 to 6m about half way in, away from the drying rocks and clear of the SW shore. Exposed to S'ly winds and gusty in strong N.W'ly winds.

A rock with a depth 1.5m is reported (2004) approximately 50m off the W shore due W of the rocks (dr. 2.1m) mentioned above.

Interest St Blane's Chapel and Monastery at Dunagoil, Standing Stones and stone circles nearby. An Iron Age fort at Dunagoil Bay and at Dunstrone at N end of Lubas Bay. At Kingarth, the ruins of St Blane's Chapel.

Kip Marina

Approach The Marina is entered through a buoyed, dredged channel in Inverkip Bay about 1/2 mile N of a conspicuous Power Station Chimney and 1 mile NE of the Power Station jetties. The channel must be approached from W'ward as the shores both N and S of the channel are shoal 2 cables off. There is 2m in the channel at LW and it is marked at its outer end by a green con Lt buoy 'KIP' Fl.G 5s. The Lt. is faint. VHF Marina Ch.M (37) Call sign 'Kip Marina'. Tel. 01475 521485.

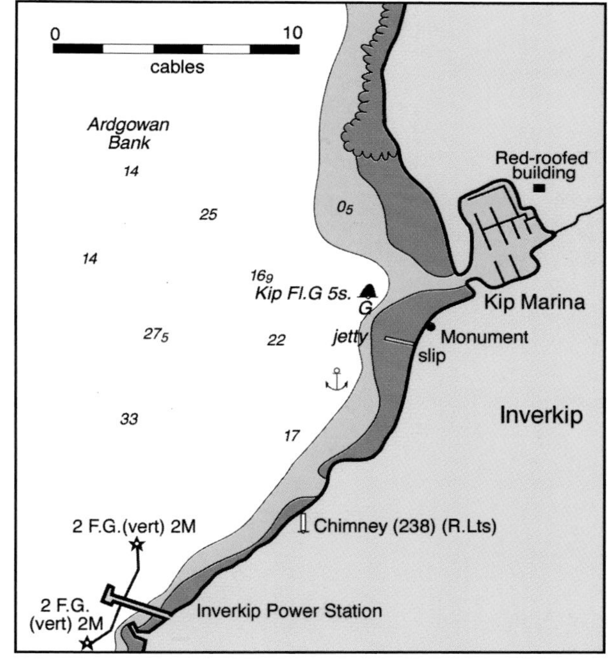

Kip Marina

Facilities Visitors pontoon berths, water and diesel, electricity, chandlery, hoist, yacht and engine repairs, electrical repairs slip for launching, showers,toilets, bar and restaurant. There are Shops, PO, tel, hotels and train connections to Glasgow at Inverkip village.

Anchorage **On the E side of the Upper Firth of Clyde**

Lunderston Bay A mile S of Cloch Point. In offshore winds or in settled conditions anchor in the centre of the N end of the bay, well N of the Y beacon and clear of cables and gas pipe line. The Warden Bank Buoy is 1 mile W of this bay and can be passed on either hand.

Inverkip Bay A little to the S of the slips about 2 cables S of the Marina entrance. Temporary anchorage in 1 to 2m. Exposed from NW through W to SW.

Wemyss Bay About 4 miles S of Cloch Point. Temporary anchorage to the N of the Ro.Ro Ferry Pier (Lts 2FG (Vert.) in 2 to 5m. Yachts may tie up on the N side of the pier clear of the ferry. Exposed from W to S. Shops and hotels. Train connections to Glasgow. The railway station is noted for its fine Edwardian architecture.

Skelmorlie Bank buoy No.32 is 1.5miles SW and is marked by a green con Lt buoy (Fl G 2s). This may be passed on either side.

Fintry Bay In settled conditions temporary anchorage may be had in Fintry Bay on the W side of Great Cumbrae Island.

Largs Channel looking towards Arran *Mike Balmforth*

Largs Channel and Fairlie Roads

Chart

(ii) 1907—Little Cumbrae Island to Cloch Point
(ii) 2221—Firth of Clyde - Pladda to Inchmarnock Northern Sheet
(ii) 2491— Ardrossan to Largs
(iv) ALF 5610·6 & 5610·7 Largs Yacht Haven ALF 5610·15(B) OS map 63

General

The Largs Channel and Fairlie Roads lie between the Cumbrae Islands and the Ayrshire shore. The shore on Great Cumbrae is clear of danger if it is given a fair offing. The shore between Largs and Fairlie is very shoal. The extensive shoal areas of Southannan and Hunterston Sands have an Ore/Coal Terminal and Platform Construction site on them. The channel near these shores is clearly buoyed as it is off Brigurd Spit.

Tides

Largs const. –0025 HW Greenock (+0050 HW Dover) Rise 3.4m Sp. 2.9m Np.

Tidal streams The tide rarely reaches 1 knot, but between Hunterston Sands and Farland Pt on Great Cumbrae the spring rate may reach about 1.5 knots and in fresh to strong winds a short but uncomfortable sea can be experienced off Farland Pt.
In Cumbrae Pass, the channel between Great and Little Cumbrae, the ingoing stream runs E and the outgoing W. It is unlikely that a spring rate of 1 to 1.5 knots is exceeded in mid channel, a greater rate may be attained off the salient points.

Lights

Largs Pier N end	2FG (vert.) 7m 5M	
Largs Yacht Haven Entrance Lt buoy	Iso 3s	Spherical red & white stripe
Largs Yacht Haven S breakwater	Oc G 10s 4m 4M	
Largs Yacht Haven W breakwater	Oc R 10s 4m 4M	
Fairlie Pier Head	2FG (vert.)	
Fairlie pier elbow	2FG (vert.)	
Hunterston Ore/Coal Jetty NE corner	2FG (vert.) 11m 5M	
	2FG (vert.) 11m 5M	
Great Cumbrae, Millport Eileans W end	QG 5m 2M	
Millport Pier Leading Lts	Front FR 7m 5M	Lights in line 333°
	Rear FR 9m 5M	

Caution

Violent squalls are experienced in E'ly weather particularly in the eastern half of the channel and in the Fairlie roads. Should these squalls occur good refuge may be had in Millport Bay.

Largs

General About 7 miles S of Inverkip Bay and 9 miles S from Cloch Point. **Temporary anchorage** in 7 to 10m N of the Pier opposite the Royal Hotel. N of there the bay is very steep-to and depths of 15m are soon achieved. Exposed to winds from N through W to S. There is an unlit Admiralty buoy just N of the Ferry Pier. Alternatively tie up at the inside of the pier which is available at all states of the tide and is sheltered from all winds except NW but keep clear of the Ferry slip.

Facilities Shops, PO, tel, hotels, Calor gas, water at pier. EC Wednesday. Indoor swimming pool. Inshore Lifeboat. Car Ferry to Cumbrae with bus connection to Millport. Train and bus connections to Glasgow. Several slips for launching small boats. The best are to the S close by Largs Sailing Club.

Interest The Pencil on Craig Bowen commemorates the Battle of Largs in 1263. Kelburn Country Centre the Estate of the Earl of Glasgow, offers spectacular views over the entire Firth of Clyde. Kelburn Castle and Sundials with 16th century towerhouse.

Largs Yacht Haven

Approach This Marina lies 1 mile S of Largs Pier opposite Ballochmartin Bay, Great Cumbrae. The Pencil, a conspicuous monument stands 3 cables to the N of the entrance. The entrance is marked by white paint and a spherical red & white SPH Lt buoy (L Fl 10s). Access may be had in any state of the tide. On entering proceed to a 'Visitor's berth'. Depth 3.5m. VHF Marina Ch M(37). Call sign `Largs Yacht Haven' Tel 01475 675333

Caution In order to keep clear of the shoal water N of the Yacht Haven keep at least 3 cables off shore and outside the buoys laid for racing NW of the entrance.

Facilities 750 pontoon berths with water and electricity, 24 hr. diesel, chandlery, 70 ton hoist, yacht and engine repairs, Marine electrics and electronic repairs, sailmaker, sail and motor yacht charter, slip for launching. Chandlery, showers, restaurant and coffee shop.

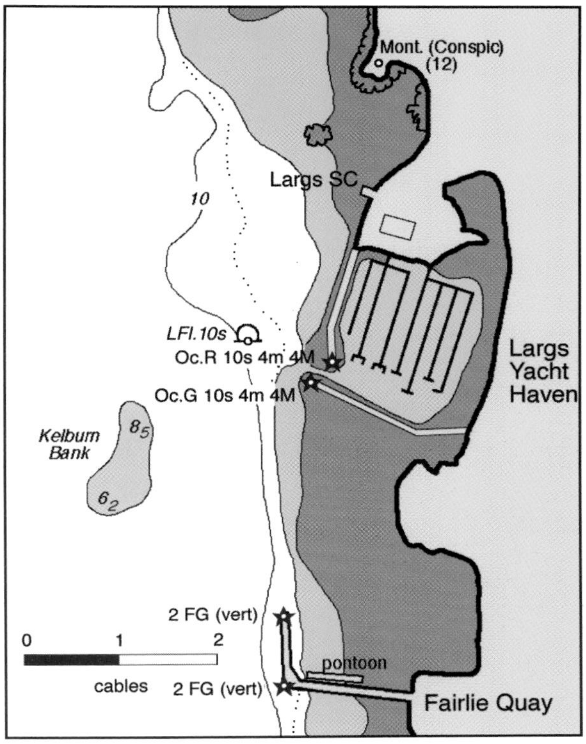

Largs Yacht Haven

Fairlie

General 2 miles S of Largs Pier, NE of Hunterston Ore/coal Terminal. Anchor in 4m to 8m clear of moorings. Keep well off as shore dries out for 2 cables at LW. If approaching from the S pass the green con Lt Buoy (Fl G 1.5s) marking the NW end of Fairlie Patch on the starboard hand. There is an unlit Admiralty mooring buoy 1 cable NE of the Ore Terminal. Much exposed to W wind although the Ore Terminal may give some protection. Shops, PO, tel, hotel, petrol. Slip at Fairlie Yacht Club, jetty suitable for dinghies.

Interest Sir T. Lipton's Shamrock I and II America's Cup yachts were built at Fairlie.

Facilities **Fairlie Quay** Laying up facilities at former NATO pier and shed operated by Kip Marina, tel. 01475 521 485.

Great Cumbrae

Anchorage **Tomont End** (Monument) At the N end of Great Cumbrae, good holding ground and well sheltered from strong SW winds. Approach White Bay and anchor In 5 to 8m over sand with the monument to eastward. Do not go too close in shore as the bay dries out for a cable at LW.

Scottish National Water Sports Training Centre At the N end of Balloch Bay near the Largs - Cumbrae Ferry. Pick up mooring if available. Anchor to the N of Centre's slip but well off shore. Visitors welcome at the Training Centre. Showers and toilets. Slip available for launching small craft. The Training Centre offers Yachtmaster courses, dinghy and diving training.

Balloch Bay One mile W of Largs Yacht Haven offering best anchorage on the E side of Great Cumbrae. Called Ballochmartin Bay on charts. There is a Grey House on the shore. Anchor anywhere nearby fairly well in shore in 8m and clear of moorings. There is an unlit Admiralty mooring buoy close by.

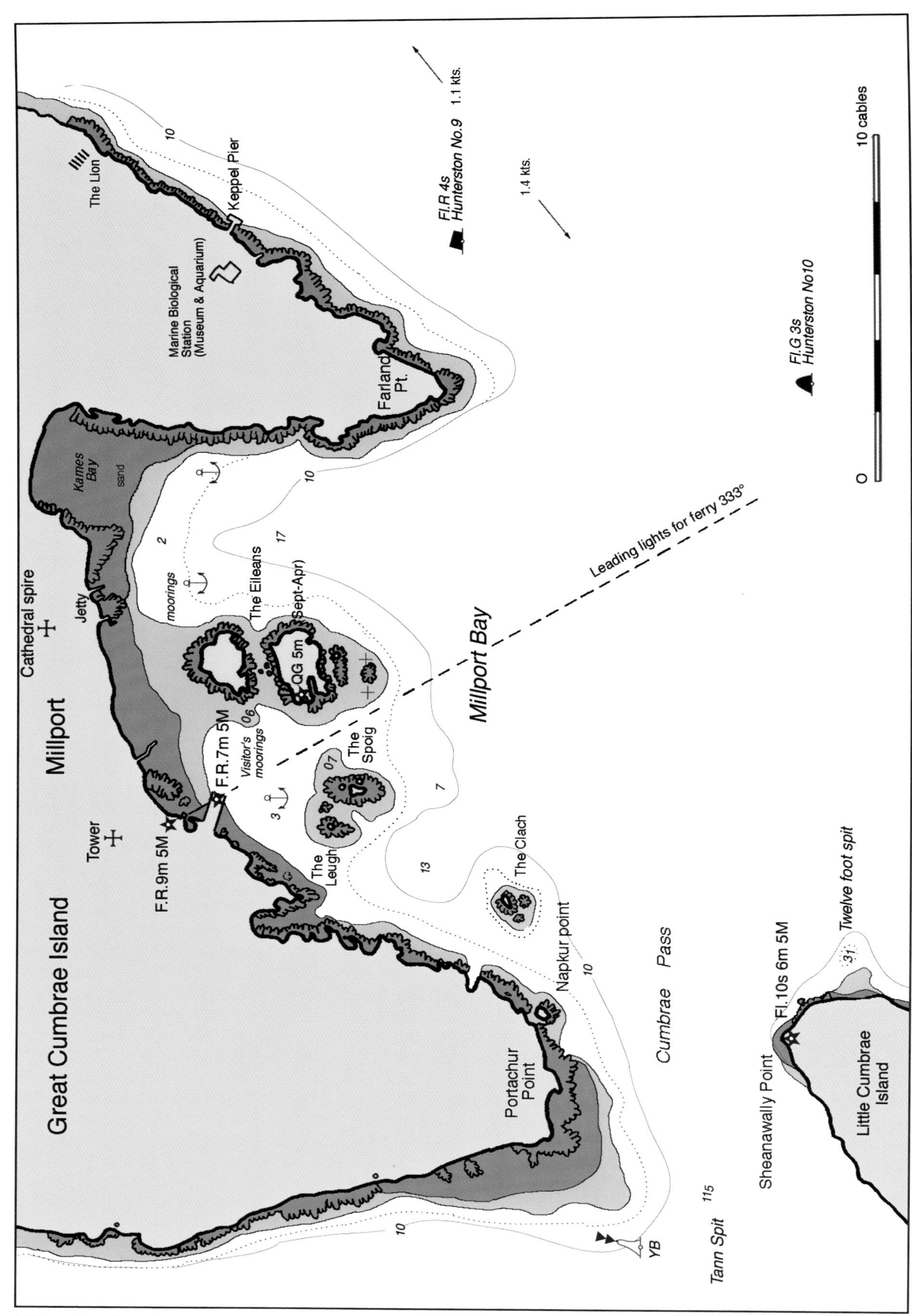

Millport Bay, Great Cumbrae

Millport

Charts (iii) 1867—Plans in the Firth of Clyde
(iv) ALF 5610·15(C)

General At the S end of Great Cumbrae the E side of Millport Bay provides good anchorage well protected from most winds. However in S to SW winds a swell sets into the bay making it untenable. Not recommended when poor weather is anticipated. In strong southerlies better protection can be had in Little Cumbrae, Balloch Bay or Tomont End (Monument).

Lights The Eileans, W end QG 5m 2M is only exhibited from September to April and may be difficult to discern due to shore lights.
Millport Pier Leading Lts bearing 333° Front FR 7m 5M. Rear FR 9m 5M.

Approach From the E give Farland Point on the SE comer of Great Cumbrae a fair berth.

From the W Millport Bay is entered through Cumbrae Pass between Portachur Pt and Sheanawally Pt. on Little Cumbrae. Portachur Spit extends 2 cables SW and is marked by a S cardinal yellow/black buoy, the Tann buoy, which should be left to port.

The W side of Millport Bay has a number of rocks, the Clach, the Spoig and the Leugh; and in the middle, the Eileans, N and S. Although all are visible above water, they should be given a fair berth.

Anchorage **Millport Bay** Anchor in 3m to 4m to the NE of the N'most Eilean, clear of the moorings and within convenient distance of the Jetty. A tripping line should be used. The E side of Millport Bay also affords good anchorage.

Visitors moorings in the bay to the W of The Eileans. Alternatively anchor in 2 to 5m W of these moorings.

Note To avoid a dangerous unmarked rock to starboard, keep end of pier on leading bearing, 333°, Yachts may tie up at the pier which is available at all states of the tide (2.1m at LW) or lie along side the Inner harbour and dry out. The passage between N'most Eilean and the shore can be navigated only after half-tide.

Facilities Shops, PO, tel, hotels, Calor gas,diesel, petrol, craft shops. Water at pier.

Strawherry Jetty and a slip at the old harbour allows small craft launching at suitable states of the tide. The Island offers many slipways for launching small craft and yachts.

Interest The Cathedral of the Isle (the smallest Cathedral in Britain), Marine Biological Station & Aquarium at Keppel Pier. Museum of the Cumbraes, Garrison House.

Little Cumbrae

Chart (iii) 1867—Plans in the Firth of Clyde
(iv) ALF 5610·7 OS map 63

General On E side of Little Cumbrae give the shore E of Sheanawally Point a wide berth to avoid a shoal patch 1 cable off, near Twelve Foot Spit. Anchor in 2 to 3m between the island on which the old castle stands and Broad Island to the N. Keep clear of moorings and nearby jetty. Well sheltered from SW to NW. In strong S'lies and in E'lies the anchorage may be uncomfortable. In such conditions move to the N end of the bay leaving Broad Island to port. This may offer more protection. This part of the bay is shoal. Anchor in 2m N of Broad Island. Landing on Little Cumbrae is no longer objected to.

Interest Little Cumbrae Castle - towerhouse destroyed by Cromwell. Old Lighthouse and Tower, also remains of 200 year old coal fired lighthouse on hilltop.

Note 1 mile to the E of Broad Island on Little Cumbrae is a yellow Lt buoy (Fl Y 5s) marking the outflow from Hunterston Power Station; give this a wide berth.

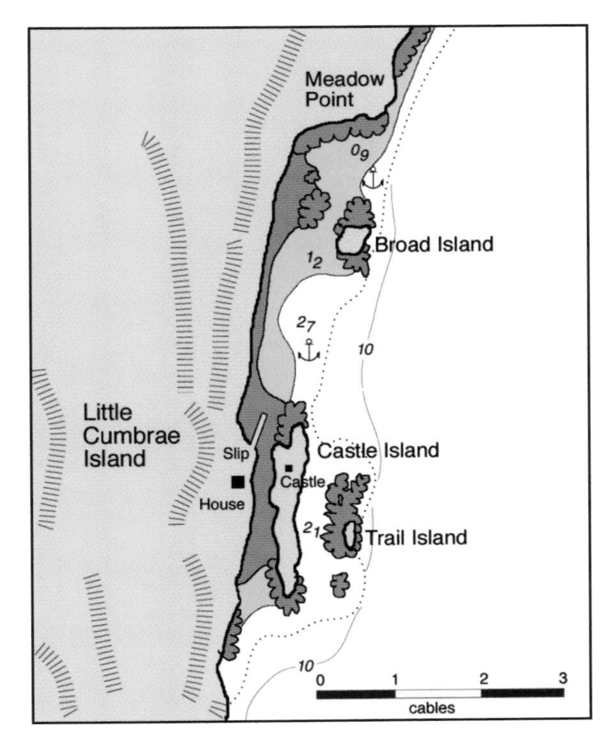

Little Cumbrae anchorage

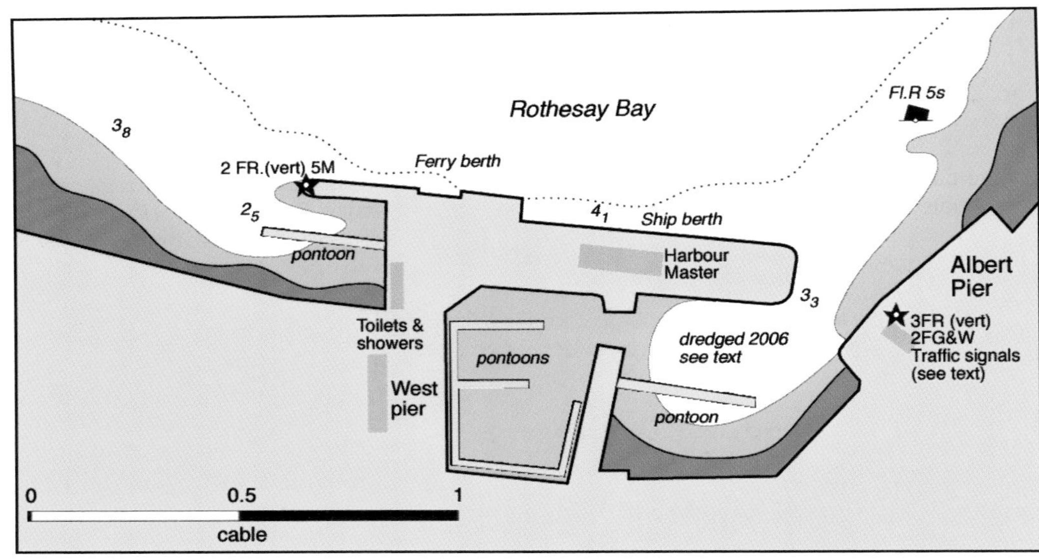

Rothesay Harbour

Rothesay

Charts	(ii) 1906—Kyles of Bute & 1907—Little Cumbrae to Cloch Pt (iii) 1867—Plans In the Firth of Clyde, (iv) ALF 5610·5 & 5610·8(A) & (C) OS map 63			
Tides	Rothesay Sound const. + 0010 Greenock (+0105 Dover)			
Lights	In Rothesay Sound;	E Sound: Toward Point Lt	Fl. 10s 21m 22M	
		Toward Point shoal	Q(3)	E Cardinal buoy (BYB), No 34
		Toward Bank (Barnhilt)	Fl.G 3s	Green con. buoy
		Bogany Point	Fl.R 4s	Red can buoy
	In Rothesay Bay:	Admiralty Mooring Buoy	Fl Y 2s	
	Rothesay Pier Lights:	W side of Front Pier	2 FR (Vert.)	
		Albert Pier (Traffic signal lights)	3FR (Vert.): No traffic.	2G&W (vert): Traffic both ways

Approach Entering Rothesay Sound **from the NE** give the shoal off Toward Pt, marked by an E Cardinal Pillar buoy No. 34, a good offing. Rothesay Bay is entered **from the S** round Bogany Pt, marked by a red can buoy, and from the west round Ardbeg Pt which should be given a good clearance. Care should be taken to clear the shallow area 1 cable offshore just N of the slipway at Ardmaleish Boatyard. Once in, there are no hazards except a few Admiralty buoys. One only is lit and is in the centre of the bay, about 3 cables off the pier. At night, all these buoys and pier lights are likely to be difficult to locate against the background of town lights all round the bay.

Anchorage **Rothesay Bay** Best anchorage may be found off the West shore outside several rows of visitors moorings but depth may be greater than 10m. Alternatively off the South shore again outside the moorings in deep water.

35 Visitors moorings on W side of bay are owned and maintained by the Bute Berthing company (Tel. 07787 365104 & 01700 500630) whose representative collects dues.

Rothesay Sound Achavoulin or Kirkmanfindlay Bay on the Toward shore just E of the abandoned Oil Platform construction yard at Ardyne Pt. Anchor in 5 to 7m, W of jetty and clear of moorings near Castle Toward. The bay shoals for about 1 cable at LW. Provides a convenient shelter in E'ly winds. Water at Toward Sailing Club.

Berthing Alongside berths may be had at the finger pontoons in the outer harbour (24 berths approx.) or at the pontoon W. of the W Pier (12 berths). From June 2009 a further 30 berths should be available in the inner harbour which has been dredged to 2m. Electricity and water available. Berthing arranged by Berthing Master, with whom depths at pontoons should be checked, Tel. (mobile) 07787 365104 or Tel. 01700 500630. **Note:** Albert Pier is not to be used.

Facilities Shops, PO, tel, hotels, chandlers, Calor gas, indoor baths. Boatyard (boat and engine repairs) near Ardmaleish Pt. Water, toilets and diesel at pier. Cruiser Yacht Charters, Ro-Ro Ferry to Wemyss Bay. Port Radio Station call sign 'Rothesay Harbour' VHF Ch 16 and 12.

Interest Rothesay Castle, early 13th century. St Michael's Chapel, 14th century. The ruined chancel of St Mary's Chapel with its ancient tombs stands near the Parish Church. The Victorian harbour-side toilets are worth a visit!

Port Bannatyne

General

About 2 miles W of Rothesay. When approaching from the S or E Ardbeg Point must be given a wide berth as it is shoal for more than a cable. Anchor in 5 to 7m between the disused pier and the marina, as the head of the bay known as Kames Bay dries out for about 2 cables at low water. Alternative anchorage can be had in the NW comer of the bay, well off shore. (ALF 5610·5). The marina is situated in the SW corner of the bay and is protected by a breakwater with a Fl.R.4s 4M light on the outer end. Entering Kames Bay from the N there is a Measured Distance (927.2m, 164°-344°) between Ardmaleish Pt and Undraynian Pt. though the shore from Ardmaleish Pt to Kames Bay should be given a wide berth. It is often shoal for more than 1 cable off.

Facilities

Port Bannatyne Marina provides 100 pontoon berths, all dredged to 2.5m, with water and electricity. Full onshore shower and toilet facilities will be in place for the 2010 season. Repairs and wintering for 120 boats. Shops, PO, tel, hotels. Golf course.

Interest

Kames Castle, a tower house, has its origins in the 14th century. Wester Kames, a 17th century keep is now restored.

Loch Striven

Charts

(ii) 1906—Kyles of Bute
(iv) ALF 5610·13 OS maps 63 and 56

Tides

Loch Striven Head –0020 Greenock (+0055 Dover)

General

A beautiful and isolated loch with lovely mountains and glens. Provides a number of temporary anchorages in settled conditions.

Caution

The mountains and glens in this narrow loch in fresh to strong winds, create such turbulence that squalls can be very fierce and erratic. Near the entrance to the loch there are two charted areas which may be subject to naval activities.

Approach

The entrance is opposite Port Bannatyne between Ardyne Pt on the E and Strone Pt on the W Navigation to the head of the loch is free from off shore dangers.

Anchorage

Inverchaolain. On the E side 2 miles N of Strone Pt. Temporary anchorage S of the burn. Alternatively 2 or 3 cables to the N around the point, in clear view of the church. Anchor in 5 to 8m. Fine views of Inverchaolain Glen and the mountains and glens towards the head of Loch Striven.

Ardbeg Pt. About 4 miles N of Strone Pt on the W side. North and south of Ardbeg Pt are a number of sandy beaches which provide temporary anchorages in settled conditions.

Lochhead The head of the loch dries out about 2 cables S from Lochhead. Anchorage may be had in 5 to 7m at the NE corner about 1 cable S of a house. The best protection from S'ly winds is to anchor in 5m, on the E side N of a trout farm on the point to the NW of Ardtaraig. The shore out from the burn in the SE corner is shoal for 1 cable.

Loch Riddon looking towards the East Kyle *Argyll Tourist Board*

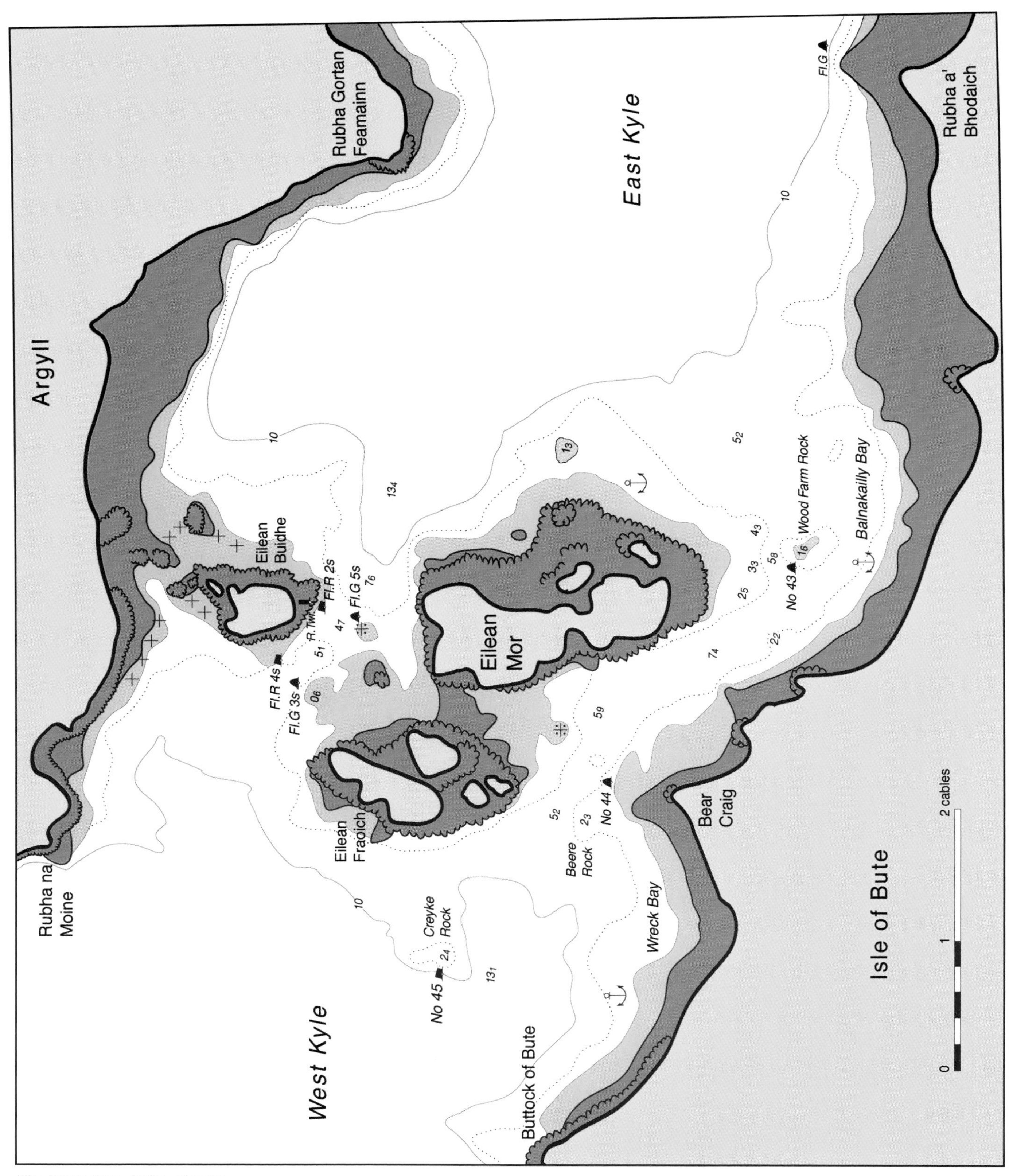

The Burnt Isles, Kyles of Bute

Kyles of Bute

Charts (ii) 1906—Kyles of Bute (iv) ALF 5610·13 & 5610·8(B) OS maps 62 and 63

General The Kyles of Bute, set between high and rugged hills on Argyll and the gentler slopes of the Island of Bute, are divided into the East and West Kyles by the Burnt Isles. The West Kyle is also known as the Kerry Kyle. These arms of the sea around the northern part of Bute offer the best protected and perhaps the most beautiful sailing waters in the Clyde Estuary. This is so particularly in the vicinity of the Burnt Isles, Caladh Harbour and Loch Riddon, where anchorages can be found which provide shelter in all winds, although, as in other channels bounded by steep slopes, fresh to strong winds can cause strong twisting gusts. The winds experienced in sailing from the Buttock of Bute to Tighnabruaich can be very flukey.

Tides Burnt Isles const. –0020 Greenock (+0055 Dover)

Tidal streams There is little tidal flow in the **East Kyle**. At Burnt Isles it attains 5 knots in the N channel and 3 knots in the S channel at springs. In the narrows at Rubha Ban it is 2 knots springs falling to 1 knot further W In the West Kyle.

Note One arm of the flood tide travels up the **West Kyle,** and then through between the Burnt Isles until it meets the other incoming flood tide coming up the East Kyle from Rothesay Sound. In settled conditions these two incoming streams meet in the vicinity of the small Church on the N shore of the East Kyle 1M S of Colintraive. In strong winds the meeting place is more uncertain. The W going stream through the narrows starts about 2 hours before HW, and the E going stream 5 hours after HW.

The buoyage priorities at the channels at the Burnt Isles and throughout the Kyles are determined by the dominant stream coming up the West Kyle.

Lights

Ardmaleish Pt on Bute	Qk Fl	N Cardinal Pillar buoy (BY)
Ru a' Bhodaich Pt. on Bute	Fl G	Green light buoy
S end of N channel at Burnt Isles.	Fl R 2s & Fl.G 5s	Red & Green light buoys
N end of N channel at Burnt Isles	Fl.R 4s & Fl G 3s	Red & Green light buoys
Off fish farm E of Rubha Ban	Fl.Y 6s & Fl.Y 4s	2 yellow buoys
Rubha Ban narrows in the W Kyle	Fl R 4s	Red light buoy
Carry Pt, N shore of W Kyle	Fl R 4s	Red light buoy
Ardlamont Pt. off Am Brideum (dr1.5)	Fl R 4s	Red light buoy

Anchorage **Colintraive** In the bay just NW of the ferry slip in 6 to 10m away from the ferry mooring buoys and clear of a cable just W of the slip. Or alternatively off the monument on the shore about 2 cables W of the ferry slip. Anchor close in as the shore is steep-to, but clear of moorings. Shop. PO. Hotel, Ferry to Bute with bus connections to Rothesay. Water at ferry slip. Visitors moorings for hotel patrons.

The Burnt Isles

Passage **The N channel** is between the S end of Eilean Buidhe, marked by a red lit buoy and a red beacon, and the N end of Eilean Mor, marked by a green lit buoy. Additionally the northern end of the channel is marked by port and starboard lit buoys. Details of the lit buoys are shown on the plan on p.30. Going W the passage, though narrow, is straight through, leaving the two red buoys on the starboard hand and the two green buoys to port.

Caution As there are many rocky patches and the remains of 2 beacon plinths SW of a line joining the 2 green buoys, keep to the recommended channel.

Once through the N channel give the N and NW of Eilean Fraoich a wide berth to avoid rocky outcrops. Depths of 4m exist through the buoyed channel but avoid passing within 5m of the southmost G buoy where there is an obstruction with a least depth of 3m.

The S channel is 'S' shaped and when proceeding NW begins with a width of less than 0.5 cable between rocky patches off the SE corner of Eilean Mor and the green buoy marking Wood Farm Rock. Enter nearer, **but not too near**, the buoy which must be left on the port hand. Swing round the channel keeping well out from the Bute shore which is shoal and out from the SW corner of Eilean Mor. Leave the green buoy off Bear Craig close to port as the channel is less than 0.5 cable wide at this point. After passing the green buoy, maintain course for 0.5 cable to avoid Beere Rock.

Caution Yachts beating through the S channel should take special care to avoid the rock NE of the Beere rock (No.44) buoy which is charted as awash at Chart Datum.

Once through the narrows the way is clear to visit Caladh Harbour, Loch Riddon or to continue passage through to the West Kyle.

Anchorage **S of Eilean Mor** in 4m. Keep clear of the rocky patch to the N.

SW of Wood Farm Rock, there is good anchorage in the bay in 3 to 4m but subject to tidal streams.

Wreck Bay between Beere Rock and the Buttock of Bute (see cover photograph). Anchor in 3 to 4m. By keeping shorewards of a line between Beere Rock and the Buttock of Bute tidal streams are avoided.

Loch Riddon

Chart (ii) 1906—Kyles of Bute. (iv) ALF 5610·13(B) & Caladh Harbour 5610·13(A) OS map 63

Approach Loch Riddon is 1/2 mile NW of the Burnt Isles and is entered between Eilean Dubh on the W and Rubha na Moine on the E. It has a length of about 3 miles but dries out for 1.5 miles at LW from Glendaruel at the head. Eilean Dearg (One Tree Island) is about 3/4 mile N of Eilean Dubh on the E side of the loch but beware of the rock (dr. 0.3m) 60m N of the island. Near HW the narrow channel between Eilean Dearg and the E shore can be safely navigated.

Anchorage **Fearnoch Bagh** (Fearnoch Bay) On the E side at the entrance to Loch Riddon. A clean bay with good anchorage in 4m at its NW side.

Ormidale On the W side of the Loch, just beyond the pier. Anchor as far inshore as moorings will allow. The loch dries out only a little further N from here. The shore shoals off the burn just to the N. This is very deceptive towards HW.

There is also a good anchorage in 4m off the E shore opposite Ormidale. To avoid entering the shoal area, do not anchor as far N as the wall on the foreshore.

Caladh Harbour

Approach A popular anchorage lying behind Eilean Dubh, at the W entrance to Loch Riddon. The **S entrance**, marked by a white beacon on its W side, opens out to a width of a cable but, passing the middle of Eilean Dubh, it narrows to 1/3 cable with rocks on either side. Keep to mid channel.

There is an islet marked by white beacon in the **N passage** leading to Loch Riddon. A red pole marks a rock on the shore N of the islet. The best passage is mid-way between the red pole and the white beacon.

Anchorage Anchor in 3m in the centre, remembering that the W side dries out some considerable way at LW.

Good anchorage can also be had off the slip in 3 to 5m outside the harbour to the S about 1/2 cable E of the white beacon. Note the spit extending 1/2 cable S just W of the entrance. Exposed to SW in which case shelter can be sought in Wreck Bay, E of the Buttock of Bute. (p.31)

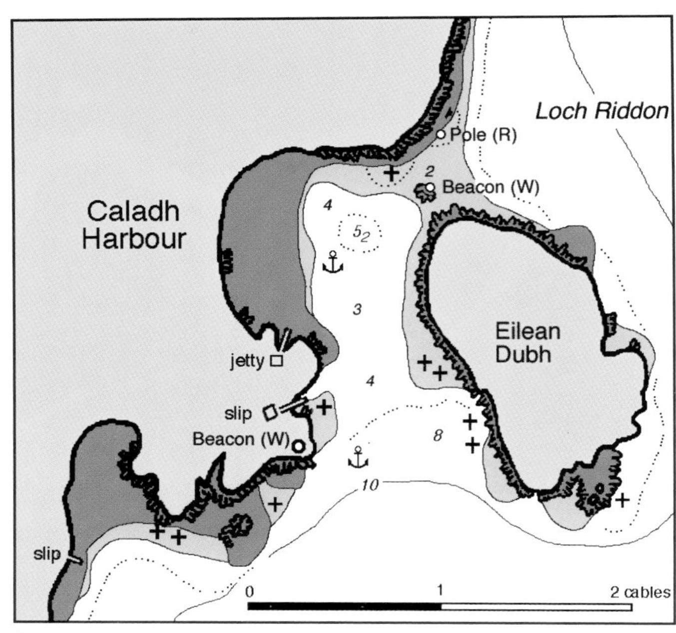

Caladh Harbour

Caladh Harbour looking North East
Mike Balmforth

The West Kyle

Chart (ii) 1906—Kyles of Bute (iv) ALF 5610·13 & 5610·9 OS map 62

General Otherwise known as the Kerry Kyle, this area provides sheltered waters and good facilities particularly for smaller craft.

Approach Keep a reasonable distance off the Buttock of Bute. There is a fish farm marked by yellow buoys between Caladh and Rubha Ban. Leave the red buoy which marks a shoal at Rubha Ban on the starboard hand when westbound. There is a spit, 3 cables S of Kames, Rubha Mor, extending offshore by 1 cable at the first power beacon on the W shore. About 2 miles S of the spit, **Carry Rock buoy,** Fl.R 4s, marks an extensive shoal off the W shore.

Anchorage **Blackfarland Bay.** On Bute, opposite Tighnabruaich. Good anchorage in 4 to 8m can be had in the centre of the bay. Approaching from the NE, keep well clear of Rubha Glas which shoals for about 1 cable, at the entrance to the bay. Sheltered from the SW. There is a rocky patch close inshore in the centre of the bay and care must be taken to avoid swinging over it if anchoring during an onshore wind.

Blindman's Bay This anchorage is about 3 miles S of Kames and is 1 mile N of Ardlamont Pt. Anchor at the S end of the bay in 6 to 8m. Anchor should be let go just before the W point of Inchmarnock closes the HW mark of the S point of the bay. Holding is not good in certain parts of the bay.

Ettrick Bay On Bute opposite Ardlamont Pt. The bay dries out for fully 2 cables at LW. Anchor near the middle of the bay in 6 to 8m. **Caution** It is to be noted that Admiralty charts warn against anchoring due to underwater obstructions. Items of interest near Ettrick Bay comprise:- stone circle about 1/2 mile NE from the shore and a stone cross near St. Colmac, also an Iron Age fort at Dunalunt about 1 mile from SE end of Ettrick Bay and Castle Cree.

The West Kyle looking North East from Kames *Margaret McBride*

Tighnabruaich

Anchorage Anchor in about 2 cables W of Rubha Ban in 6m off the slip. The shore is steep to. Moorings may be available; enquire at boatyard. Well protected from all winds. Alternatively, tie alongside the pier about 1/2 mile to the SW.

Facilities Shops in village and at pier, PO, tel, yacht and engine repairs at boatyard, Chandlery, Sailing School. EC Wednesday. Visitors moorings off hotels. Water at pier. Golf course

Interest 2 miles N there is a Wildlife Centre and Forest Trail. The Caladh Castle Forest Trail provides views over Caladh Harbour and the Kyles of Bute.

Kames

Anchorage Anchor anywhere between Tighnabruaich pier and Kames disused pier. Exposed to SW winds when Blackfarland Bay is much preferred. In E winds good anchorage can be had in the bay SE of Rubha Dubh keeping well clear of rocky outcrop at the N end.

Facilities Shops, PO, tel, hotel. Moorings available for hotel patrons.

Interest On Bute about 1 mile S of Rubha Dubh there is an old chapel and a chambered cairn.

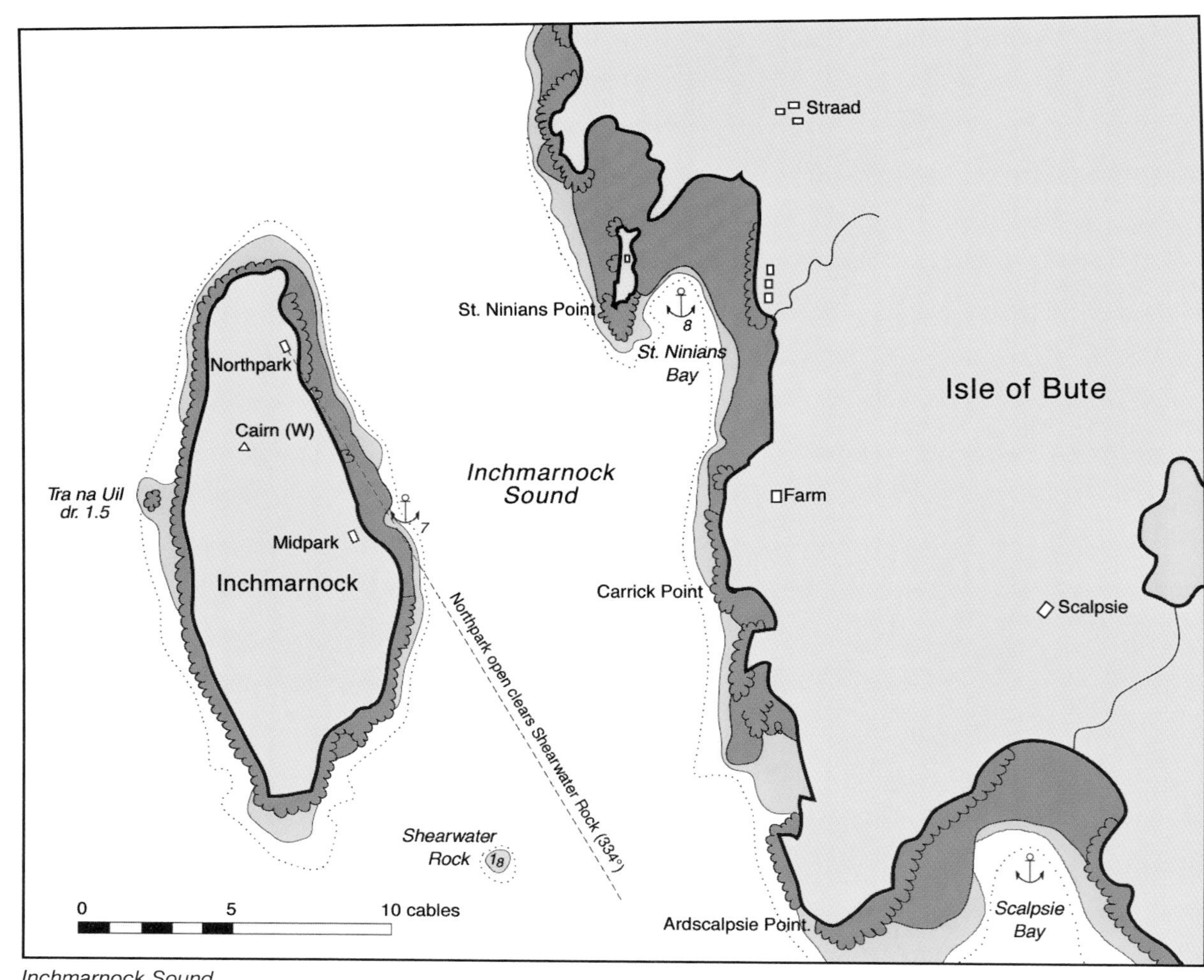

Inchmarnock Sound

Inchmarnock Sound

Charts

(ii) 2221—Firth of Clyde. Pladda to Inchmarnock Northern sheet
(ii) 2383—Inchmarnock Water
(iv) ALF 5610·6(A) & 5610·9 OS map 63

General

Inchmarnock Sound is 2 miles S of the sheltered waters of the W Kyle and between Inchmarnock Island and the SW shore of Bute.

Shearwater Rock, (min depth 1.8m) 1/2 mile SE of Inchmarnock should be given a clear berth when entering and leaving the Sound. See clearance bearing on plan. In a S'ly swell the rock could prove dangerous. **The NE point of Inchmarnock** requires to be given a berth of 1 cable to avoid a sandbar which appears to be extending.

Tides

Const. —0015 Greenock (+0100 Dover) Spring rise 3.1m Neap rise 2.2m

Anchorage

Inchmarnock On the E side of the island about 1 mile S from its N end, off Midpark Farm. Anchor in 6m. Sheltered from NW and W.

St Ninian's Bay On Bute, opposite Inchmarnock. On entry keep well clear of a spit S of St. Ninian's Pt. The head of the bay dries out for 3 cables at LW. Do not anchor N of a line joining the old buildings on the W side of the bay to the cottages on the E side. Anchor in 6 to 8m. Exposed to SW.

Scalpsie Bay On Bute, about 2 miles S of St. Ninian's Pt, NE of Ardscalpsie Pt. Approaching from the N Ardscalpsie Pt should be given a very wide berth as it shoals out 3 cables to the SE. Anchor near the centre of the bay and well off shore. Sheltered in winds W through N to E. Of interest are 2 cairns and 1 Dun at the head of the bay and a fort 1/2 mile to the W. Fort at Ardscalpsie Pt.

Dunagoil Bay just N of Garroch Head on W side of Bute. Clear sandy bay. St Blane's Chapel is nearby.

Interest

There is a ruined chapel just N of St. Ninian's Point, standing stones at NW corner of the bay and another chapel 1/2 mile to the N of the standing stones.

Lower Loch Fyne

Charts (ii) 2381—Lower Loch Fyne & 2382—Upper Loch Fyne
(iv) ALF 5610·9 & 5610·14 OS maps 55, 56 & 62

General Loch Fyne is deep and generally free from off lying dangers although there are a number of dangerous rocks which cover, close inshore.

Tides At East Loch Tarbert and Ardrishaig Const. –0005 Greenock (+0110 Dover)
At Loch Gair Const. 0000 Greenock (+0115 Dover)
At Inveraray Const. + 0010 Greenock (+0125 Dover)

Tidal streams are weak generally. In the middle of the narrows at Otter Spit the tidal stream is little more than 1 knot in either direction. Nearer the beacon on the spit it may reach a maximum of 2 knots under flood conditions.

Lights

Ardlamont Pt Red can light buoy	Fl R 4s	
Skipness Pt Red can light buoy	Fl R	At W side of entrance to Loch Fyne
Sgat Mor Light (Skate island)	Fl W 3s 9m 12M	At E side of entrance to Loch Fyne
East Loch Tarbert Entrance beacon	Fl R 2.5s	
Ardrishaig Approach sector Lt	L.Fl WRG	

Approach Entering Loch Fyne from the West Kyle, give Ardlamont Pt, from which extends a long rocky ledge, a wide berth. The point is marked by a red buoy Fl.R. 4s. Resist any temptation to cut inside the buoy. A rock with less than 2m lies 2c SW of the buoy. Giving the shore a reasonable offing clears all hazards until Sgat Mor (Skate island) which is 4 miles from Ardlamont Pt.

Sgat Mor has extensive rocky patches around it, particularly a rocky patch 1.5 cables from its E side. There is a dangerous underwater rock 1.5 cables E of the white round tower light on the S end of Sgat Mor. The channel between the island and the peninsula Eilean Aoidhe is almost 2 cables wide and a safe passage may be easily made by keeping to mid channel.

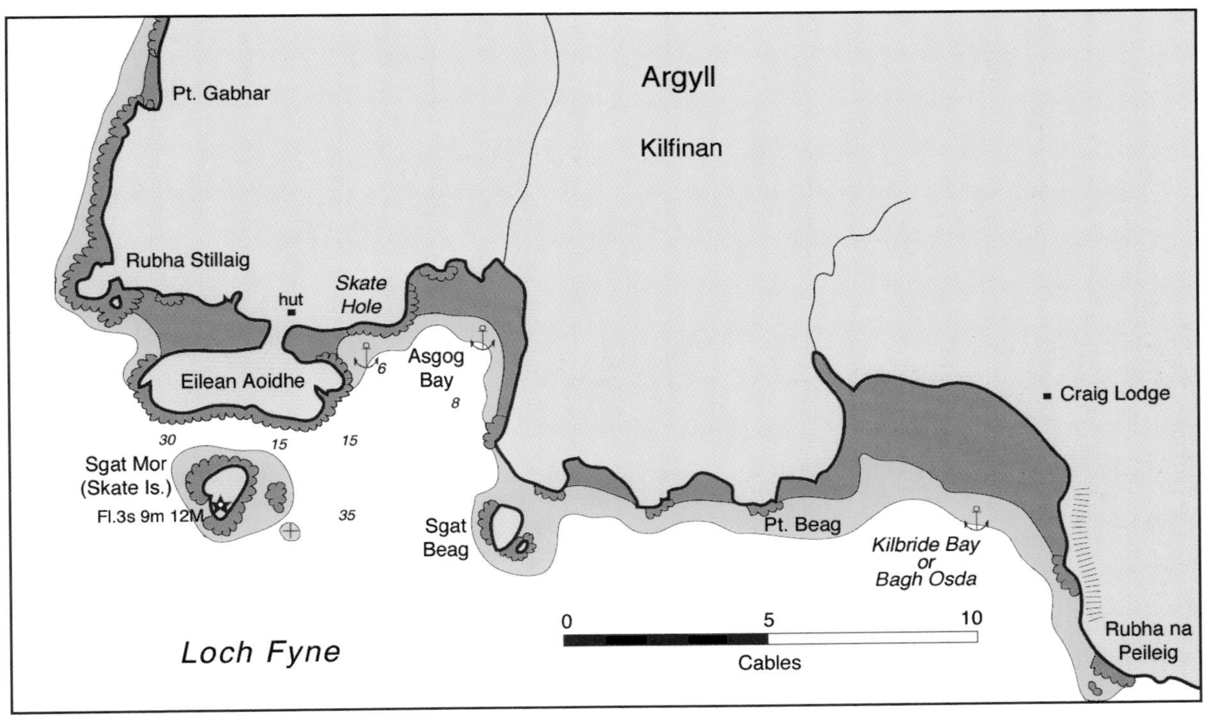

Skate Hole & Asgog Bay

Anchorage **Kilbride Bay** or **Bagh Osde.** This wide bay about 2 miles from Ardlamont Pt provides temporary anchorage in offshore winds. Anchor at the centre of the bay in 6 to 8m. The head of the bay dries out for 3 cables.

Skate Hole and **Asgog Bay** About 4 miles from Ardlamont Pt. These anchorages are both entered between Sgat Mor (Skate Island) and Sgat Beag (Little Skate Island). Keep well off Sgat Mor. As Asgog Bay opens out, enter mid-channel giving Sgat Beag a reasonable offing. In **Asgog Bay** the head dries out for at least a cable. In **Skate Hole** the anchorage is in 4m, just inside the points of this little bay. The greater part of the bay dries out. It is a reasonably protected anchorage but is exposed to the S. **Interest**: Nearby Cairn, Standing Stone and Standing Stones. Old Chapel near Stillaig Farm.

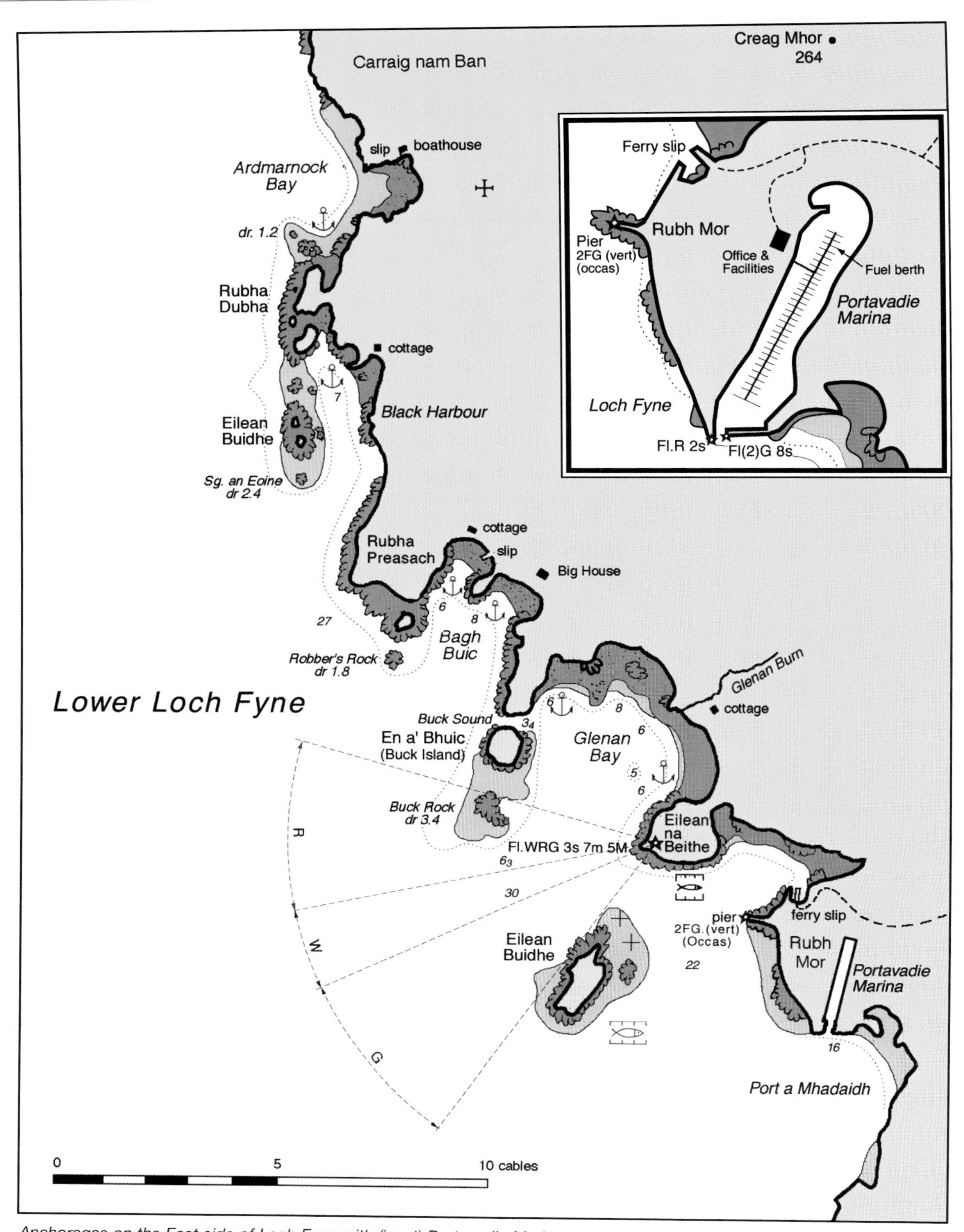

Anchorages on the East side of Loch Fyne with (inset) Portavadie Marina.

Lower Loch Fyne - East side

Chart (ii) 2381—Lower Loch Fyne (iv) ALF 5610·14 OS map 62

Marina **Portavadie Marina,** 1.5M N of Sgat Mhor. This new marina has been created from a dock originally built for oil rig construction but never used. Following recent development it now offers 230 fully serviced berths for boats up to 21m loa. Onshore facilities include toilets, showers and laundrette with a bar, restaurant, chandlery and self catering apartments due for completion during 2008. There are no obstructions in the approach which is between breakwaters (LD 4.5m) lit as shown on the inset plan above. Diesel, petrol, gas, slip, and winter storage. Contact on VHF ch. 80, Tel 01700 811075.

Lower Loch Fyne - East Side (continued)

Anchorage

Port a Mhadaidh. The bay to the S of Portavadie Marina is exposed, shelves quite abruptly and is not recommended for anchoring. The bay to the N of Rubh Mor, SE of Eilean na Beithe, is almost wholly occupied by fish cages, their moorings and marker buoys, and the only clear but narrow channel is required for the Tarbert - Portavadie vehicle ferry for access to the slip NE of the pier. The pier light 2FG (vert) is rarely lit but there is a fish farm floodlight to the S usually lit. The Lt beacon on W"ly point of Eilean na Beithe shows sectored light Fl WRG

Glenan Bay Opposite E Loch Tarbert, 2 miles N of Skate island. If entering between Eilean Buidhe and Buck Rock, give the latter a wide berth. Buck Rock covers only at HW springs but would be difficult to see at night. Anchor in 6 to 8m. If entering the bay coming from Port a Mhadaidh keep well off the E side of Eilean Buidhe as it has rocky outcrops for more than a cable, also keep clear of fish farm S of Eilean na Beithe. The bay can also be entered through Buck Sound which is a narrow channel, depth 3.4m, between Eilean Bhuic (Buck island) and the mainland. The anchorage is exposed to SW winds.
In suitable conditions anchorage may be had in the E corner of the bay N of Eilean na Beithe. Here the shore shoals out a significant distance. **Interest**: Follow Glenan Burn to ruined village There is a forest walk E of the bay, S of the holiday cottage.

Bagh Buic (Buck Bay) Connected to Glenan Bay by way of Buck Sound. Entering from the N there is a drying rock (Robber's Rock) off Rubha Preasach. Once inside the bay it is safe to proceed to anchor in 4 to 6m in the SE corner, or in 4 to 6m in the NW. Exposed to SW winds. **Interest**: Vitrified fort nearby.

Black Harbour 1 mile N of Glenan Bay. At the entrance a rock, Sgeir an Eoine off the S end of Eilean Buidhe, dries 2.4m and must be given a wide berth. Entering from the S follow the E shore from Rubha Preasach towards the cottage. This approach clears Sgeir an Eoine and the numerous rocks around Eilean Buidhe. Anchor in 5 to 7m with the cottage still in view. Exposed to SW winds. **Caution** Approaching Black Harbour from the N the danger of mistaking the numerous gaps between the islets for the entrance, can be avoided by entering at Rubha Preasach as for S approach. **Interest**: Long cairn E of Black Harbour.

Ardmarnock Bay (Auchanachar Bay) 1/2 mile N of Black Harbour. The W side of the bay is protected by a series of islets and rocks extending for 2 cables N of Rubha Dubh. The most N'ly rock dries 1.2m and must be given a good clearance when entering from the S. The boathouse on the shore kept under a dip on the N shoulder of Creag Mhor bearing 062° clears N of the rock (dr. 1.2m). Anchor in 2 to 5m just E of the protecting rocks. Exposed to winds from SW to NW.

Auchalick Bay and **Kilfinan Bay** offer good anchorages in offshore winds or settled conditions. These bays are 1 and 3 miles respectively N of Ardmarnock Bay. Exposed to the SW. Note there are fish cages moored offshore between Auchalick and Kilfinan Bays.

Caution

Glenan Bay, Buck Bay, Black Harbour and Ardmarnock Bay should be approached with care as their appearance is similar and they could easily be taken for each other.

Lower Loch Fyne - Scottish Series *Mike Balmforth*

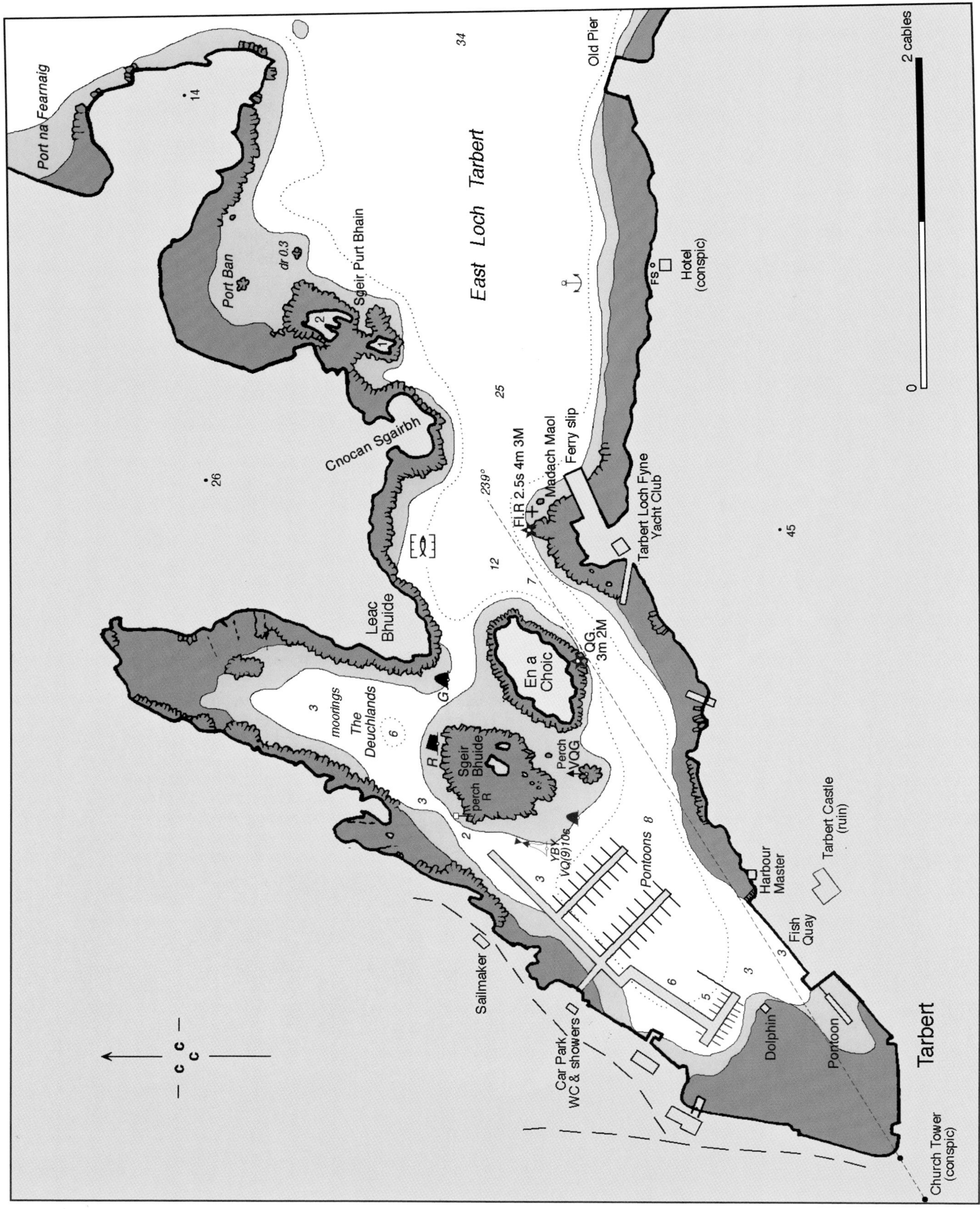

East Loch Tarbert

East Loch Tarbert

Chart (ii) 2381—Lower Loch Fyne
(iv) ALF 5610·12(D)

General East Loch Tarbert is on the W side of Loch Fyne about 7 miles N of Skipness Pt which should be given a good offing. It is a perfect natural harbour but its entrances are narrow. Within the entrances, Eilean a Choic (Cock Island) and Sgeir Bhuide divide the anchorage into two, the main harbour and the Deuchlands (Dubh-chaol Linne).

Lights At entrance, Madadh Maol Fl R 2.5s 4m 3M
Eilean a Choic (Cock Island) QG 3m 2M
G. Perch SW of En a Choic VQG

Tarbert Harbour *Ronald M Cowan ABIPP*

Approach (i) **Main Harbour** The entry to the main harbour, although narrow is well marked. Speed limit 5 knots. After passing the old steamer pier on the S shore, make for the red beacon marking the rocks extending from the point, where the ferry slip is situated. Pass N of this beacon and then turn to port to pass S of the Green Perch, QG, S of Cock Isle. Also pass S and W of the next green beacon, VQG, marking the rocks to the SW of Cock Isle.

(ii) **The Deuchlands**. (Dubh-choal Linne) Entering the Deuchlands passage keep well off the N end of Cock Island and leave the green buoy, marking the rocky outcrops off Leac Bhuide, to starboard. To enter the Deuchlands, alter course northwards when the submerged rocks off Leac Bhuidhe can be safely cleared and pass mid channel with the red buoy on the port hand. A rock which covers at HW lies towards the head of the Deuchlands and beyond this the bay shoals. There is a passage between the main harbour and the Deuchlands passing to the N of Sgeir Bhuidhe. Give the red W cardinal perch a prudent offing.

Anchorage Tarbert Harbour Authority provides pontoons for yachts on the N side of the harbour and berthing facilities have recently been expanded to accommodate over 120 visitors in addition to residents. Large yachts may use the SW end of the fish quay by arrangement with H.M. VHF ch.14 and tel. 01880 820344. The Harbour Authority also provides a few swinging moorings in the middle of the main harbour. The Deuchlands is very full of private moorings and the anchoring space there is difficult to find. If anchoring in the main harbour keep clear of moorings and fairway to fish quay. A tripping line is essential.

Facilities Shops, PO, hotels, tel, craft shops, Sailmaker, Chandlery, Calor gas, petrol and diesel. Water and electricity at pontoons. Toilets and showers. EC Wednesday. Bus connection to Glasgow and Campbeltown. Slip at Yacht Club. Chart Agent. Leitch, the Sailmaker. Yachts may dry out at Dolphin or in the inner harbour. Car ferry to Portavadie leaves the slip by the Y.C. The car ferry to Islay and Jura leaves from West Loch Tarbert. Doctor, Dentist. Golf Course at West Loch Tarbert 1 mile.

Interest Above the Harbour stands the ruin of the tower built by James 1V in the late 15th century, as an extension to the original castle which in the 14th century had been used by King Robert the Bruce. The remains of the two drum towers may be seen.There is a forest walk past the castle, access to which is opposite the fish quay by the old police house.

Lower Loch Fyne (West side)

Anchorage **Tarbert Harbour entrance** There is a relatively exposed anchorage outside the narrow entrance to Tarbert Harbour in 6m off the Columba Hotel, W of the old steamer pier. Well sheltered in all but easterly winds.

Barmore Island This peninsula is about 1.5 miles N of East Loch Tarbert and has good temporary anchorages in both the north and south bays. Visitor's moorings in N bay for patrons of Stonefield Castle Hotel.

South Bay: Entry presents no difficulty. Anchor not far within the bay as it dries out fully half way at LW.

North Bay: Great care must be taken entering or leaving North Bay to avoid the group of rocks, Sgeir Mhaola Cinn (dries 1.8m), which lies about 2 cables off the N end of Barmore Is. and have frequently trapped the unwary. There is a BY perch with a CCC triangular topmark on this rocky patch. Give this perch a wide berth as the rocks extend some distance N of it. Anchor anywhere in the bay clear of the moorings provided by the hotel for its patrons. Soundings are deep. The rocks Sgeir nam Bo (dries 2.5m) 1 cable E and Sgeir Leathan 1 cable NE of Barmore Island can be avoided by keeping well out from the peninsula.

Note There is an unlit Admiralty buoy off Ard nan Ron about 1 mile N of Barmore Is.

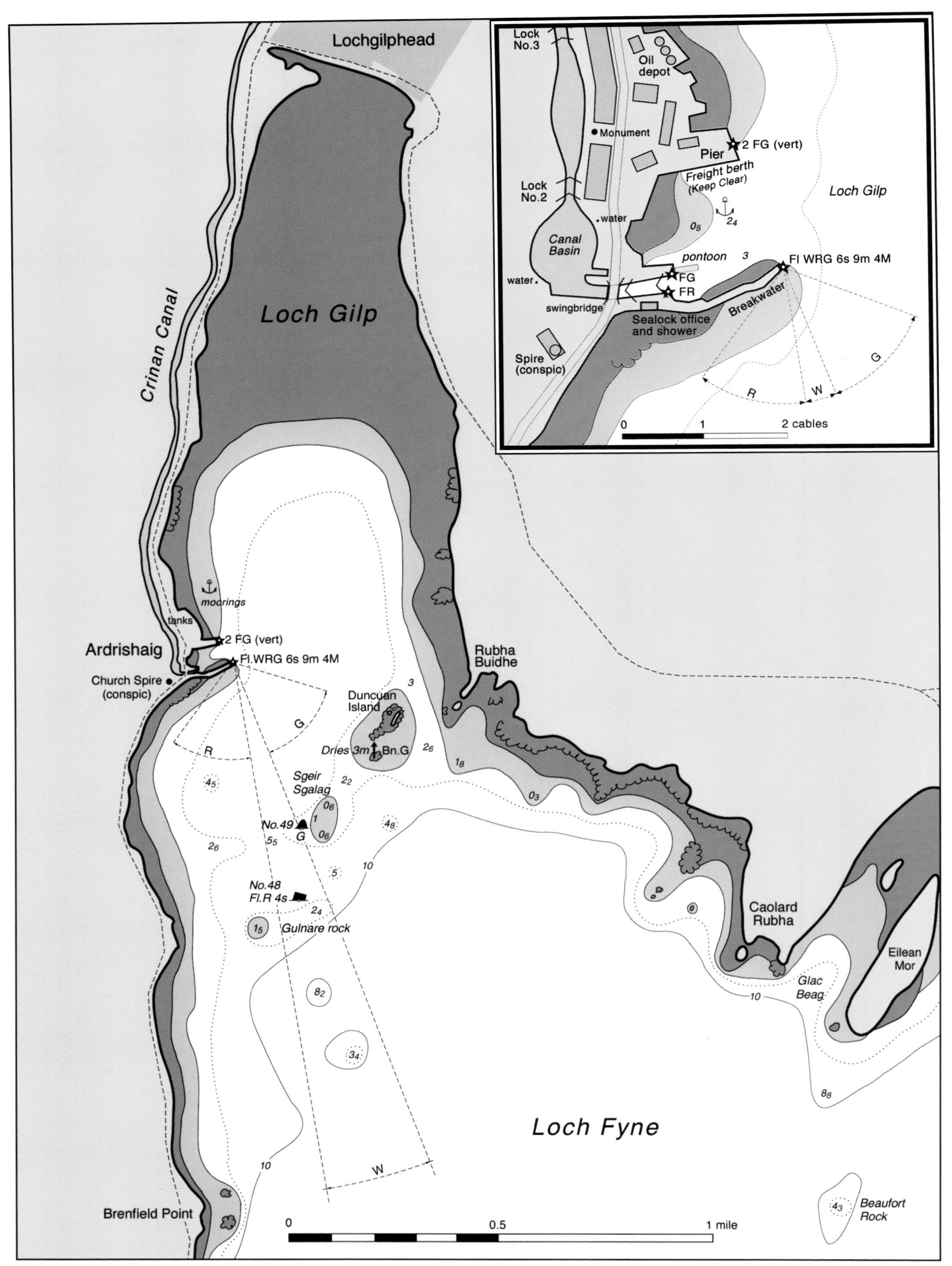

Loch Gilp and Ardrishaig Harbour (inset)

Loch Gilp & Ardrishaig

Charts (ii) 2381—Lower Loch Fyne.
(iv) ALF 5610·14(B) & (C) OS map 55

General Ardrishaig marks the E entrance to the Crinan Canal which is entered through the sealock behind the breakwater.

Lights

Ardrishaig breakwater	L Fl WRG 6s 9m 4M	White Tower
Ardrishaig pier	2 FG (vert)	
Entrance channel	Fl R 4s	Red can buoy
	Unlit	Green conical buoy No.49

Approach From the S leaving Barmore Island well to port, there are no dangers for almost 5 miles until Big Rock, with 2m over it, 1 mile NE of Rubha Mhinidhe Beag. Within a mile of Ardrishaig breakwater there are many dangerous rocks and shoal patches to be avoided. The most S'ly of these is a rocky patch with 3.4m over it about 3/4 mile from the breakwater. A red lit buoy marks the Gulnare Rock (2.4m over it) on the E side of a rocky shoal whose least depth is 1.5m. A green lit buoy marks Sgeir Sgalag (0.6m over it). Another rock (dries 3m) marked by a G Bn. lies on the S side of a rocky spit extending nearly 4 cables off Duncuan Island. The preferred approach to the breakwater at Ardrishaig is to leave the red buoy on the port hand and the green buoy on the starboard hand.

Note: It is advisable to leave Loch Gilp using the channel marked by the green and red buoys. However if going in the direction of the Narrows at Otter Spit, there is a channel of less than 2 cables width and a least depth of 2.2m between the green beacon off Duncuan Island and Sgeir Sgalag (with 0.6m over it). Keep closer to the beacon side which must be left to port.

Cautions At night follow the white sector of the Ardrishaig breakwater Lt and leave the red lit buoy to port, then make towards the breakwater light. The red sector light approximately covers the Gulnare Rock and shoal patch. The green sector light covers Sgeir Sgalag to Duncuan Is. Note this light is 20m from the end of the breakwater and is difficult to distinguish from a street light.
If approaching Loch Gilp from the E beware of the Beaufort Rk (4.3m over it) about 1/2 mile S of Eilean Mor. The Beaufort Rk, like Big Rk, could present dangers in a S'ly swell.

Anchorage Good anchorage in 4m can be had off the oil depot, 2 cables N of the pier among the moorings. Do not anchor much beyond the Argyll Hotel near the small landing jetty with steps, as Loch Gilp dries out at LW from about 1/2 mile N of the breakwater right to the head of the loch. In strong SW winds shelter should be sought behind the breakwater or better within the Canal sealock which is always kept open at night.

Facilities Shops, PO, tel, hotels, Calor gas, petrol, diesel at garage, boatyard, chandlers, water at taps round canal basin and at pier. EC—Ardrishaig—Wednesday, Lochgilphead—Tuesday. Bus connections to Glasgow and Campbeltown. Taxi, Ardrishaig 07850 645671.

The Crinan Canal

General The Crinan Canal is open seven days per week in peak season, Monday to Saturday during spring and autumn and Monday to Friday during the winter. Locking may commence in either direction at 0800, except in winter when it commences at 0900. Details of exact dates and times should be confirmed with the Canal office or lock keepers (see below) as these may be subject to variation from time to time.

The canal is largely a do-it-yourself one except for the bridges, lock 14 and the sealocks which are fully manned at intervals throughout the day. The Passbill, the periods of working hours, charges, conditions and a copy of the "Skipper's Guide" describing the operation of locks etc. are obtainable from the Canal office at Ardrishaig (Tel: 01546 603210) or the lock-keeper at Crinan (Tel: 01546 830285). Yachtsmen are advised to obtain this information beforehand. The likely passage time is about 5 hours but water shortage or other circumstances could result in delays. Canal dues are paid at both sea locks. Lock keepers at sea locks listen Channel 74.

Tides Ardrishaig const. –0005 HW Greenock (+0110 HW Dover) Sp rise 3.3m Np 2.8m
Crinan const. –0045 HW Oban (–0605 HW Dover) Sp rise 2.4m Np 1 .7m

Approach Approaching the sealock, steer a course parallel but not close to the breakwater as the channel of entry is narrow and shoal on either side. It is helpful if yachtsmen intending to use the canal tie up inside the sealock, which is always kept open overnight and can be entered at any state of the tide. Alternatively tie up at the pontoon outside the sealock or anchor between the breakwater and the pier.

Max length Length overall 88ft (26.8m), breadth 20ft (6.1m), draft 9ft (2.9m), maximum height under cables 95ft (29.2m)

Safety For details of British Waterways Boat Safety Scheme see conditions printed in Appendix 1.

The Crinan Canal (continued)

Passage

The passage from Ardrishaig to Crinan is 9 miles. The canal consists of 15 locks and 7 bridges. It may be convenient to see it as divided into the following sections.

The rise to the summit:
a. Sealock, bridge, basin, 2 locks and a third lock with bridge ending 1/2 mile from Ardrishaig.
b. A run for 3.5 miles through the E long reach to Cairnbaan with 1 bridge (Oakfield Wharf Bridge near Lochgilphead).
c. A bridge and 4 locks to the summit.
d. The summit reach for about 1/2 mile to lock 9 at the fresh water loch.

The descent to Crinan:
a. 5 locks with Dunardry Bridge about 3.5 miles from Crinan
b. Two clear passages of about a mile each to Bellanoch Bridge and then to Crinan Bridge.
c. A final mile to lock 14, basin and sealock at Crinan.

Note

Before entering the canal
1. Before entering the sealock, have fenders on each side to protect the boat from rubbing the walls of the canal or other vessels.
2. Have ready two check ropes of at least 16 to 18m each with a 1/2 m diameter bowline on the throwing end with the other end attached to bow or stern.
3. At the sealocks only, throw the line at the bow first to check the effects of the outflow due to water spill. At all other inland locks the stem rope should be thrown first to assist checking the boat's forward motion.

During the locking operation
1. To protect your own vessel and others, the boat should remain in a fixed position within the lock. This is not always easy to achieve as the changing water level necessitates frequent rope adjustments through fairleads.
2. During the climb to the summit, the rush of water filling the locks can seem alarming and unless the boat is kept fixed firmly It may move with possible resultant damage.
3. To counter the effect of this fast flow, keep the vessel's bow into the lock side. This can best be done by leading the bow rope to an anchor or sheet winch and keeping it tight.

On leaving the lock
1. During the climb to the summit, release the bow rope after the stern one as the water flow is against the direction of the boat's motion.
2. During the descent from the summit, release the stern rope last as the stream is with you.

Throughout the passage of the canal
1. It is necessary for 1 or 2 members of the crew of each vessel to go ashore at each set of locks to assist in the lock operation. These duties include securing and releasing ropes, operating sluice gates and manually opening and closing lock gates. Whilst it is possible for a family to take their vessel through on their own, it is very helpful and quicker to be part of a team of boats working together, sharing the operations.

Caution

The presence of fresh to strong winds will affect increasingly the ease with which boats may enter or leave the locks. Occasionally it may be necessary to warp boats between the locks which are close together.
The canal narrows over the last mile or so to Crinan and the corner after Crinan Bridge should be taken carefully at reduced speed as many boats moor there.

Facilities

Ardrishaig: Shops, hotel, PO, tel,Calor gas, petrol, boatyard, yacht charters. Water at taps around basin. Shower facilities at pier square. EC Wednesday. Bus connections to Glasgow and Campbeltown. Taxi, Ardrishaig 07850 645671

Lochgilphead: Shops, EC Tuesday.

Cairnbaan: Hotel at lock 5 and shop at lock 8.

Bellanoch Bridge: Shop, PO, tel, petrol

Crinan: Hotel, tel, Calor gas, diesel and petrol. Water at taps round basin. Boatbuilders engineers and chandlers. Call Crinan Boats office hours only VHF Ch 16/12. Slip for dinghies below hotel. Long term berthing (1 week to 1 year) can now be purchased on arrival at the sea locks.

Boat park facility is now available for winter storage at lock 5, Cairnbaan.

Toilet/showers are provided alongside the canal at 4 locations; Ardrishaig pier; lock 5, Cairnbaan; lock 11 and Bellanoch bridge. A "Watermate" key is provided upon payment of canal dues.

Anchorage

1. The vessel in passage through the canal is entitled to free mooring for 1 night. Overnight mooring may be had at the Jetties provided.
2. On leaving the sealock at Crinan, anchorage may he had to the E of and clear of the canal entrance. Anchorage is also available in Crinan Harbour to the W and S of the entrance. Moorings in Crinan Harbour may also be hired.

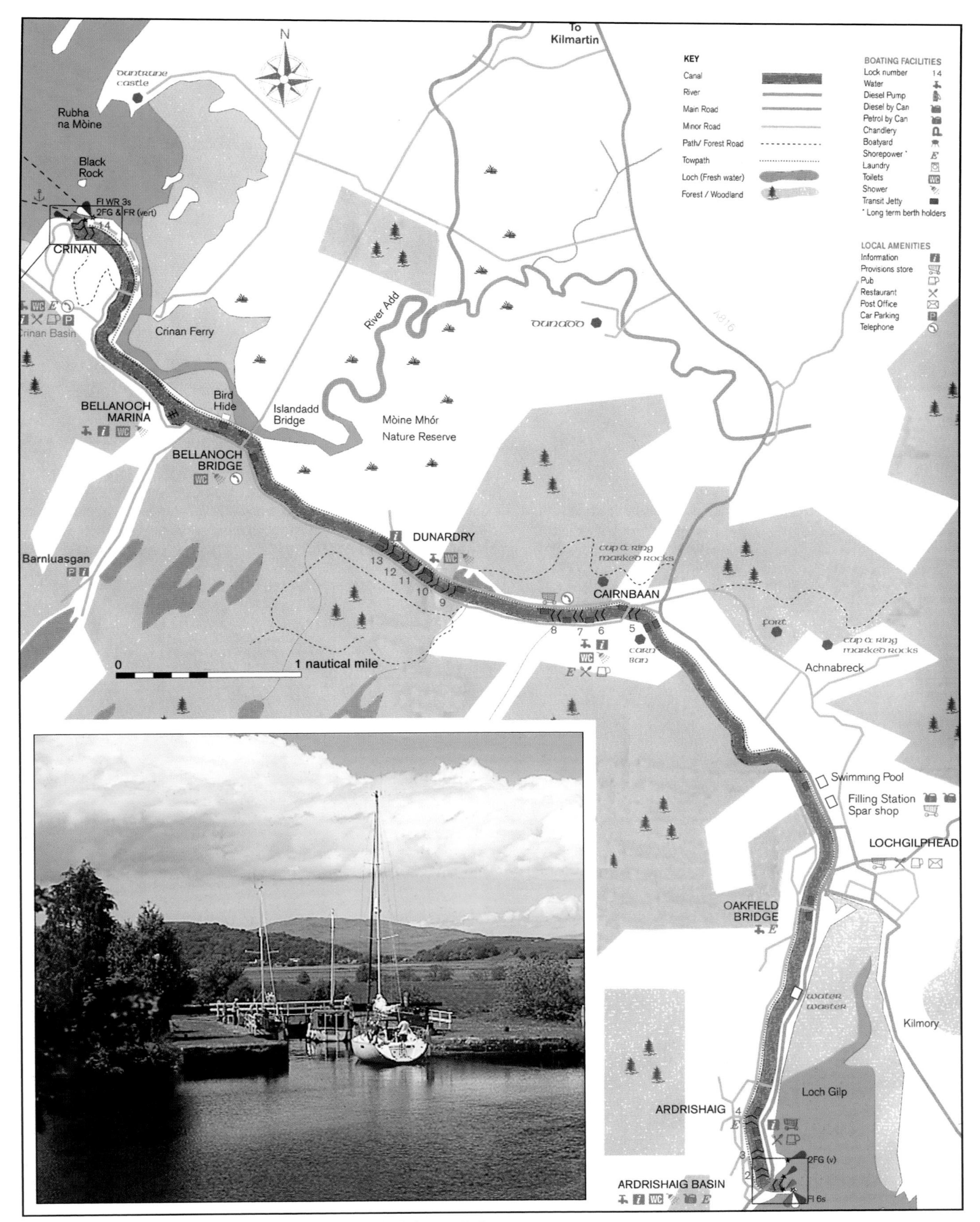

Crinan Canal © British Waterways and reproduced with their permission

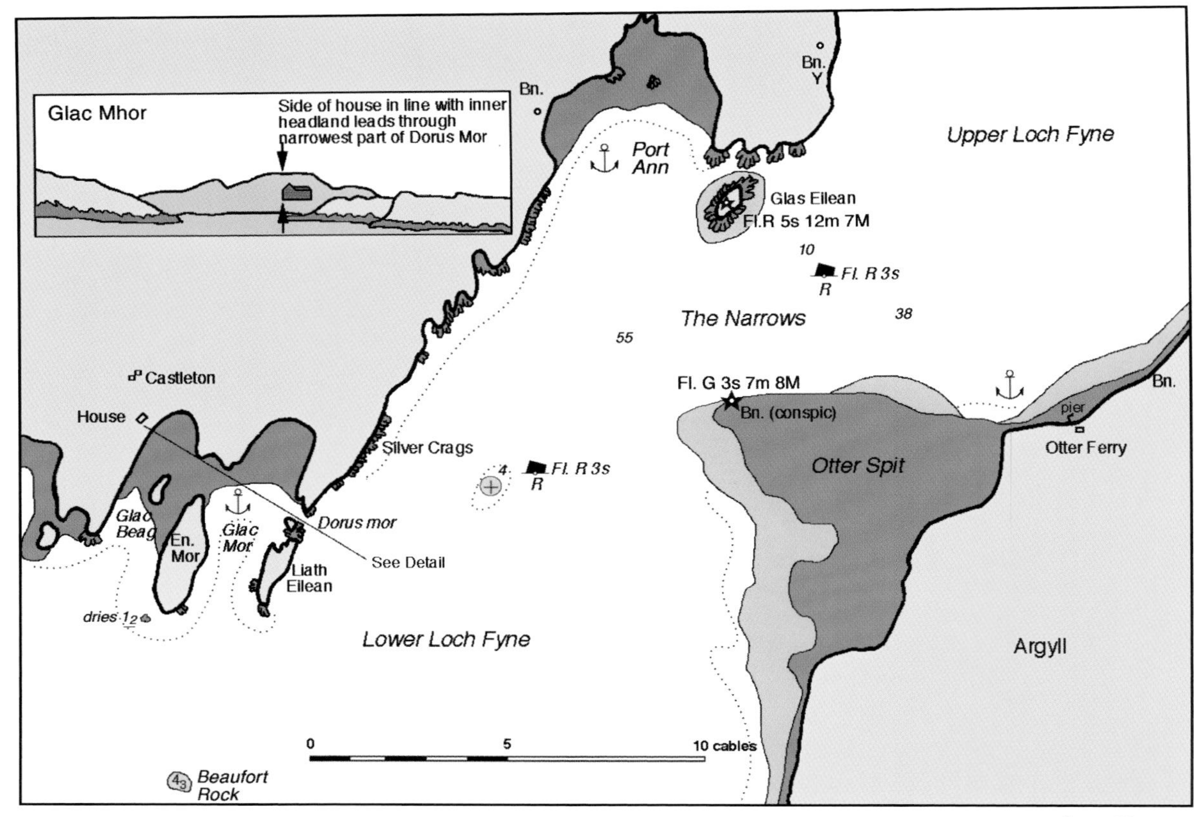

Otter Narrows

Otter Narrows

Charts (ii) 2381—Lower Loch Fyne & 2382—Upper Loch Fyne.
(iv) ALF 5610·14 OS maps 55, 56

Tides Inveraray Const. +0010 Greenock (+0125 Dover)
Tidal streams not more than 2 knots at springs.

Lights

SW of the Narrows	Fl R 3s	Red can light buoy
Otter Spit Beacon	Fl G 3s 7m 8M	Green tank on concrete pyramid.
Glas Eilean Beacon	Fl R 5s 12m 7M	Red column on pedestal
NE of the Narrows	Fl R 3s	Red can light buoy

Approach Upper Loch Fyne is entered through the Narrows between Otter Spit to the S which extends more than 6 cables out from the E side, and Eilean Glas to the N. Both are marked by beacons. The channel is at least 4 cables wide and the tide near Eilean Glas is never more than 1 knot. Nearer the Spit it may reach 2 knots. It is reported (2009) that a shallow shingle bank extends some distance WSW of the Otter Spit beacon which should be therefore be given a berth of at least 250 m. The two red buoys before and at the Narrows mark shoal patches. They may both be passed on either hand but keep well off the southern buoy if passing to the W of it.

Anchorage **Otter Ferry** About 1 mile from the Narrows on the E side of the loch. Anchor in 5m behind the moorings near the stone pier. There are **5 visitors moorings** and a dinghy pontoon. Exposed to N to NW winds but well protected from SW winds. Shop, PO, tel, water at craft shop (old Primary school). Pub/Restaurant. A small boat could be slipped from the beach. Landing at LW easier than at Loch Gair.

Glac Mhor (Castleton Bay) The larger of two bays about 2 miles E of Ardrishaig.The smaller bay, Glac Beag, dries out almost to its mouth at LW. Enter between Eilean Mor and Liath Eilean. Keep well clear of the S end of Eilean Mor and avoid a rock which dries 1 2m. Proceed mid channel between the two islets until a house opens out on the port side and the 2 channels separating Liath Eilean from the shore, on the starboard side, are abeam. Anchor in 3 to 5m well out from the house. Both arms of the bay shoal badly. Exposed from the S to SW. This anchorage may also be entered from the E through Dorus Mor passing slightly N of mid channel to avoid a reef on the islet side, altering course to port when through to miss the sand spit extending W from the Sliver Craigs side. Beautiful and remote view of Loch Fyne and beyond to Arran.

Port Ann Opposite Otter Spit. Approaching from the S keep at least 1.5 cables off the shoal patch marked by the red buoy. Glas Eilean, which has a red beacon on its S end helps enclose the E side of the bay. The head of the bay dries out for at least a cable but good anchorage can be found off the W shore In 5m to 8m. The channel to the N of Eilean Glas is about 1/2 cable wide and has a least depth of 8m. As the islet and the shore have rocky outcrops, keep mid channel.

Largimore A chalet village about 1 mile NE of Otter Ferry is a temporary anchorage which may provide moorings for visiting yachtsmen. Shop, petrol, water at shop. Concrete slip for launching yachts and small craft.

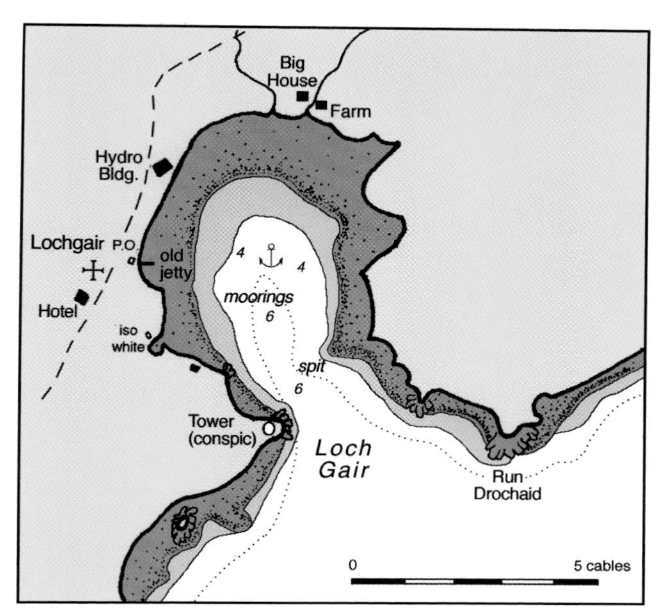

Loch Gair

Loch Gair

Chart (ii) 2382—Upper Loch Fyne. (iv) ALF 5610·14(E) OS map 55

Approach On the W side about 3 miles above the Narrows. Approaching from the S keep well away from the shore to avoid Clach Garbh (Carraig Geur, dr. 1.5m) one cable offshore and about 1 mile N of Glas Eilean.

The SW side of the entrance to Loch Gair is marked by a conspicuous square tower. Both sides of the entrance channel have shoal banks extending from them which reduce the width to about 1 cable. To enter, hold to the W side of the channel. By now the Big House should be seen over the spit. Set a course for the Hydro Plant building towards the NW corner of the loch. **Entering from the N** keep well off Run Drochaid at the entrance to the loch as rocks, which cover, extend from it.

Anchorage This is a well sheltered anchorage. The shores of the loch dry out at low water for about a cable. Anchor in 4m in the centre of the loch among the moorings well off the village. Alternatively to be clear of moorings, anchor E of a line between the Big House and the Square Tower. Row ashore to the old stone jetty until about mid-tide. It is then easier to row to the shore near the Hydro building.

Facilities Hotel caters for yachtsmen, PO, tel, water available near PO.

Loch Gair anchorage *Edward Mason*

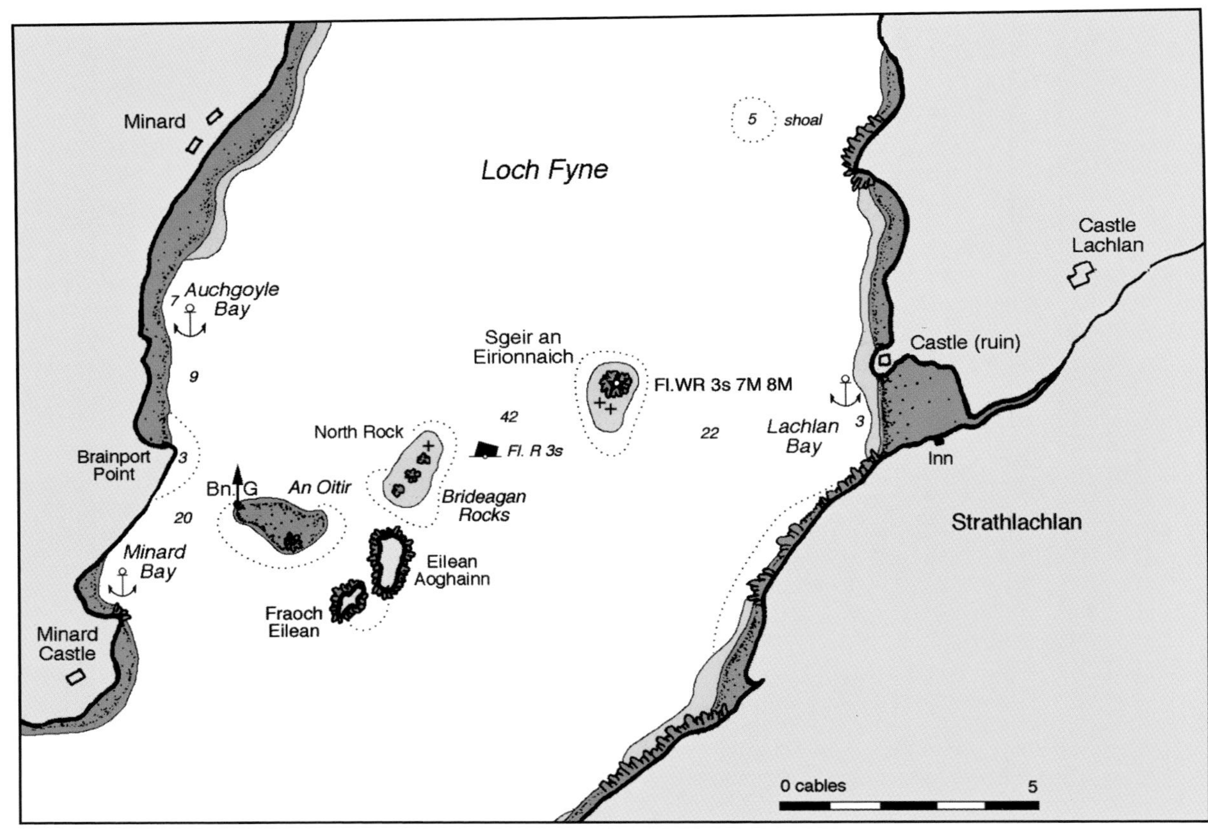

Minard Narrows

Minard Narrows

Chart (ii) 2382—Upper Loch Fyne. OS maps 55 and 56

Lights

Sgeir an Eirionnaich (Paddy Rock)	Fl.WR 3s 7m 8M	Bk. framework twr. on base - Wh. stripes
Brideagan Rocks	Fl.R 3s	Red can Lt buoy

Tides Tidal streams in the Minard Narrows are unlikely to exceed 1 knot.

Approach With reasonable care there are three easy passages to choose from between the islets, rocks and shoal patches which obstruct the fairway of the loch off Minard. Going North these are:

i) A channel on the W side of the narrows of at least 1 cable between the green beacon near An Oitir (Otter Rock) and the shore at Brainport Point. Pass close to mid channel, slightly nearer the beacon, leaving it on the starboard hand.

ii) A channel of at least 2 cables between the red lit buoy E of North Rock and Sgeir an Eirionnaich (Paddy Rock). Pass close to mid- channel slightly nearer the red lit buoy, leaving it to port.

iii) A channel on the E side of the narrows of at least 4 cables between Sgeir an Eirionnaich (Paddy Rock) and the E shore of the loch.

Anchorage **Minard Bay** At the narrows on the W side of the loch. Enter the bay keeping well clear of the S entrance. Anchor in 8m. Sheltered from the SW

Lachlan Bay 1.5 miles on the other side of the loch from Minard, should be visited only in settled weather as it offers only temporary anchorage at N end of the bay in 2-3m with NW edge of castle bearing 055°. The bay is noted for Old Castle Lachlan, 15th century keep and bailey. A nearby inn offers hospitality.
Caution: If making for Lachlan Bay from Minard Bay and a N passage is chosen, beware of the North Rock (depth 1.5m over it) and the shoal patch extending about 1/2 cable N of it. The red buoy marking those hazards is 1 cable due E of North Rock.

Auchgoyle Bay On the W side just N of the Narrows. Anchor in 8m anywhere suitable along this shore. Close by the S end of Crarae Pt beneath the conspicuous flag staff but W of the burn may offer some protection from NW winds. Exposed to SW. Shop, PO, tel, water available in Minard village. Neolithic chambered Cairn at Crarae in Lodge gardens. These famous woodland gardens are open to the public.

Upper Loch Fyne

Chart (ii) 2382—Upper Loch Fyne. (iv) ALF 5610·14 & 5610·14(D) OS maps 55 & 56

General Above Minard Narrows gives access to the upper reaches of Loch Fyne, an area which is generally safe and free from off-shore dangers, although there can be violent directional changes of wind in fresh to strong winds. The winds however in Upper Loch Fyne are in general less fierce than can be experienced in the lower reaches of the loch and shelter may be had from the prevailing wind by suitable choice of anchorage or, if under passage, suitable choice of loch side. The usual effects of wind on water allows one to choose the calmer side. Inveraray is 10 miles and Cairndow, near the head of the loch, is about 14 miles from Minard Narrows.

Anchorage **Newton Bay** About 4 miles N of Minard Narrows on the E side of the loch. Entering give the islet at the W entrance a reasonable clearance. The little bay just E of the islet offers good temporary anchorage. The best anchorage may be had off the village out from the moorings in 8m. Good protection from the SW.

Strachur Bay 3 miles NE of Newton Bay. The best anchorage, although exposed, may be had near the moorings at the S of the bay. The N shore shoals badly and an obstruction has been reported at the edge of the shoal area. There are **2 visitor's moorings** for use by patrons of the Creggans Inn. Showers may also be available at this hotel. Hotels, PO, tel, shops at Clachan, Calor gas. EC Wednesday.

St Catherine's On the E side 4 miles N of Strachur. Slip for small boat launching at hotel. Shops, PO, tel.

Calrndow The head of the loch dries out 3 cables at LW. Anchor to the S of the point before Cairndow opposite Ardkinglas House well offshore in 6m.The shore is very shoal NE of this and the whole bay off the village of Cairndow dries out at LW. Extensive fish farming operations extend across much of the loch off Ardkinglas house. Small cardinal buoys indicate the navigable passages between the obstructions and each shore. It would appear that vessels should not use the apparently unobstructed passage through the centre of the fish farm to reach the upper part of the loch.

Good anchorage exists opposite the Memorial about 1 mile NE of Ardklnglas House. Shops, PO, hotel which caters for yachtsmen. Interest: Kilmorich Kirk (Gothic style church and tower). Ardkinglas House mansion in the Scottish style, designed by Sir Robert Lorimer. Dundarave Castle built in 16th century and Strone Gardens.

Moorings have been laid off the W shore opposite Cairndow, about 3 cables S of the Loch Fyne Oyster Bar restaurant and shop. These are free for the use of patrons of the shop and restaurant.

Caution It is forbidden to anchor or fish in the charted area in the vicinity of Ardnagowan, 2 miles N of Strachur. There are two unlit Admiralty buoys within this area.

Inveraray

Approach On the W side 4 miles N of Strachur. **Caution:** Coming from the S, An Oitir (Upper Otter Spit) which runs almost 2 cables off shore 1/2 mile S of the pier, must be guarded against.

Anchorage Good anchorage can be had off the mouth of the river, just NW of the pier well off shore in 5m. Exposed to SW. An unlit Admiralty buoy lies 4 cables E of the pier. Yachts which can take the ground can get good shelter alongside the stone pier.

Facilities Shops, hotels, PO, tel, Calor gas, water at tap near pier, bus connections to Oban, Glasgow and Campbeltown.

Interest Inveraray is a town of Georgian buildings, the ancient capital of Argyll and contains Inveraray Castle built in the Scot's Baronial style. The castle contains in its Drawing Room and State Rooms, a display of Beauvais Tapestries, fine paintings and a vast collection of swords and firearms. The grounds too are attractive with garden and woodland walks. Inveraray Jail and the maritime museum in the Arctic Penguin are well worth visiting.

Inveraray *Argyll Tourist Board*

Kilbrannan Sound

Charts

(i) 2131—Firth of Clyde and Loch Fyne & 2126—Approaches to the Firth of Clyde
(ii) 2221—Firth of Clyde-Pladda to Inchmarnock - Northern Sheet
(iii) 1864—Harbours and anchorages in the Firth of Clyde.
(iv) ALF 5610·9 & 5610·12 OS maps 62 and 68

General

Kilbrannan Sound is a clear stretch of water extending for 20 miles from Skipness Point to Campbeltown Loch. There is a heavy overfall with the S going stream (the ebb) on the Erins Bank which lies towards mid channel off Whitefarland Point on Arran. When progressing south from Carradale Harbour (also known as Port Crannaich) beware of a rocky ledge known as Crubon Rock off Carradale Point, marked by a red can light buoy. 1.5M NNE of Davaar Island lies Otterard Rock marked by a pillar buoy (BYB) and inshore of this lies Long Rock and Smerby Rocks marked by a red can buoy.

Tides

Skipness Point const. –0025 Greenock (+0050 Dover)
Campbeltown const. –0030 Greenock (+0045 Dover)

Lights

Skipness Pt	Fl.R 4s	Red can light buoy
Port Crannaich Harbour Lt	Fl.R 10s 5m 6M	On metal column
Carradale Pt	Fl.(2) R 12s	Red can Lt buoy
Otterard Rock	Qk Fl (3) 10s	E Cardinal Pillar buoy (BYB)
Davaar Island Lt Ho	Fl.(2) 10s 37m 23M Horn (2) 20	
Skipness Range (1 mile N of Skipness Pt)	Iso R sector Lt. 292°–312° (20°) 8s 7m 10M	

Anchorage

Skipness Bay Entering the bay, Skipness Point must be given a wide berth as there are a number of off-lying rocks and tidal streams run strongly in both directions. A red buoy Fl.R.4s marks the outer end of these rocks. When approaching this bay keep well to the W and S of the red buoy to avoid rocks and a shoal lying 2 cables due W of the buoy. Temporary anchorage in 4 to 8m in N'ly winds can be had anywhere to the S of the point, from the ruined castle and chapel to the houses. It is shoal closer in towards the houses. Shop, PO, tel, water at village hall. EC Tuesday. Bus connection to Tarbert. Ferry from Claonaig to Lochranza (Arran) with bus connection to Brodick.

Interest Old chapel possibly on the site of St. Brendan's chapel and 14th century castle with 13th century curtain walls. Skipness House and Gardens. There is nearby a dun, a standing stone and a dunan. In clear and settled weather Skipness offers a spectacular panoramic view of Bute, Arran and the Mull and one of the finest views of Arran.

Grogport 3 miles N of Carradale Harbour. Visitors mooring available to those using restaurant. Water.

Saddell Bay 5 miles S of Carradale Bay. Temporary anchorage in 4 to 8m in the centre of the bay. Interest: Saddell Castle. with its 10th century keep and remains of Saddell Abbey nearby, founded in 12th century by Somerled Lord of the Isles. Walks in Carradale Forest.

Kildonald Bay 2 miles S of Saddell Bay. Temporary anchorage in 6m sheltered from S'ly winds. Drying rocks lie in the S side of the bay. Small vessels can, with local knowledge, pass between Ross Island and shore avoiding the rock which dries 2.3m on the NW side of the island

Carradale Harbour and Kilbrannan Sound *Barrie Waugh*

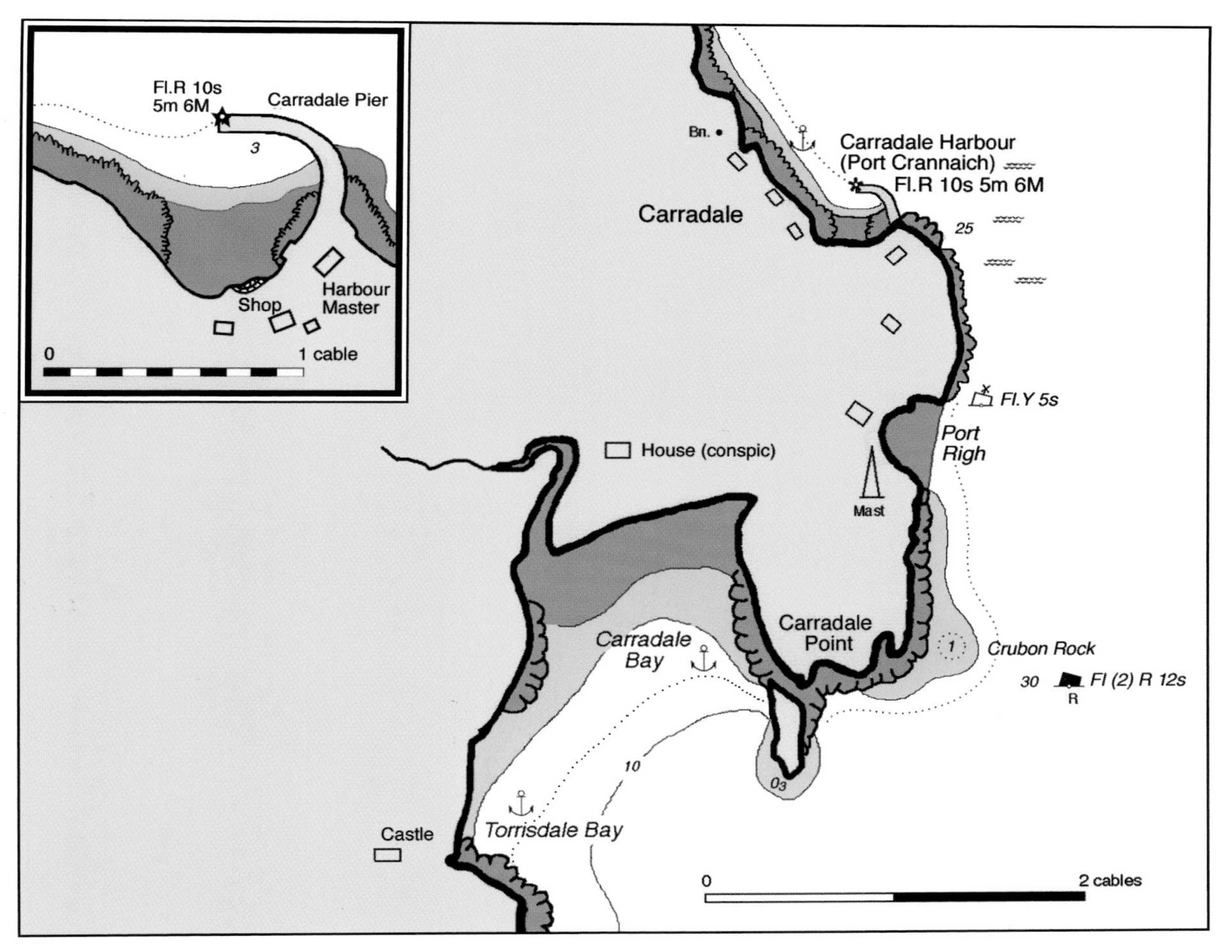

Carradale Bay with (inset) Carradale Harbour

Carradale

General This well sheltered harbour, also known as Port Crannaich, is well used by yachtsmen and can be entered at any state of the tide. Though there are rocks close inshore in the SE and the NW approaches to the harbour, giving each side a sensible offing clears them. The entrance is narrow and once inside manoeuvrability is restricted. A fishing fleet is based here. Tie alongside in a depth of about 3m (LW) and contact the harbourmaster. Sheltered in all winds though a N'ly gale causes a swell. In certain states of the tide there are overfalls in an area within 1/2 mile E of the harbour entrance. It is the intention of the NLB to discontinue the Cruben Rock buoy (Fl.(2) R 12s)

Lights Harbour breakwater, Fl.R 10s 5m 6M, Metal column

Anchorage **N of Carradale Harbour** Good anchorage is reported just N of the harbour in 3 to 5m with the power beacon on shore bearing not less than 280° to avoid the submarine power cables.

Carradale Bay Good anchorage may be obtained in 4m anywhere at the head of Carradale Bay. Subject to swell.

Torrisdale Bay Anchor in 8m just off Torrisdale Castle (dark stone), in the SW corner of the bay but well clear of two (reported) red buoys which have very heavy chains and anchors.

Facilities Shops, PO, tel, hotel, petrol, diesel and Calor gas. Water at pier. EC Wednesday. Golf course (9 hole). Forest walks.

Interest There is a vitrified fort at Carradale Point.

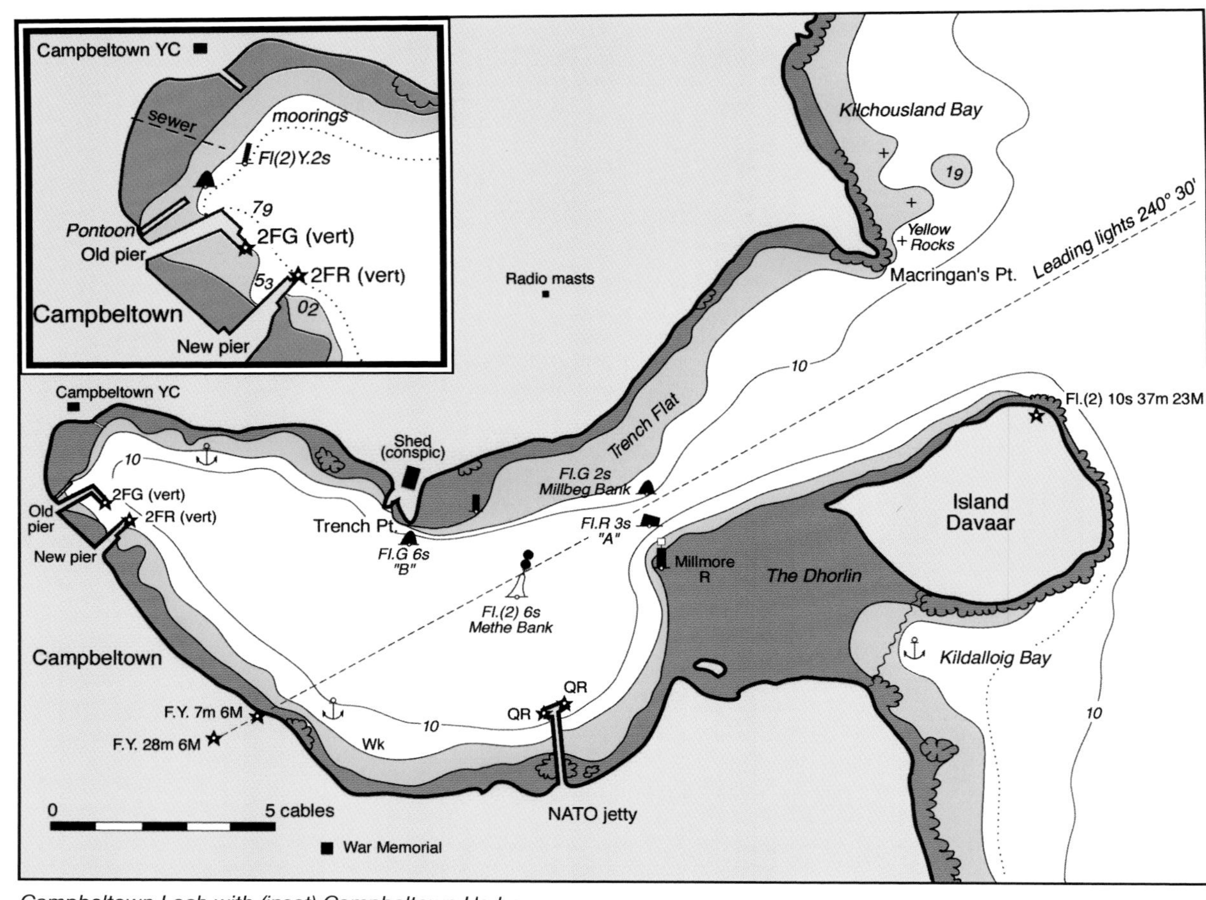

Campbeltown Loch with (inset) Campbeltown Harbour

Campbeltown

Charts (i) 2126—Approaches to the Firth of Clyde (iii) 1864—Harbours and Anchorages in the Firth of Clyde. (iv) ALF 5610·11 & 5610·12(B) & (C)

Tides Campbeltown const. –0030 Greenock (+0045 Dover)
Tidal streams run strongly E of Davaar Island with overfalls on the S going stream.

Lights

Otterard Rock (least depth 3m)	Qk Fl (3) 10s	E Cardinal Pillar buoy (BYB)
Long Rock (dries 1.5m)	(unlit)	Red can buoy
Davaar Island	Fl (2)10s 37m 23M	Wh. Twr. and balcony.
Harbour lights shown on plan.		

Approach **From the N** 1.5 M N of Davaar Island lies Otterard Rock and Long Rock with Smerby Rock. The passage between Otterard and Long Rocks has a least width of 4 cables and a depth of over 10m.

Approaching give Macringan's Pt a good offing and pick up the 2 orange leading lights bearing 240° 30' then keep to the navigation channel to avoid Millbeg Bank and Trench Flat to the north and Millmore and Methe Bank to the south.

From the S entering Campbeltown Loch is straightforward leaving Davaar Island to port

Anchorage **Campbeltown Harbour** A pontoon with min. depth 3m is situated NW of the old pier. It is administered by Campbeltown Loch Berthing Co. By arrangement with the harbour master, larger yachts may use the inside face of the old (NW) quay or the inside face of the new (SE) quay where depths allow. Depths up to 2.5m may be found. It may be busy with fishing boats. Yachts may anchor to the N of the harbour or to the SE of it. Good holding in mud.

Campbeltown Loch In N'ly winds anchor to the E of the Sailing Club. In S'ly winds anchor off the war memorial.

Kildalloig Bay On the S side of Davaar Island. Anchor in 6m off Dhorlin Shoal which connects Davaar Island to the mainland. Temporary anchorage in NW winds. Caution - underwater cable.

Facilities All facilities available at Campbeltown. Bus and air connections. EC Wednesday. Visitors' pontoon with water and electricity. Boat and engine repairs, chandlers, petrol, diesel. Hotels. Sailing Club. Aqualibrium Leisure Centre with swimming pool, showers, gymn and bistro. Launching slip for small craft. Coastguard. Lifeboat.

Interest 2 golf courses, Museum, Walk to Davaar Island at low tide to see picture cave.
3 miles S of Davaar Island is the cave of St Kiaran who pre-dated St Columba.

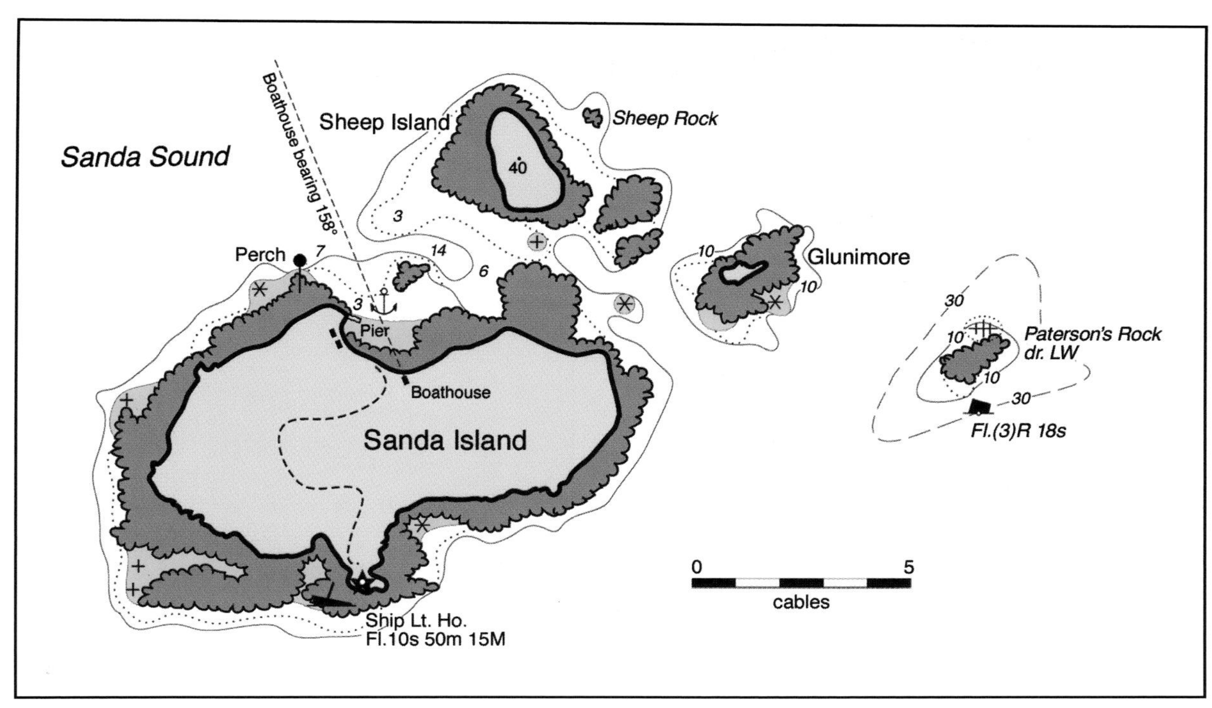

Sanda Island

Sanda

Charts (i) 2126—Approaches to the Firth of Clyde & 2199—North Channel, Northern Part
(iv) ALF 5610·11 & 5610·11(A)

Tide Const. –0040 Greenock (–0040 Dover). Sp rise 2.4, Np 2.0.

Lights

Ship Lt.	Fl.10s 50m 15M	Wh. Twr. and buildings
Paterson's Rock	Fl.(3) R 18s	Red can buoy

Anchorage There is a strong tide setting across the entrance to the bay with possibly an E-going eddy on the ebb. Note the reef extending N from the point N of the pier, marked by a black perch with ball topmark. **Caution:** Note that this perch is not on the edge of the reef and should be given a wide berth. Note also the rocks in middle of the bay which dry 1.2m. The recommended approach course into the bay is 158° towards a boathouse on the beach. Anchor just E of the pier.

Caution **Paterson's Rock** This dangerous rock, which is steep-to, is marked on its S side by a Red can buoy. Approaching from the N keep **well** to the E of the buoy which, due to the deep water and scope of its mooring chain, can move off-station.

Facilities Pub & restaurant established 2003. Holiday cottages

Ship Light, Sanda (Ailsa Craig in background) *Mike Balmforth*

Mull of Kintyre

Charts (i) 2724, 2126, 2798 and 2199 (for titles see chart index p.6)

General Making passage round the Mull within 2 or 3 miles of the coast requires great care and with due regard to appropriate wind conditions and the times of tidal streams and eddies. Races exist S and SW of the Mull and dangerous breaking seas occur in fresh to strong S winds especially when opposed by the E-going (incoming) tidal streams. By keeping at least 3 miles offshore and well S of Sanda Island the confused, and at times dangerous, tidal conditions can be avoided.

Tides There are two distinct tidal streams off the Mull of Kintyre:-

The **offshore stream** occurs S and W of Sanda Island and the Mull and attains at springs a rate of over 3 knots. During the last 2 hours of the W-going off-shore stream a dangerous race forms off Sron Uamha (Deas Point). This race can be violent and dangerous to yachts in fresh to strong S'ly winds.

The **inshore stream** passes in both directions through Sanda Sound and close to the S and W shores of the Mull and turns one hour earlier than the offshore stream. This stream achieves 5 knots in each direction just W of the Mull and in the Sound of Sanda. At times in the tidal cycle and also where wind and swell conditions are adverse the boundary between this inshore stream and the main offshore stream can be an additional cause of turbulent seas.

The extract on the opposite page from the Admiralty Tidal Atlas for the Firth of Clyde and Approaches, reproduced with the permission of the Hydrographer of the Navy, is of particular value in understanding the timing and direction of these streams.

There are several races in Sanda Sound and its NE approaches. Races also extend W and SW of Sanda Island. None of these races should present problems in conditions suitable for rounding the Mull.

In amplification of the information given in the tidal diagrams the following are times for the changes in direction of the inner stream:-

In Sanda Sound (mid-channel)
W-going stream begins –0110 HW Dover (–0230 HW Greenock)
E-going stream begins +0500 HW Dover (+0340 HW Greenock)
5 knots springs in either direction.

Close W of Mull of Kintyre
N-going stream begins –0130 HW Dover (–0250 HW Greenock)
S-going stream begins +0430 HW Dover (+0310 HW Greenock)
5 knots springs in either direction.

Passage For full details of passage making N'wards round the Mull see CCC Sailing directions Part 2, Mull Of Kintyre to Ardnamurchan. Conditions can deteriorate rapidly and the timing of passage making, whether north or southbound, is most important. **Small craft unless properly equipped and able to batten down all hatches should not attempt this passage in unsettled weather.**

Campbeltown Harbour (yacht pontoon on right, see p.50) *Argyll Tourist Board*

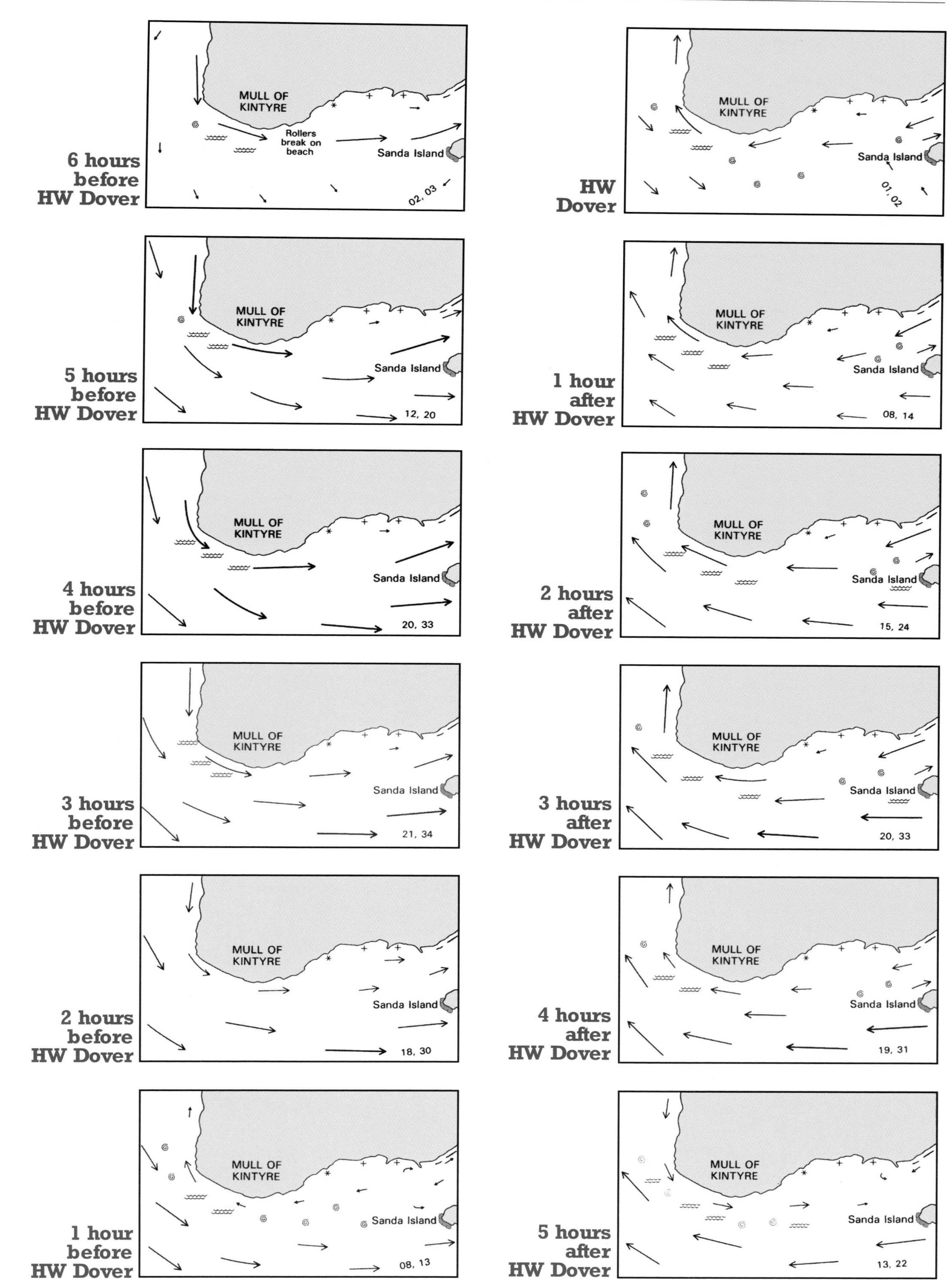
MULL OF KINTYRE
Rollers break on beach
Sanda Island
02, 03
6 hours before HW Dover
HW Dover
01, 02
5 hours before HW Dover
12, 20
1 hour after HW Dover
08, 14
4 hours before HW Dover
20, 33
2 hours after HW Dover
15, 24
3 hours before HW Dover
21, 34
3 hours after HW Dover
20, 33
2 hours before HW Dover
18, 30
4 hours after HW Dover
19, 31
1 hour before HW Dover
08, 13
5 hours after HW Dover
13, 22

West Coast of Arran

Charts (i) 2126—Approaches to the Firth of Clyde, (ii) 2221—Firth of Clyde, Pladda to Inchmarnock - southern sheet (iv) ALF 5610·9, 5610·11 & 5610·12

Constant Skipness Pt const. –0025 Greenock (+0050 Dover)
Carradale Bay const. –0030 Greenock (+0045 Dover)

Lights

On Kintyre Shore		
Skipness Pt	Fl.R 4s	Red can light buoy
Port Crannaich Harbour Lt.	Fl.R 10s 5m 6M	On metal column
Carradale Pt	Fl.(2) R 12s	Red can Lt buoy
Otterard Rock	Qk Fl (3) 10s	E Cardinal Pillar buoy (BYB)
Davaar Island Lt Ho.	Fl.(2) 10s 37m 23M Horn (2) 20	Wh. Twr.
On Arran Shore		
Iron Rock Ledges	Fl G 8s	Green con Lt buoy

Tides In the Kilbrannan Sound, over the Erins Bank between Imachar Pt and Whitefarland Pt, a bad tidal rip or overfall is sometimes experienced. This extends for about 1 mile off the Arran shore.

Anchorage The anchorages on the W side of Arran, excepting Loch Ranza, are all much exposed and are tenable only in E winds or in settled weather conditions.

Catacol Bay 2 miles S of Loch Ranza. Temporary anchorage to the S of the Glen Catacol burn at the S end of the bay in 12m. Exposed from NE to W. Gives some shelter from S winds. Hotel.

Whitefarland Bay About 6 miles S of Loch Ranza. Temporary anchorage in 6 to 12m. The bay at Whitefarland Pt shoals for 2 cables off shore for about 1/2 mile N. Exposed from N to SW. Shop at Pirnmill 1 mile N.

Machrie Bay About 11 miles S of Loch Ranza. Approaching the N end of Machrie Bay keep well clear of Iorsa Patch which has 0.3m over it at LW. It lies 3 cables W of a prominent jetty. Temporary anchorage in 3 to 7m anywhere in the bay. The shore shoals for about 1 cable for mile on either side of the Machrie Burn. Exposed from SW to NW. **Interest**: Auchagallon Stone circle, Bronze Age burial cairn surrounded by 15 standing stones. Numerous similar stones and stone circles are found near Machrie Bay. Between Machrie Bay and Drumadoon Pt the King's Cave can be seen on the seaward side of the red sandstone face of Torr Righ Mor.

Blackwaterfoot About 14 miles S of Loch Ranza. From the N enter Drumadoon Bay round Drumadoon Pt with its prominent rock pinnacle. This bay is rocky in places for about 3 cables off shore and very exposed from W to S winds. A hazardous rock lies in the bay 3 cables off shore S of a church and close by a flag staff on the W side of the Black Water Burn. To clear this rock, keep almost 1/2 mile off shore until S of a beacon a little to the E of the church and flagstaff and then go N for about 1/2 mile towards the beacon giving the E shore a reasonable offing. Anchor in 4m near the burn mouth. **Facilities**: Shops, PO, tel, hotels, indoor swimming pool. Bus to Brodick. Golf course. **Interest**: A large number of standing stones, forts and burial chambers of the Iron and Bronze Ages.

Caution Proceeding S towards Pladda avoid the dangerous **Iron Rock Ledges** which extend 8 cables from the shore (See p. 57).

Loch Ranza

Approach About 2 miles W from the Cock of Arran at the N end of the Kilbrannan Channel. Enter between Newton Pt, at the NE end of this small loch, and Coillemore Pt. Give Newton Pt a wide berth to avoid the Screda Reef and the Cairn an unmarked rock at its southern tip.

Anchorage The most popular anchorage is to the N of the castle ruin in 4 to 6m but it is rather shoal in this area and not good holding ground in strong winds. In strong S'ly winds the gusts from the glen are very fierce. In such conditions it is better to anchor in 10m well out from the S shore, which shoals badly, clear of a line from the pier to the N end of the castle spit and clear of the visitors' moorings. In most conditions the anchorage is good but the loch is exposed to N'ly winds. Conditions may be endured in NW'lies but in NE winds it is very uncomfortable. The pool behind the castle virtually dries out at LW.

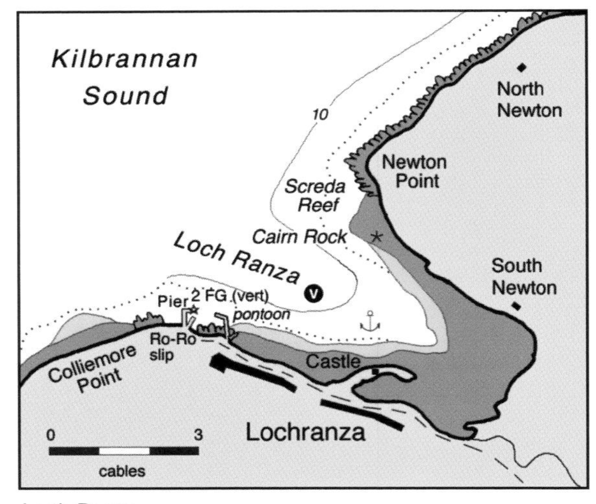

Loch Ranza

Facilities **12 visitors moorings** in the centre of the loch and a pontoon for dinghies and short term berthing 200m E of the pier. Shops, tel, hotel, restaurant, craft shop, Youth Hostel, Calor Gas, petrol at Pirnmill. Water from tap at ferry slip. Golf course. Slipway for launching small craft E of ferry slip. Ferry to Claonaig on Kintyre, bus service to Brodick.

Interest: Lochranza Castle (14th C. - 16th C.), Ossian's Cave and Fairy Dell within walking distance. Distillery welcomes visitors

East Coast of Arran

Charts

(i) 2126—Approaches to the Firth of Clyde
(ii) 2221—Firth of Clyde, Pladda to Inchmarnock-northern sheet
(ii) 2220—Firth of Clyde, Pladda to Inchmarnock-southern sheet
(iii) 1864—Harbours and Anchorages in the Firth of Clyde.
(iv) ALF 5610·9 & 5610·10

General

An attempt to circumnavigate Arran, a distance of about 50 miles, should use Lamlash Harbour and Loch Ranza as the only relatively protected anchorages. All others are temporary and should be used only in settled conditions.

Caution Coming from Loch Ranza on the northern end round the Cock of Arran and down the E side, the squalls off the mountains are exceptionally fierce in strong winds.

Measured distance Between Sannox and Corrie the poles marking two consecutive measured miles are lit (courses 322° or 142°)

Lights

On SE of Holy Island. Pillar Rock Point Lt.house	Fl (2) 20s 38m 25M	Wh. square Twr..
On SW end of Holy Island, Lighthouse	Fl G 3s 14m 10M	Wh. Twr.
Off SE end of Arran, Pladda LIghthouse	Fl (3) 30s 40m 23M	Wh. Twr.
N Channel entrance to Lamlash Bay	Fl R 6s	Red can Lt. Buoy
S Channel entrance to Lamlash Bay	Fl (2) R 12s	Red can Lt. Buoy
Off SW end of Arran, Iron Rock Ledges	Fl G 6s	Green Con Lt. Buoy

Tides

For about 1 mile SW of Pladda off the SE of Arran, there is a tide rip which is bad in strong wind against tide conditions.

Anchorage

North Sannox About 1/2 mile N of Sannox between the most S'ly of the measured mile posts, offering an outstanding view of Goat Fell, Cir Mhor and Caisteal Abhail (the Castles). Anchor in 3m over the sandy bottom just N of the burn close in towards a small field. Temporary anchorage exposed to NE to SE winds.
Interest: Cairn and Iron Age Fort nearby. The vast boulders of the Fallen Rocks are 1 mile N at the shore.

Sannox Bay 5 miles S of the Cock of Arran close by the most southerly of the measured mile transit posts. Temporary anchorage off the old stone pier In 6 to 12m. Sannox Rock with a least depth of 1.5 m over it is 2 cables off shore near the centre of the bay. Much exposed from NE to SE wind. Offers a beautiful view of Glen Sannox, Goat Fell and Caisteal Abhail (the Castles). **Facilities:** Cafe tearoom, PO, tel. Golf Club welcomes visitors. Pony trekking up Glen Sannox. Draw water from burn nearer its source than the houses.

Corrie 1 mile S of Sannox. A temporary anchorage in 4 to 8m in off shore winds, off either of the old stone harbours N and S of Corrie Point. **Facilities:** Shops, PO, tel, hotels, craft shop. Water available. Bus connections to Brodick.
Interest: Stones for the building of the Crinan Canal were taken from a nearby quarry.

Brodick Bay

Charts

(iii) 1864—Harbours and Anchorages in the Firth of Clyde.

General

From Merkland Point, Brodick Old Quay near Brodick Castle on the W side of the bay past the long sandy beach to Glenrosa Water and Brodick at the S end of the bay, there are no hazards if a reasonable distance is kept offshore. Most of the bay, though open, provides good anchorage but is much exposed to E'ly winds.

Lights

Brodick Pier 2FR (vert.) 4M Grey post
Admiralty Mooring Buoy No.2, Fl Y 2s
Spherical Buoy, Fl (4) Y 10s

Goat Fell from the South East — *Mike Balmforth*

Anchorage

Good anchorage can be had in 3 to 5m about 2 cables W of the pier, well offshore clear of moorings and the Ro-Ro Ferry. Shelter may be sought within the limited area provided by the inner pier. Whilst at the pier, the ferry blocks the entrance. Tie up alongside the pier and report to the harbourmaster. Subject to swell in E'ly winds. In NW winds anchorage can be had anywhere between Brodick Old Quay and Merkland Pt in 3 to 5m. **Visitors moorings** in SW corner of the bay.

Facilities

Shops, PO, tel, hotels cater for yachtsmen. Calor gas, Ro-Ro Ferry to Ardrossan. Slip near pier Golf course.

Interest

Brodick Castle, gardens and Country Park. The Rosaburn Heritage Museum. The immediate vicinity of Brodick is rich in archeological remains such as standing stones, a stone circle and 2 chambered cairns.

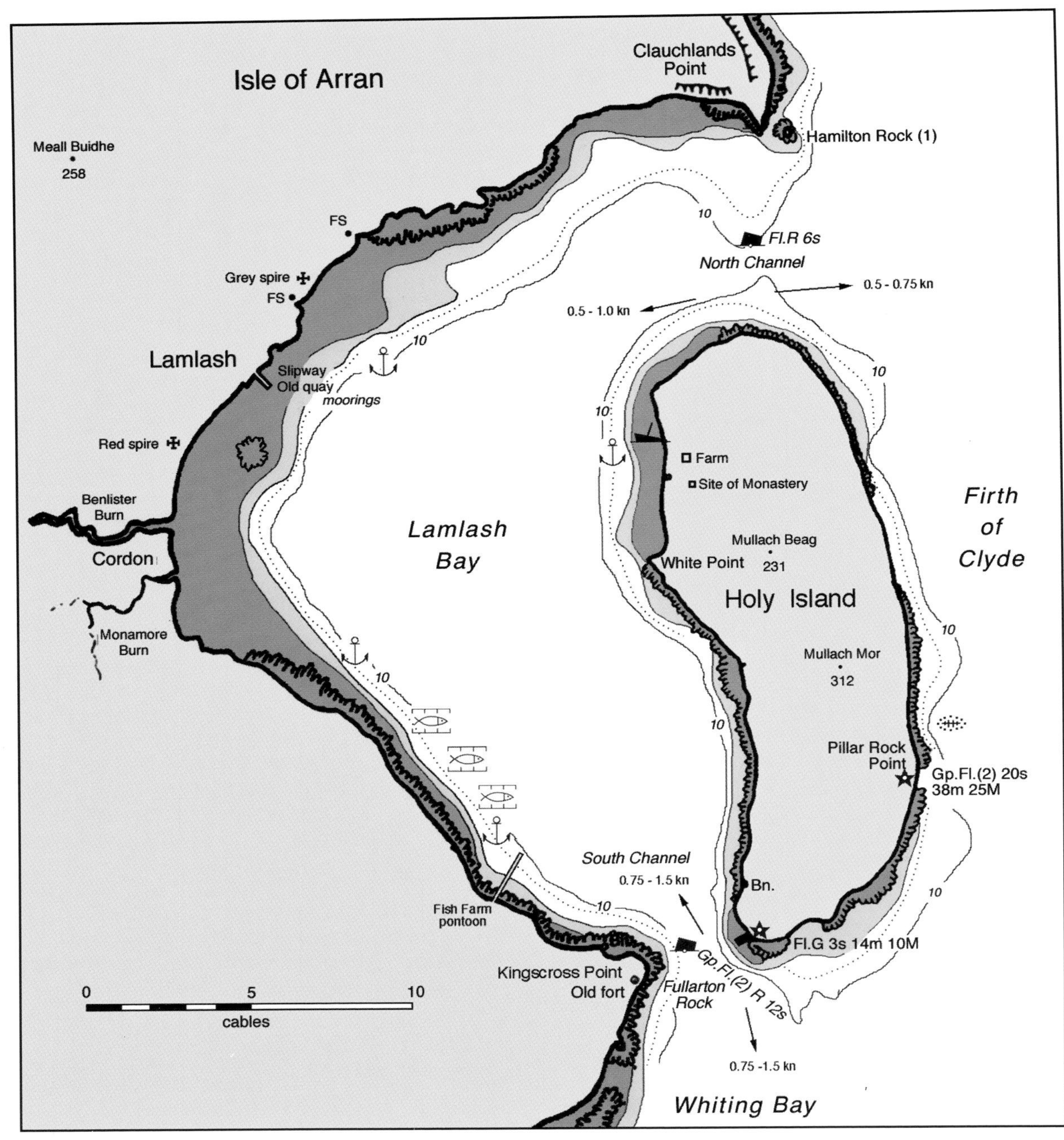

Lamlash Bay

Lamlash Bay

Charts (iii) 1864—Harbours and anchorages in the Firth of Clyde. (iv) ALF 5610·10

General Lamlash Bay is a splendid natural harbour protected on its E side by Holy island and which provides during a circumnavigation of Arran the only shelter from wind from all directions.

Constant –0025 Greenock (+0050 Dover)

Lights

At entrance to N channel	Fl R 6s	Red can Lt. buoy.
At entrance to S channel	Fl G 3s 14m 10M	Wh. Twr. SW end of Holy Is.
Off Kingscross Pt, Fullarton Rk.	Fl (2) R 12s	Red can Lt. buoy.

Tides The incoming tide flows N between Kingscross Pt and the Holy Island and achieves 1 knot at springs. On the S going stream it flows at 1.5 knots.

Approach **Entering from the N Channel** Hamilton Rock, which is always above water, lies off Clauchland Pt and should be given a reasonable berth on the starboard hand. A red can light buoy is moored in deep water between Hamilton Rock and Holy Island.

Lamlash Bay (continued)

Approach (cont.)

Entering from the S Channel pass between the red can light buoy marking the Fullarton Rock about 1 cable E of Kingscross Pt with a least depth of about 2m over it, and the lighthouse on the SW end of Holy Island. The red can Lt. buoy should be left on the port hand on entering. Caution: In strong NW winds the effect on the wind of the mountain glens makes it gust fiercely and can make entry to Lamlash Bay difficult through the S channel. In such winds entry through the N channel is comparatively easy.

Anchorage

Lamlash Anchorage can be had in 4 to 6m E of the stone pier and slip which dries out at LW. There is a large number of moorings out from the pier and the bottom slopes quite steeply which restricts anchoring. This anchorage is exposed to NE winds and is subject to swell in which case shelter may be found opposite at Holy Island. Approaching Lamlash in the dark from the N channel, difficulty may be experienced locating the moorings with attached yachts, until disconcertingly close, because of the ribbon of lights stretching from the town. **Facilities:** Shops, PO, tel, hotels, craft shops, water near pier, Calor Gas, diesel. Slipway, RNLI Inshore lifeboat. **Visitors moorings**: 20 moorings operated by Arran Yacht Club, tel. 01770 600333. **Interest**: Standing stones. Ruins of Kilbride Chapel.

Holy Island Good shelter can be obtained by anchoring well in shore off the farmhouse but well to the S away from the jetty, nearby mooring and wrecks. Anchor in 6 to 8m. Bottom is pebble and weed. The most convenient place to land is at the jetty. Owners of Holy Island have made it a religious Retreat. Walkers permitted in certain areas. Dogs and fires prohibited. **Interest**: Site of 12th century monastery by Somerled, Lord of the Isles. Evidence of Viking occupation, Runic inscriptions in St Molaise Cave.

Cordon to Kingscross A shoal caused by the Benlister and Monamore Burns extends 2 to 3 cables off Cordon. From SE of the shoal to Kingscross this shore offers the best shelter from W through S to SE winds. In a S'ly gale the best place to anchor is off the old ferry jetty NW of the slipway, clear of the moorings and fish farm pontoons and about 1/2 mile from the point. A large fish farm is established on this shore marked by yellow (flashing) buoys. **Interest:** Dun and cairn at Kingscross Pt.

Whiting Bay About 1 mile S of Kingscross Pt provides temporary anchorage well off shore in 4 to 8m. Small jetty indicates position of the old pier. Much exposed from NE to S. **Facilities**: Shops, PO, tel, hotels, craft shop, water near jetty.

Mike Balmforth

Pladda

Light

Pladda LIghthouse Fl (3) 30s 40m 17M Wh. Twr.

Anchorage

At the SE end of Arran, about 4 miles from Whiting Bay. This island provides anchorage on its E side well in towards the shore just N of the lighthouse landing jetty. Anchor in 5 to 8m, a sandy bottom with thick weed. Sheltered from N to W winds. May offer some shelter from SW winds.

Caution

The channel between the N end of Pladda and the Arran shore has many dangerous rocks and a spring tidal rate of 3.5 knots in each direction and should not be navigated without local knowledge. The shore near Kildonan has many rocky spurs stretching 2 cables off shore and should be given a wide berth.

If proceeding W from Pladda an overfall may be experienced SW of Pladda during the outgoing southerly stream. The **Iron Rock Ledges** extend 8 cables from the SW end of Arran some 7 miles from Pladda. They dry in several places and their outer end is marked by a green con Lt buoy Fl G 6s. To avoid this dangerous reef keep Pladda in view until Imachar Pt on the W side of Arran can be seen clear of Drumadoon Pt.

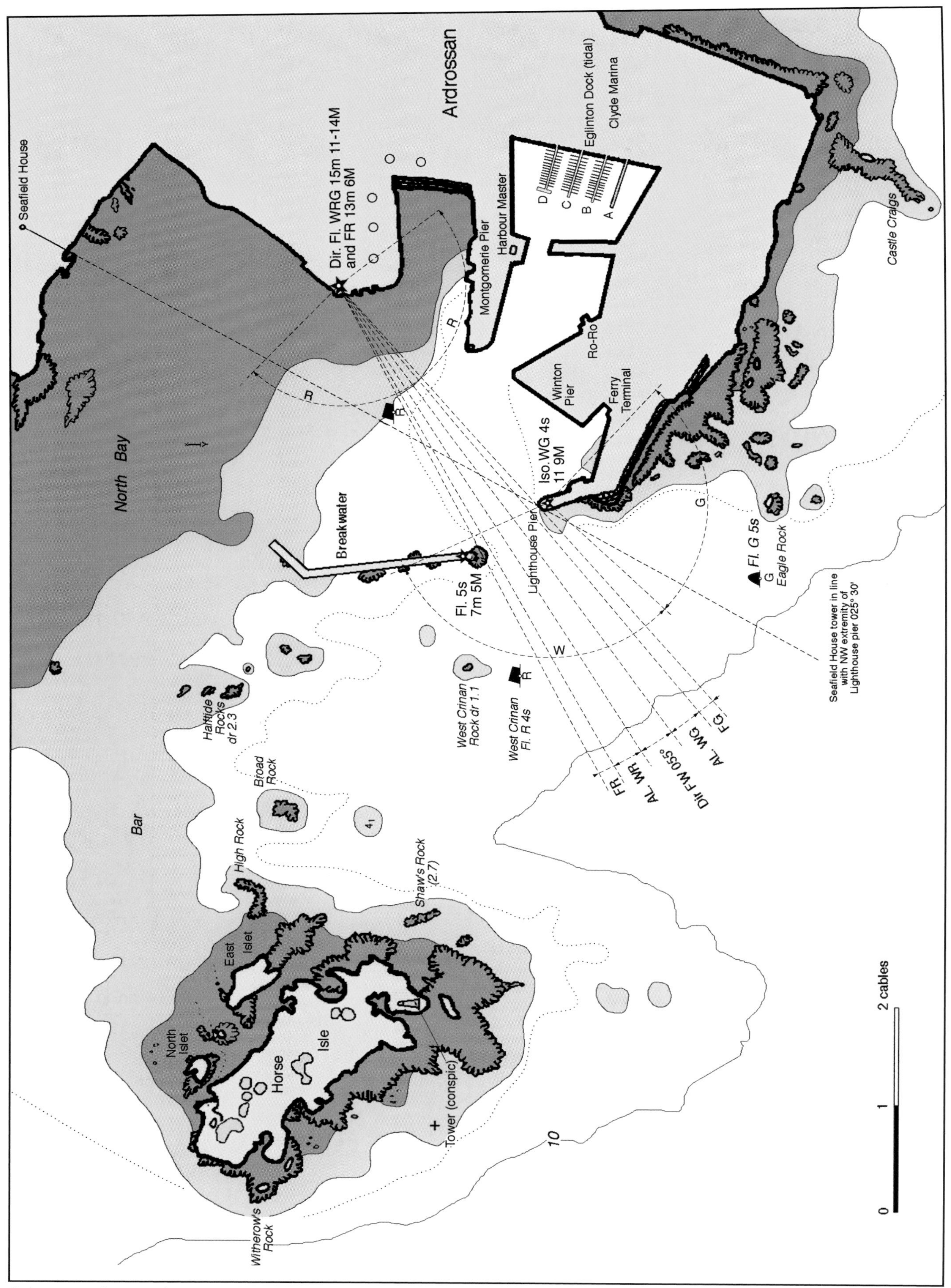

Ardrossan and approaches

Farland Point to Heads of Ayr

Charts

(i) 2126—Approaches to the Firth of Clyde
(ii) 2221—Firth of Clyde, Pladda to Inchmarnock – northern sheet
(iii) 1866—Harbours in the Firth of Clyde (iv) ALF 5610·9 & 5610·10

General

This stretch of coastline S of Hunterston and the Great Cumbrae shoals gradually from sandy beaches and has numerous outlying boulders and dangerous shoal patches, unmarked, which stretch well off shore. In strong W and NW winds, this area is characterised by breaking seas well off shore.
From S of Farland Point to the approaches to Troon, keeping 2 miles off shore clears all dangers, but beyond there lies Lady isle, a small rocky island 2 miles W of Troon. It has 2 towers, the larger showing the navigation light. There are sunken rocks all around and the island should be given a wide berth, particularly the N end.

Constant

Ayr const. –0025 Greenock (+0050 Dover)
Rise 3.2m MHWS, 2.7m MHWN, 1.9 MTL

Tides

Clear of headlands the tidal stream is less than 1/2 knot.

Lights

Cumbrae Elbow	Fl.6s 28m 14M	Wh. Twr
Lady Isle	Fl.(4) 30s 19m 8M	Wh. Bn.
Turnberry Pt Lt	Fl.15s 29m 24M	Wh. Twr.
Ailsa Craig	Fl.4s 18m 17M	Wh. Twr. Vis. 145° – 028° (243°)
On E side of Arran		
Holy Isle, Pillar Rock Pt.	Fl.(2) 20s 38m 25M	Wh. Sq. Twr.
Pladda	Fl.(3) 30s 40m 23M	Wh. Twr.

Ardrossan

Chart

(iii) 1866—Harbours in the Firth of Clyde (iv) ALF 5610·9 & 5610·10

General

The harbour is a ferry terminal and commercial port. A yacht marina is situated in the inner part of Eglinton Dock.

Lights & marks

West Crinan Rock	Fl.R 4s	Red buoy between Horse Isle and Breakwater.
Eagle Rock	Fl G 5s	Green buoy S of Harbour entrance
Leading Lights	Dir F WRG 15m 9M FR 9m 9M	Metal framework Twr.
Breakwater	Fl.R 5s 12m 5M	Red gantry – N side of harbour entrance
Lighthouse Pier	Iso WG 4s 11m 9M	Wh. Twr. – S side of harbour entrance.
Horse Isle	Unlit	Grey stone beacon on its S end.

Signals

Signals are shown from the control tower at entrance to Eglinton Tidal Basin as follows;

3 F.R.(vert)	Harbour and Marina closed; no entry for commercial and pleasure vessels
3 F.G.(vert)	Marina open, Harbour closed to commercial vessels; pleasure craft may enter/exit Marina; no commercial movements.
2 F.R. over 1 F.G.	Harbour open, Marina closed. Commercial vessels may enter/exit subject to approval of Harbour Control. Contact on VHF Ch 16,12 and 14. Call sign 'Ardrossan Harbour' or 'Harbour Control'. Pleasure craft must clear the approach channel, the ferry turning area and the Outer Basin.

Approach

It is 4.5 miles from Farland Point to the harbour entrance which lies approximately 1/2 mile behind Horse Isle, a low rocky islet about 3 cables long with a grey stone beacon on its S end. The stone beacon forms a good sea mark for picking up the harbour. Keep well S of Horse Isle to clear rocky shelves and shallow patches extending more than 3 cables from its S end. Nearer the harbour entrance go between the red and green buoys marking the West Crinan Rock and the Eagle Rock respectively but pass closer to the red. At night keep to the white sector light bearing between 053° to 056° to avoid these reefs. Do not attempt the passage N of Horse Isle without local knowledge. In very strong SW winds entry to the harbour would be difficult, and may be closed in severe conditions.

Marina

The Eglinton Dock with a least depth over sill of 4.9m has 250 fully serviced berths plus visitors. Call sign 'Clyde Marina' Ch 80 from 0900 - 1800 hrs or tel 01294 607077. After hours call Harbour Control Ch 12 or 14. Toilets, showers, laundrette and new bar and restaurant opening spring 2008. 50 ton boat hoist. Undercover storage. Engine and electrical repairs. Diesel, gas and chandlery.

Anchorage

Temporary anchorage can be obtained behind the breakwater in 4 to 8m. As it is shoal inshore of this, anchor within comfortable swinging distance of the breakwater.

Facilities

All available in the town. EC Wednesday. Ro-Ro ferry to Arran. Train and bus connections.

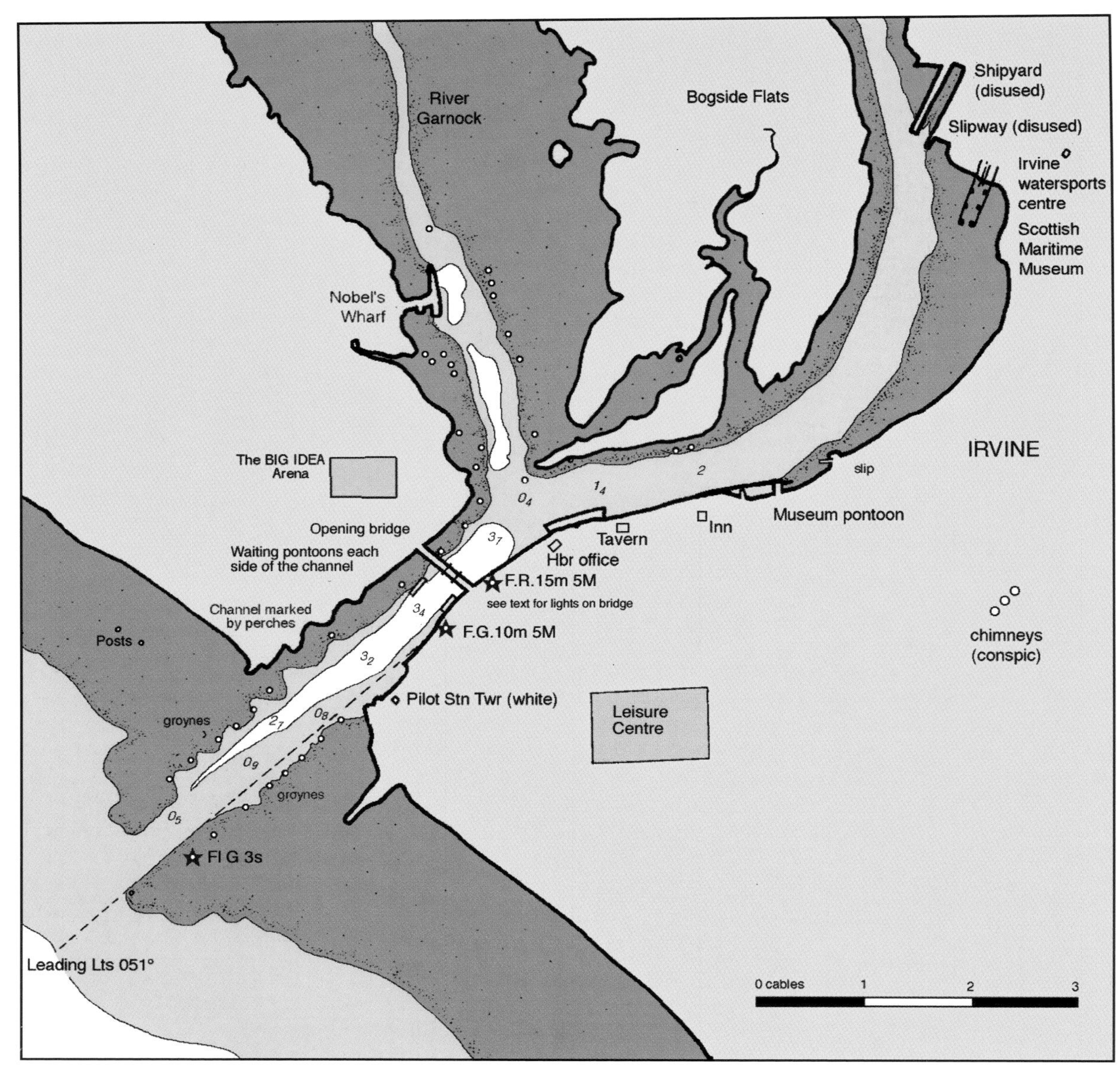

Irvine Harbour

Irvine

Chart (iii) 1866—Harbours in the Firth of Clyde. (iv) ALF 5610·10

General Irvine Harbour which is no longer a commercial port has a difficult entrance which has a tidal set across it during S or N winds. **Caution:** A pedestrian bridge across the entrance channel has been constructed immediately S of the inner leading light structure to give access to the site of the 'Big Idea' Exhibition Centre on the NW side of the River Irvine. See plan above and text opposite for operating details.

Tides Constant –0025 Greenock. MHWS 3.1, MHWN 2.6, MTL 1.8, MLWN 0.9, MLWS 0.4

Lights Harbour entrance Lts:
S side Fl G 3s 6m 5M Green metal column with platform

Harbour Leading Lts (Bearing 051°)
Front FG 10m 5M Green mast
Rear FR 15m 5M Green mast

Harbour Bridge Lts: (see opposite page: Bridge)

Outflow Pipe Marks:
About 2 miles W of the harbour entrance and about 1 mile off shore
Yellow light buoy Fl Y 10s and Yellow Light buoy Fl Y 5s
About 1 mile SW of Harbour entrance Yellow Light buoy Fl Y 3s

Irvine *Alister Firth*

Irvine (continued)

Approach Although the coastline is low lying, the tall white pilot house, surmounted by a signal mast, and 5 tall blocks of flats indicate the entrance to the river. Irvine can be seen from well off shore. The town lies about 1/2 mile up the river. The bar at the entrance is very shoal having a depth of less than 1m LWS. The river is narrow and after heavy rainfall may hinder a small craft's entry. An auxiliary engine is necessary to navigate the river. The channel which leads up to the wharfs is marked by perches on each side. In all but off shore winds, do not attempt to enter above Force 4.

Bridge A new bridge with a central opening sliding span has been built over the harbour entrance channel formed by the River Irvine. The bridge is situated at 55°36'.17N 4°42'.00W just SW of the inner leading light (FR 15m 5M) indicated on the plan. Currently (January 2004) the 'Big Idea' Exhibition is closed indefinitely.

Until the 'Big Idea' Centre is reopened the bridge will normally be left open. When closed the air draft at MWHS is 5 metres. Vessels requiring the bridge to be opened should contact the bridge operator by VHF on channel 12 or telephone 08708 403123. If no reply contact HM. (tel: 01294 487286)

The full open position provides a horizontal clearance of 18 metres, but vessels will be asked to state what width of opening will be sufficient for them as this may substantially cut down the time to open and close the bridge. The bridge will normally be opened on 5 minutes notice.

Two 'waiting pontoons' 18 metres in length are positioned on each side of the channel on the seaward side of the bridge for the use of vessels unable to contact the bridge operator.

FR and FG lights are exhibited in the support pillars at each of the opening span of the bridge. Leave FR to port and FG to starboard when approaching from seaward. Additionally two vertical red lights are exhibited on the centre of the opening span. When the bridge is open these vertical lights are separated. The bridge structure is also lit with white lights for pedestrian access.

Berthing Tie up at visitors wharf just beyond the second leading light by the Harbour Office to the seaward side of the Scottish Maritime Museum pontoons and report to the Harbour Master. Depth alongside 2.2m MLWS. Bottom soft mud. Nearby are the premises of the Irvine Water Sports Club who welcome visiting yachtsmen. (tel: 01294 274981)

Facilities Usual facilities in the town. No boat repairs. Train and bus connections. EC Wednesday. There is a slipway, restricted usage, for boat launching. Sailmaker. Magnum Leisure Centre.

Interest Scottish Maritime Museum, pontoons for floating exhibits. A Royal Burgh of 13th century origins. Eglinton Castle, Seagate Castle, Adam mansion of Perceton House. The 'Big Idea' is a major millennium project promoted by the Nobel Exhibition Trust.

Saltcoats Harbour

Anchorage The ground is shoal and rocky. Yachts, except those with bilge keels should anchor outside.

Facilities Available in town. Slipway ideal for launching and retrieving small shallow draft boats and others, in suitable tidal conditions.

Interest Fossil trees visible in the harbour at LW. Harbour built between 1686 and 1700.

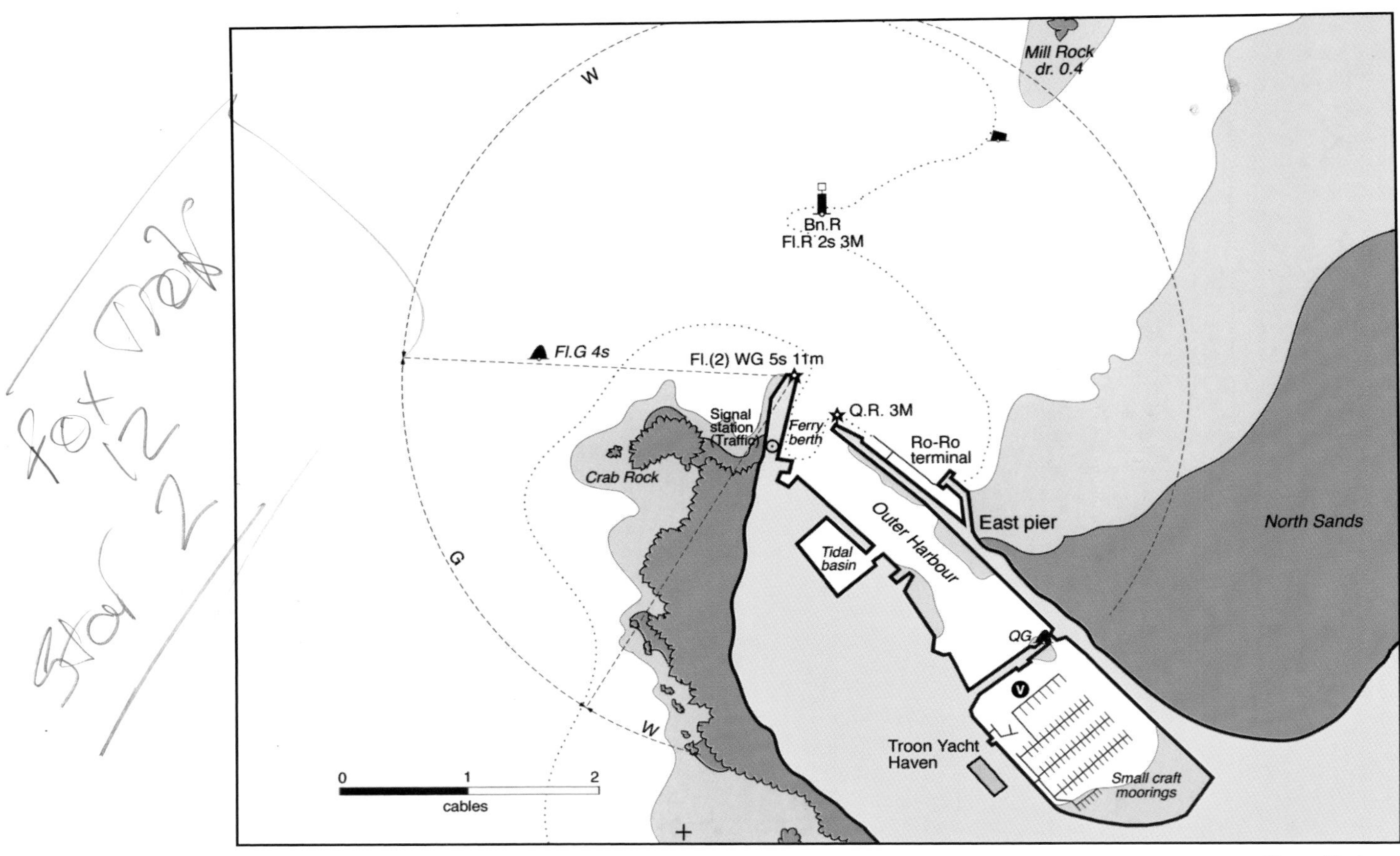

Troon Harbour

Troon Harbour & Marina

Chart (ii) 2220—Pladda to Inchmarnock, S. Sheet (iii) 1866—Harbours in the Firth of Clyde (iv) ALF 5610·10

Lights

Lady Isle	Fl. 2s 19m 11M	Wh. Bn. Racon (T)
Troon Harbour N approach Bn.	Fl.R 2s 3M	Red metal pile
W Pier Head	Fl.(2) WG 5s 11m 9M	Wh. Twr.
E Pier Head (Dolphin)	QR. 3M	Grey lattice Twr.
Troon spit	Fl G 4s.	G Con Buoy
Pipe outflow mark	Fl Y 5s	Nr. Lappock Rock, 2 M N of Harbour entrance, Y Lt. buoy

Signals Yachts should observe the lights at the signal station on the West Pier and listen out on Ch16/14 and obtain clearance from the Harbour Master before leaving or entering harbour. HM also broadcasts ferry arrivals and departures 10 and 20 minutes beforehand on Ch16/14.

Approach Troon is about 15 miles from the Little Cumbrae and the harbour is more easy to access than any other harbour on the Ayrshire coast. From the NW keeping well off shore to avoid Lappock Rock 1mile to the N and marked by a dark cement beacon with a green barrel on top, there are no dangers. The shoal ground to the W of the entrance is marked by a green con buoy 1 cable off the Crab Rock, which on entry must be left on the starboard hand. Mill Rk, about 4 cables NE of the entrance is marked by a red can buoy and must be left on the port hand. A tubular steel beacon painted red has been positioned 2 cables N of the harbour entrance. Outside the entrance the shore becomes shoal and must be avoided.

In good visibility the conspicuous shipyard shed indicates the position of Troon but it must be remembered that the harbour entrance is several cables to the N and there are rocks extending about 2 cables W of the West Pier. At night the harbour lights are very difficult to distinguish from the surrounding town lights.

Approaching Troon Harbour from the S safe passage may be had on either the W or E side of Lady Isle but give its N end a wide berth to avoid Scart Rock which lies 2 cables off, and shallow patches up to 1/2 mile off. Troon Rock with 5.6m over it lies about 1 mile W of the entrance and could be hazardous in a heavy swell. Access to the harbour is difficult in SW gales and hazardous in NW winds over Force 6.

Berthing **Temporary shelter** can be had in the **Outer Harbour**, tying up at a suitable berth. Although the tidal basin is used by commercial traffic and a fishing fleet, the HM (tel 01292 313412) may allow its temporary use by yachtsmen. Those wishing to stay for a longer term should do so in the **Marina** (tel 01292 315553) which is situated in the inner harbour. A G con. buoy (QG) is located just to stbd. of the entrance to the marina. On arrival moor up at the end of B pontoon or call up on VHF Ch 80 just before arriving. 20 berths are reserved for visitors. Depth 3m.

Facilities Water and electricity, showers, laundrette service, saunas, licensed restaurant. All repairs, slipway up to 50 tons, shipwrights, chandlery, electronic and engine repairs, diesel, Calor gas. Frequent bus and train connections.

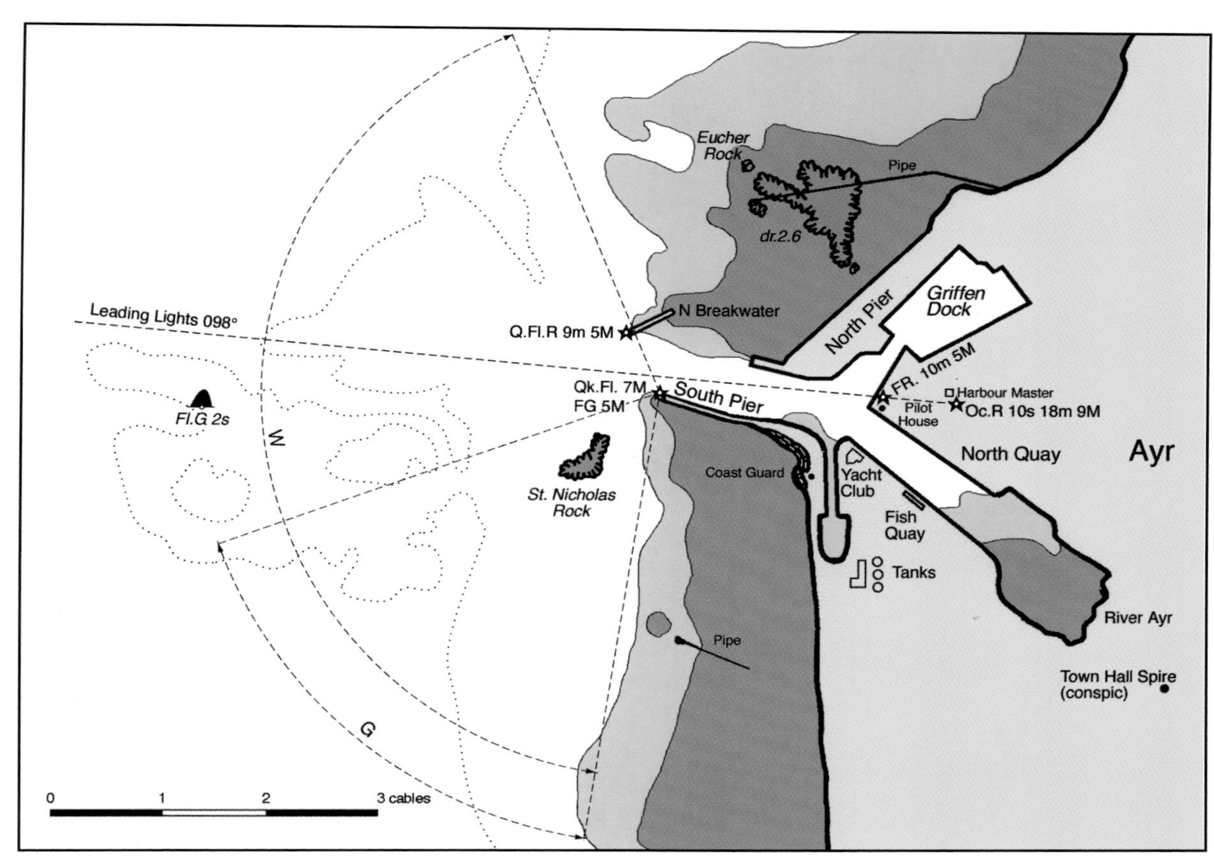

Ayr Harbour

Ayr

Chart (i) 2126—Approaches to the Firth of Clyde
(ii) 2220—Pladda to Inchmarnock, S. Sheet
(iii) 1866—Harbours in the Firth of Clyde (iv) ALF 5610·10

General Ayr Harbour, about 20 miles from the Little Cumbrae, is a commercial port which also has a fishing fleet. Although it can be entered at any state of the tide, entry could prove difficult in strong onshore winds.

Tides Const. –0025 Greenock (+0050 Dover) MHWS 3.0, MHWN 2.6, MTL 1.8, MLWN 1.1, MLWS 0.5

Lights

N Breakwater	Q.Fl.R 9m 5M	Wh. metal framework Twr.
S Pier Head (sectored Lts.)	Q.Fl. 7M over FG 5M	Wh. Twr.
Front Leading Light	F.R. 10m 5M	Red Twr. (near Pilot House)
Rear Leading Light	Oc.R 10s 18m 9M	Masonry Twr. (near Harbour Office)

Signals Two red vertical Lts (2 black balls by day) shown on mast on N pier indicates 'Harbour closed'.

Approach The whole of Ayr Bay from Troon to the Heads of Ayr has many shoal patches and should be navigated with great care keeping well off shore. Ayr lies in the centre of this bay. The Heads of Ayr, a bold rocky headland about 50m high with cliffs dropping sheer into the sea, lies to the south and forms a good landmark. From some distance off, Ayr has no outstanding features to indicate its position.

Closer in there are many shoals and in all but settled conditions, Ayr Harbour may best be approached from the W from 2 to 3 miles out to avoid the Saltpan Patches, an extensive shoal lying about 2 miles NW of the entrance. A green conical buoy near the harbour entrance marking the St. Nicholas Rocks must be left on the starboard hand on entry. It is not advisable to attempt entry in onshore winds above a Force 5.

Berthing Tie up at the Pilot Station on the N side and report to the harbour master, VHF Ch 16, 14 Call sign 'Ayr Pilots' (tel 01294 278132). A suitable berth may be available at the Quay or within the Griffin dock. If the harbour master is not available tie up anywhere along the Fish Market Quay on the S side. The harbour is subject to swell in W'ly winds and shelter may be sought in the Griffin Dock.

Facilities Shops, PO, tel, hotels, Calor gas, diesel, chandlers, crane slippage, all repairs. Prestwick Airport. Train and bus connections. Water at Pilot's Station on N quay or at the Fish Market on the S quay. Small boats may be launched at the public slip.

Interest Heart of Burn's country. Tam O'Shanter Museum. Auld Brig of Ayr from 13th Century. Brig O'Doon and its lovely river.

Heads of Ayr to Loch Ryan

Charts

(i) 2126—Approaches to the Firth of Clyde
(i) 2199—North Channel Northern Part

General

S of the Heads of Ayr to the entrance of Loch Ryan the coast is high and rocky with some sandy beaches. Keeping a mile off shore clears all dangers including the Brest Rocks (marked by a green iron cage beacon) which extend more than 1/2 mile from Turnberry. The coast offers no shelter from fresh to strong on shore winds and the entrance to Girvan Harbour is difficult in such conditions.

The coastal strip between Dunure and Maidens, including Culzean Bay with its long stretch of sand at Croy Beach, provides good facilities for day sailing for trailer sailers and other small craft which can take the ground.
For larger yachts, it should be remembered that both Dunure Harbour and Maidens Harbour virtually dry out at LW.

Constant

Girvan const. –0035 Greenock (+0040 Dover)
Stranraer const. –0020 Greenock (+0055 Dover)

Tides

Bennane Head, marked by a conspicuous silo, is a prominent headland between Girvan and Loch Ryan. There is a considerable tidal race off it which can be in excess of 2.5 knots springs in either direction. Give Bennane Head a wide berth.

The tidal streams outside Loch Ryan run along the coast towards and from Bennane Head as follows:
SSW-going stream begins + 0425 HW Greenock (+0540 Dover)
NNE-going stream begins –0140 HW Greenock (–0025 Dover)
The streams may reach 2 knots at springs.

Lights

Turnberry Pt	Fl.15s 29m 24M	Wh. Twr.
Ailsa Craig	Fl.4s 18m I7M	Wh. Twr. Vis. 145° – 028° (243°)
Corsewall Pt	Fl.(5) 30s 34m 22M	Wh. Twr.
Girvan Harbour Lights:		
N groyne	ISO W 4s 3m 4M	
S Pier	2FG (Vert.)8m 4M	
Loch Ryan off Milleur Pt	Qk Fl	N Cardinal Pillar buoy BY

Dunure Harbour

General

About 2 miles SW of the Heads of Ayr. Although well sheltered, it almost completely dries out at LW and is unsuitable for yachts which do not take the ground. Dunure provides facilities for small pleasure boats including an excellent launching and retrieving slip. An ideal place in settled conditions for day sailing to Culzean Bay, landing on sand at Croy beach 2 miles S or to Maidens Harbour which lies 5 miles S round Barwhin Pt in Maidenhead Bay.

A ruined castle on a knoll just to the S of Dunure harbour forms a good landmark. For boats of shallow draft, the approach is simple but the entrance is narrow and local advice should be sought. Exposed to all on shore winds from SW to N.

Dunure Harbour

Facilities

Shops, PO, tel, pub. Slipway.

Culzean Bay

General

2 to 3 miles SW of Dunure. Although the bay is open, good anchorage may be had in off shore winds in 6m within the S corner in clear view of Culzean castle to the SW but well out from a nearby white house. Some shelter from S'ly winds but exposed to N.

Facilities

At nearby caravan sites; Shop, water, Calor gas. Small boats can be launched or retrieved on Croy beach where the sand is generally firm.

Interest

Culzean Castle and Country Park.

Maidens Harbour

General

About a mile NE of Turnberry Point at the S end of Maidenhead Bay. A breakwater and a line of rocks, Maidenhead Rocks, protect the harbour. The entrance is between the Maidenhead Rks. and the Keown Rock (dr.1.5m) towards the N end of this sandy bay. The approach to the entrance has numerous sunken rocks and sandbanks and is subject to siltation. **Local knowledge is required for using the shallow entrance channel.** This is being deepened by excavation (2004). Harbourmaster tel: 01655 331665, Mobile: 07715072215. The village has facilities for small pleasure craft providing plenty of well sheltered harbour room for trailer sailers and bilge keelers. Trips N round Barwhin Point, 3 miles to Croy Beach at Culzean Bay, and 5 miles to Dunure Harbour.

Facilities

Shops, PO, tel, hotel, Calor gas, petrol. Slip for small craft off sloping shore at the village end of basin.

Interest

Stone Age fortress nearby. Shanter Farm, the traditional home of Robert Burns' hero Tam O'Shanter. Turnberry Castle-once home of Countess of Carrick, mother of Robert the Bruce. Turnberry Hotel and Golf Courses.

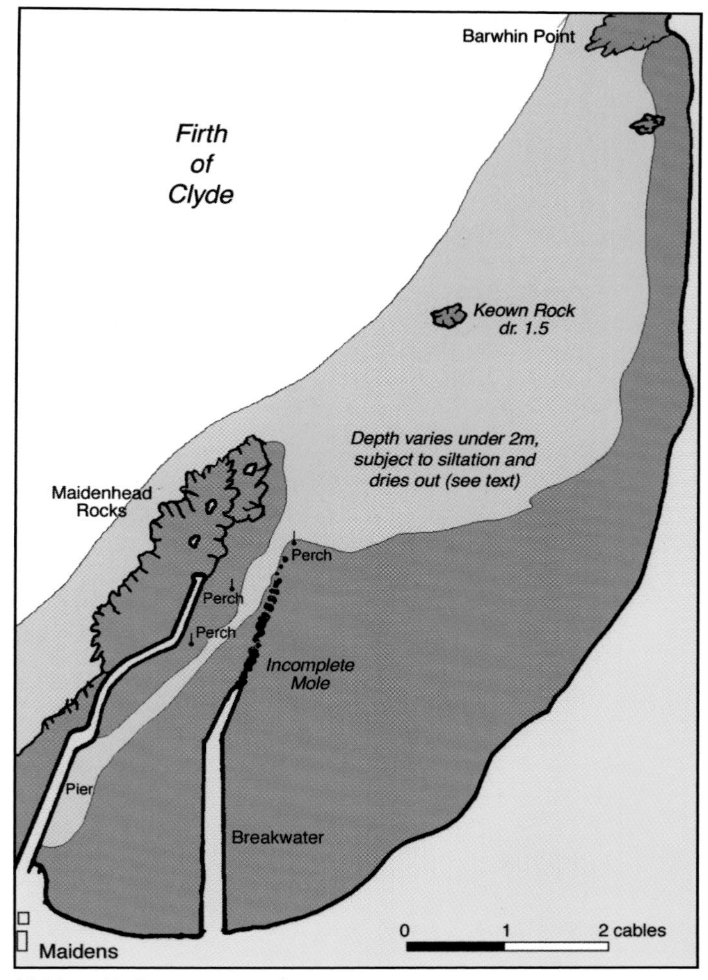

Maidens Harbour

Maidens Harbour Alister Firth

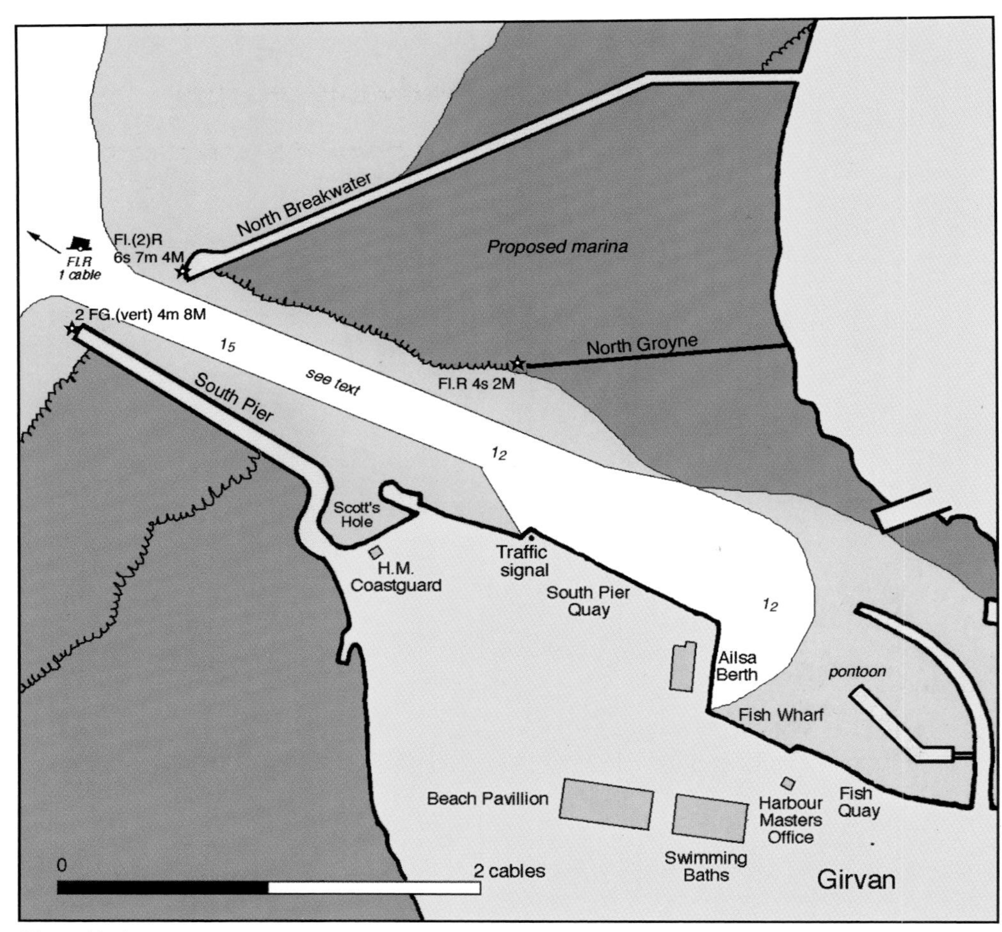

Girvan Harbour

Girvan

Chart (iii) 1866—Harbours in the Firth of Clyde.

General Girvan Harbour is used by fishing vessels and yachts. It is perhaps the most difficult to enter on the Ayrshire coast but once inside it is very sheltered. Girvan is an attractive town in pleasant surroundings and there is a proposal for a marina.

Lights

Turnberry Pt	Fl.15s 29m 24M	Wh. Twr.
Ailsa Craig	Fl.4s 18m 17M	Wh. Twr. Vis. 145° – 028° (243°)
Girvan Harbour Entrance Lts:		
N Breakwater	Fl.(2) R 6s 7m 4M	Pole on concrete base
S Pier	2 FG (vert) 8m 4M	Metal mast on Wh. Twr.
N Groyne Head	Fl.R 4s 2M	Column

Tides Const. –0032 Greenock (+0043 Dover) MHWS 3.1, MHWN 2.6, MTL 1.8, MLWN 0.9, MLWS 0.4

Signals The following signals are shown at the seaward end of South Pier Quay when the harbour is closed.
By day — Two black discs horizontal
By night — Two red lights horizontal

Approach From Turnberry Pt to Girvan Harbour, the 5 miles of coastline is studded with rocks all of which except the Brest Rocks (dr 1.1m) which extends more than 1/2 mile off shore, are close inshore. The Brest Rocks are marked by a green iron cage beacon. Bennane Head, 8 miles S of Girvan is a bold headland easily recognised. Ailsa Craig lies about 8 miles W of the harbour entrance.

A conspicuous TV mast stands on a hill behind Girvan. There are shoals to the N and S of the harbour entrance particularly the Girvan Patch with 2.0m over it which extends 1/2 mile off shore to the S. These shoals are hazardous in strong winds especially from the NW.

The harbour entrance is liable to silting, and after heavy rain the effect of the river Girvan can be very noticeable. Depths in the channel can be significantly less than those shown on the chart, possibly only 1.2m with less than 2.0m on the bar. Entry is not recommended 2 hours either side of LW and even in fresh NW winds may be difficult. On entering pass between the S pier and the old breakwater. Keep closer to the pier. Proceed up the river channel past Scott's Hole to the screen jetty or pontoon close to the fish quay. Harbourmaster VHF Channel 16,12 (0900-1700hrs Mon-Fri) Call sign 'Girvan Harbour' (tel. 01465 713648).

Girvan (continued)

Berthing

Pontoons for the use of yachts have been installed. Depth alongside 1.7m at LWS.

Facilities

Calor gas, diesel, petrol, ship repairs, slips available. EC Wednesday. Water (contact harbourmaster). Bus and train connections.

Ian Michie

Ailsa Craig

General

This remarkable rock, about 340m high and about 2 miles in circumference is very precipitous all round except on the NE side where limited access is available. It forms a distinctive leading mark on entering the Firth of Clyde, and is known as 'Paddy's Milestone'. A lighthouse is built on the most E'ly part of the rock and there is a jetty and landing place nearby. Ailsa Craig is a volcanic core. Home of thousands of seabirds. Source of granite for curling stones. Ruins of old castles are evident.

Light

East side of Craig, Fl.4s 18m l7M
Wh. Twr. Vis. 145°–028° (243°)

Anchorage

Temporary anchorage may be obtained in settled conditions and in calm seas close in shore near the lighthouse. No boat should be left unattended.

Turnberry Light and Ailsa Craig — *Alister Firth*

Ballantrae

General

About 11 miles SW of Girvan, 2 miles S from Bennane Head. The shores are rocky, particularly off Lendalfoot. Keeping well off shore avoids all hazards including the tidal race. From the S Ballantrae can be identified by a church spire and a square castle tower. There is a small pier which dries out at LW and offers no protection on this exposed shore. There is good anchorage to be had in 8 to 10m in offshore winds off the village, S of the pier and well clear of the River Stinchar.

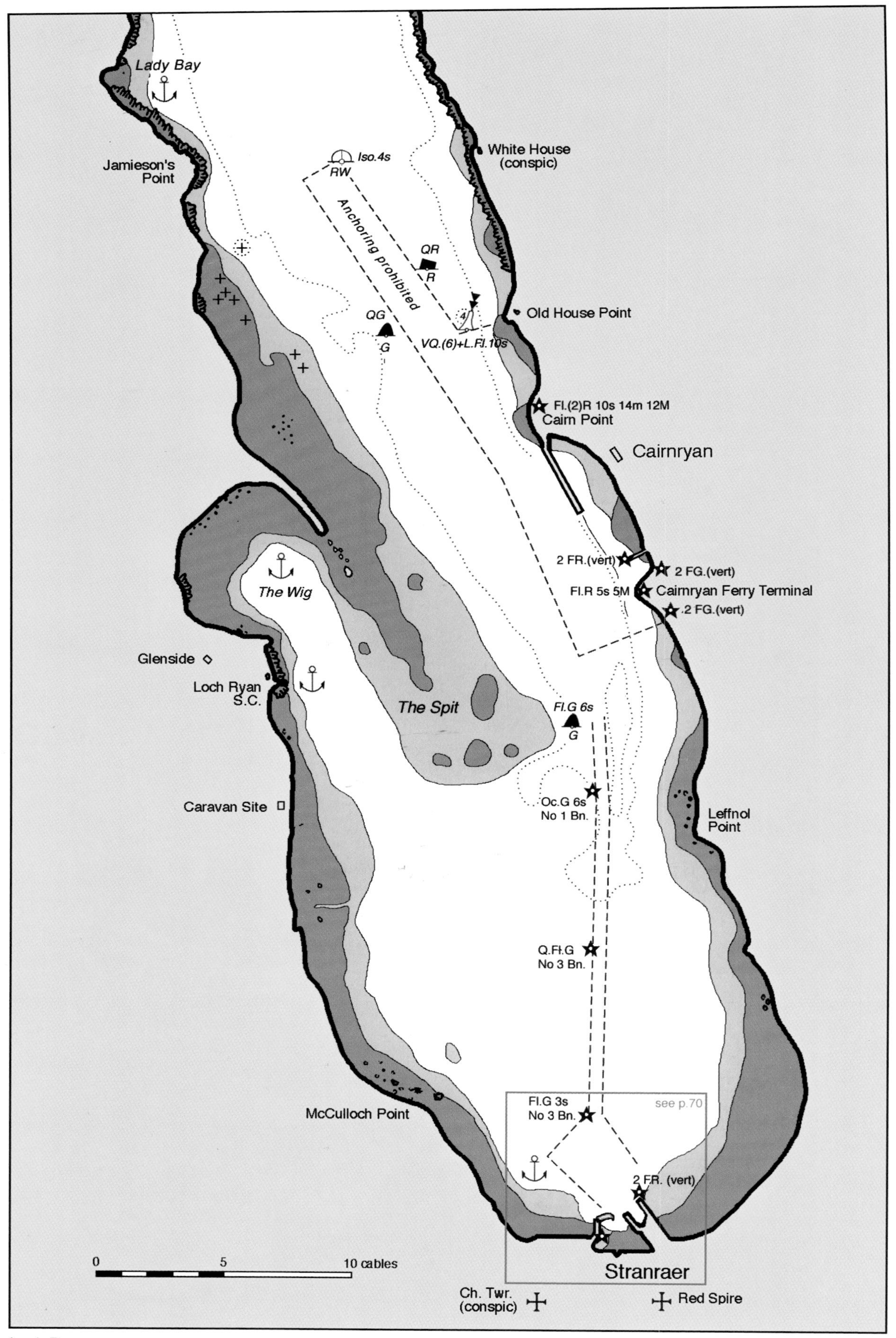
Lady Bay
Jamieson's Point
Iso.4s
RW
Anchoring prohibited
White House (conspic)
QR
R
QG
G
Old House Point
VQ.(6)+L.Fl.10s
Fl.(2)R 10s 14m 12M
Cairn Point
Cairnryan
2 FR.(vert)
2 FG.(vert)
Fl.R 5s 5M
Cairnryan Ferry Terminal
2 FG.(vert)
The Wig
Glenside
Loch Ryan S.C.
The Spit
Fl.G 6s
G
Oc.G 6s
No 1 Bn.
Caravan Site
Leffnol Point
Q.Fl.G
No 3 Bn.
McCulloch Point
Fl.G 3s
No 3 Bn.
see p.70
2 FR. (vert)
0
5
10 cables
Stranraer
Ch. Twr. (conspic)
Red Spire

Loch Ryan

Loch Ryan & Approaches

Charts (ii) 2199—North Channel Northern Sheet.
(iii)1403—Loch Ryan. OS map 76,82

General Loch Ryan is about 7 miles in length From about Jamieson's Pt, a shoal increasingly extends from the W shore. Although shallow (about 3 to 4m) in its southern half, with the SE end of the loch drying out for almost 1/2 mile, it offers shelter from all directions.

Constant Stranraer const. –0020 HW Greenock (+0055 HW Dover) Rise 3.0m Sp 2.6m Np.

Lights

Ailsa Craig	Fl.4s 18m I7M	Wh. Twr. Vis. 145° – 028° (243°)
Corsewall Point	Fl.(5) 30s 34m 22M	Wh. Twr. Vis. 027° 257° (230°) (AIS)
Milleur Point (W ent. to L. Ryan)	Qk Fl	N Cardinal Pillar buoy (BY) (AIS)
Jameson's Point	Iso.4s	RW Sph. buoy
W shore, SE of Jamieson's Point	Fl QG	Green con buoy
E shore, NW of Old House Point	Fl QR	Red con Lt buoy
E shore, W of Old House Point	VQ (6) + L.Fl.10s	S. cardinal buoy (YB)
SE end of The Spit	Fl G 6s	Green con Lt buoy
E shore, Cairn Point Light House	Fl (2)R 10s 14m 12M	Wh. Twr. with balcony
Cairnryan, N Breakwater	2FR.(vert)	Pole on concrete box
Cairnryan Ferry terminal	Fl R 5s 5m 5M & 2FG(Vert)	On Ramp Twr.

Tides Less than 1.5 knots in either direction in the channel between the shoal extending from the W shore and 2 cables off the E shore between Cairn Pt and Cairnryan Ferry Terminal. The streams are weak further within the loch beyond The Spit. However when rounding The Spit making for The Wig a strong set of tide on to it can be experienced. This is especially so with an ebb tide, and The Spit must be given a **wide** berth.

Caution 1. Entering Loch Ryan in NW gales the heaviest seas are encountered just outside the entrances especially during the N going stream.
2. Offshore in the North Channel and in the approaches to Loch Ryan and Larne on the Antrim coast there is a potential danger from close encounters with fast cross-channel ferries. A good lookout should be kept to ensure that one is not caught out by a closing bearing situation or by the wash from these vessels.
3. The Loch is a busy ferry terminal and a constant look out should be kept to keep clear of large vessels moving in restricted channels. It is recommended that a watch is kept on VHF in order to give prior warning of ferry movements, especially the high speed ferries which operate out of Cairnryan. These can generate large waves which can have a serious impact on small craft close to the shoreline and on shallow off-lying banks.
4. The rounded hill Knockdollan, 2 miles NE of Ballantrae, has an outline very similar to Ailsa Craig and can be mistaken for it. Knockdollan is commonly called the "False Craig".

Approach **From the N** the coast beyond Ballantrae to the entrance of Loch Ryan, a distance of about 6 miles is high and steep. **From the S** give the N shore of the Rhinns of Galloway a good berth as it is rocky and some drying rocks extend off it.

Enter between Milleur Point and Finnarts Pt and keeping about 2 cables off either shore clears a number of drying rocks including 1 off Milleur Pt and 1 off the Beef Barrel. From Jamieson's Pt the W shore is increasingly shoal until beyond The Spit which extends about 1.5 miles SE of Kirkcolm Pt. This extensive shoal has both its N and S ends marked by green con buoys. It is reported that silting is continuing to extend the shoal eastwards. Keep well over to the E side between Cairn Pt and Cairnryan Ferry Terminal. S of this the loch is free of dangers once clear of The Spit.

Anchorage **Lady Bay** On W side of the loch about 1mile S from the entrance. Anchor anywhere in the bay in 3 to 4m. Good holding ground. Protected from SW to NW winds. Exposed to NE winds. A convenient place to wait for suitable conditions for crossing to Ireland. Exposed to wash from ferries. (see Caution above)

Finnarts Bay On the E shore about 1mile S of Finnarts Pt. Gives protection in SE or E winds. The holding ground is not so good and in strong NE winds the gusts down Glen App make this bay uncomfortable.

The Wig Making for The Wig, go past the buoy marking the end of The Spit, and when half way to the No 1 beacon (see the warning under Tides above), head for the Agnew monument (323m) on the W shore. Do not turn northwards until Ailsa Craig can be seen in the Loch entrance. Anchor in 2 to 3 m clear of the moorings off the slip. This is the headquarters of **Loch Ryan Sailing Club** whose clubhouse is open most evenings and at weekends during the summer. Showers may be available. In N to NE winds anchor in the NE corner of the Wig but not too far in as it dries out 2 cables offshore at LW.

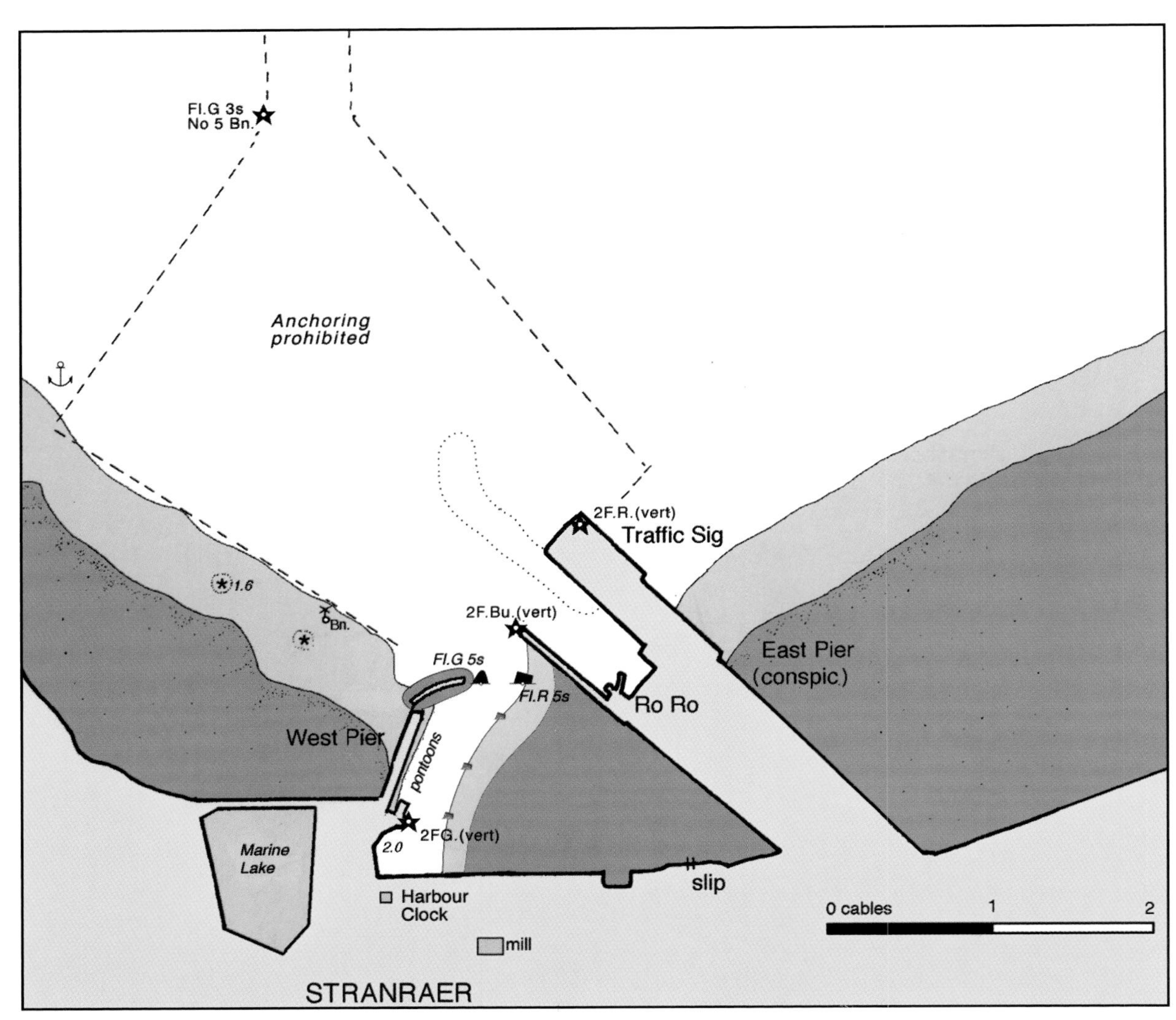

Stranraer Harbour

Stranraer

Lights

Channel lights:	No.1 beacon	Occ G 6s,
	No.3 beacon	Qk. G,
	No.5 Beacon	Fl G 3s
Ferry Terminal	Centre Pier	2 F.Bu. (vert.)
	East Pier	2 F.R. (vert.)
	Entrance to harbour	Fl.R 5s R can buoy
		Fl.G 5s G conical buoy
	At knuckle of W pier	2 F.G.(vert))

Anchorage A new breakwater has been constructed at the outer end of the W pier and an area to the E of this pier is being dredged to 2.5m. Entry to the dredged area is between the port and starboard buoys off the end of the breakwater and the extent of the dredging beyond is marked by three red can buoys. **Pontoons** with water and electricity and visitors' berths are planned to be in place by June 2008. Contact HM on VHF Ch. 14 or tel. 07734 073421. Larger draft yachts may lie on the NE face of the E pier by arrangement with HM.

Anchor off a conspicuous church, in 2 to 3m about 3 cables NW of the west pier, well off shore but clear of the prohibited area. This area is used by the ferry on its approaches to the East Pier.

Facilities Shops, PO, tel, Hotels, Calor gas, petrol water at pier. Limited boat and engine repairs. Train, bus and ferry connections. EC Wednesday. Inshore lifeboat in summer. Hire car and visit this beautiful area Pony trekking.

Interest Northwest Castle Hotel once home of Sir John Ross who discovered the Northwest Passage.

Passage planning

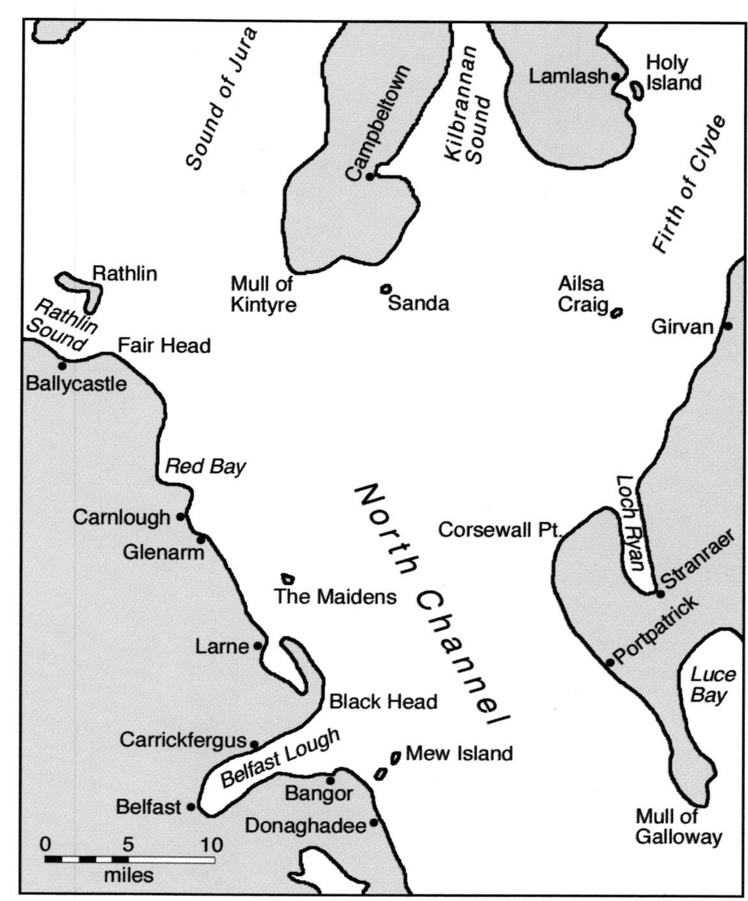

The North Channel

Charts

(i) 2126 – Approaches to the Firth of Clyde
(i) 2198 – North Channel, Southern Part
(i) 2199 – North Channel, Northern Part
(ii)1237 – Larne Lough and Approaches

General

The following notes are limited to passages from the Firth of Clyde to Belfast Lough and to the Antrim Coast. For further information, particularly for passage making between the N Irish coast and the islands of Islay, Jura and Gigha , the *Irish Cruising Club Sailing Directions for the East and North Coasts of Ireland (2002)* should be referred to. These Directions link with Part 2 of the CCC Sailing Directions for Kintyre and Ardnamurchan (Edition 2000 with updates).

Tides

The strength and direction changes of the tidal streams in the North Channel and Rathlin Sound can be best understood by reference to the Admiralty Tidal Atlas for the Firth of Clyde and Approaches (NP 222). Broadly stated the flood tide runs S'wards commencing 6 hours before HW Dover, and the ebb N'wards, 1 hour after HW Dover. Each can reach 3.5kn at springs. The tidal stream diamonds on Charts 2198 and 2199 give specific information related to HW Belfast (+0012 HW Dover). When considering a passage between Campbeltown and the E or N Coasts of Antrim account must be taken of the tidal turbulence to be experienced off the Mull of Kintyre (see p.52), and in Rathlin Sound (see p.73) if proceeding to Ballycastle or Church Bay, Rathlin.

Approaching or leaving the Irish East Coast the following sets of tide should be noted :-

(a) South from Fair Head the tidal streams along the Irish coast average 3kn increasing to 4kn off the headlands, The Maidens and the Hunter Rock off Larne. Between Fair Head and Torr Head the inshore streams can exceed 6kn.

(b) The Highlander (Highland Rock) 1.5M north of The Maidens should be given a wide berth to the E as the tide reaches 4.5 kn causing a bad race. On the W side of the Highland Rock the tide sets over Russels Rock and Allens Rock and the passage between the Highland Rock and The Maidens should be avoided.

(c) Three miles SSW of The Maidens the tide sets over the Hunter Rock (Q.Fl) at 3.5kn and it should be given a wide berth. **Note:** there is a **magnetic anomaly** in this area of up to plus or minus 4°.

(d) Off Larne and S to the Isle of Muck tidal streams are strong. For more specific details see tidal diamonds on chart 1237. The tidal streams offshore in that area can reach 5kn at springs.

(e) Opposite Black Head and 2 miles offshore the main S-going (flood tide) commences at –0500 HW Belfast (–0515 HW Dover) and the N-going (ebb tide) at +0100 HW Belfast (–0050 HW Dover). At springs the tidal rates reach 3–5kn at springs. When coasting between the Isle of Muck and Black Head advantage may be taken of the eddies which occur after half-tide both on the main flood (S- going stream) and on the ebb (N-going stream).

(f) Tidal streams are weak in **Belfast Lough** and offshore are less strong than further N and, accordingly, the direct passages between Lamlash or Loch Ryan and Belfast are more straightforward than crossings made further N.

(g) East of Mew Island, the Ram race, extending E'wards for 1M and S'wards for 2M, lasts from 2.5hrs before to 0.5 hr after HW and reaches 4kn. In unsettled weather keep 1.5M to the E.

Neither **Donaghadee Sound** nor **Copeland Sound**, where tides of 5kn and dangerous mid-channel rocks are present, should be attempted without chart 3709 and preferably with the *Irish Cruising Club Sailing Directions.*

Note

For tidal information relating to the Scottish Coast between Corsewall Point and the Mull of Galloway see p.80 of these Directions and the Admiralty Irish Sea Tidal Atlas (NP) 256.

Caution

There is potential danger from close encounters with fast cross-channel ferries. A good lookout should be kept to ensure that one is not caught out by a closing bearing situation or by the wash from these vessels.

Passage planning (continued)

Lights

Scottish Coast

Mull of Kintyre	Fl (2) 20s 91m 24M	Wh Twr on Wh Bldg
The Ship Rock, Sanda	Fl 10s 50m 15M	Wh Twr and Bldgs
Corsewall Point	Fl (5) 30s 34m 22M	Wh Twr
Crammag Head	Fl 10s 35m 18M	Wh Twr
Mull of Galloway	Fl 20s 99m 28M	Wh round Twr

Rathlin

Altacarry Head	Fl (4) 20s 74m 26M	Wh Twr black band, Racon (G)
Rue Point	Fl (2) 5s 16m 14M	Wh octagonal Twr, black bands

Irish Coast (principal lights)

Red Bay, Pier	Fl 3s 10m 5M	Metal pole
Carnlough Harbour N Pier	Fl G 3s 4m 5M	Wh Column
Carnlough Harbour S Pier	Fl R 3s 6m 5M	Wh Column, black bands
Glenarm Harbour Entrance	Fl R 3s 6m 3M	Metal pole with red can topmark
Glenarm Harbour Entrance	Fl G 3s 8m 3M	Metal pole with red can topmark
Maidens	Fl (3) 20s 29m 24M	Wh Twr, black band, Racon (M)
Maidens Aux Lt (on same structure)	Fl R 5s	Vis 142°-182° over Russel and Highland Rock
Larne	Iso WR 5s 23m 16M	Grey Twr
Black Head	Fl 3s 45m 27M	Wh octagonal Twr
Mew Island	Fl (4) 30s 37m 24M	Blk Twr Wh band, Racon (O)
Carrickfergus Marina and Harbour	For details of lights see p.78	
Bangor Marina and Harbour	For details of lights see p.79	
Donaghadee (S pierhead)	Iso.WR 4s 17m 14M	Wh Twr
South Rock Lt Ship	Fl (3) R 30s 20M	Red hull 'South Rock', Racon (T)

Directions

Campbeltown to the Antrim Coast. This passage of 35M or thereby must be planned to take account of the tides off Sanda Island and the Mull of Kintyre (see p.52). Unless a stop is made at Sanda (see anchorage details p.51) it is preferable to pass to the E and S of Sanda and to take advantage of the main W-going stream. However, unless proceeding to the N Antrim Coast and to avoid being set too far to the W and N, it is wise to use only the last 2 hrs of the ebb; that is arriving S of Sanda not earlier than 4 hrs after HW Dover. The strength of the tide, which can reach 3.5kn in mid-channel, and prevailing weather will determine the courses to steer. Several of the nearer anchorages provide good shelter in offshore winds at Cushendall and Waterfoot in Red Bay with the small harbour at Carnlough and the Marina at Glenarm offering security. (see pp. 75-76)

Campbeltown to Ballycastle. Ballycastle (see p.74) has a well sheltered marina with good facilities within relatively easy reach from Campbeltown (37 miles). Provided the passage planned (see also above) takes full account of favourable tides, and winds are not in excess of force 5, the passage can be completed without difficulty. However it is advisable to aim at arriving off Fair Head not earlier than 4.5 hrs after HW Dover which will avoid the worst turbulence as Rathlin Sound is entered. This will still allow 2 hrs of favourable tidal conditions for reaching Ballycastle. For a summary of the tidal streams in Rathlin Sound for the approach to Ballycastle see p.73 opposite. Reference to the Admiralty Tidal Atlas for the Firth of Clyde and Approaches (NP 222) is helpful.

North Antrim Coast to and from Kintyre, Islay and Gigha. It is strongly recommended that reference be made to the *Irish Cruising Club Sailing Directions for the East and North Coasts of Ireland*.

Lamlash/Loch Ryan to Belfast Lough. This passage can be undertaken with no great difficulty if account is taken of the prevailing S, SW and W winds and the tidal conditions. In fresh to strong winds, especially S of Corsewall Point, a fair sea can be set up. Clearly it is desirable to pass well E and S of The Maidens. A stop-over in Loch Ryan is a worthwhile option either at Lady Bay about 1M from the entrance on the W side of the loch or in Finnart Bay on the opposite E shore. The Wig is an alternative but a further 5M into the loch. (see p.69)

Distances
- Lamlash to Loch Ryan entrance - 31M
- Loch Ryan to Bangor Marina - 30M
- Loch Ryan to Carrickfergus Marina - 32M

Portpatrick to Belfast Lough and S towards Strangford Lough. Principally cross-tide conditions will prevail and provided due account is taken of the dangers in the vicinity of Mew Island (see Tides para (g) on p.71) and, if heading S the offshore rocks between Mew Island and the South Rock Lt Ship, these cross channel passages present no unusual difficulties.

Note

Coastal pilotage guidance for the Irish Coast from Mew Island Southwards to Strangford, Ardglass and beyond is covered in the *Irish Cruising Club Sailing Directions*.

Rathlin Sound

Chart (i) 2798—Lough Foyle to Sanda Island including Rathlin Island

General Rathlin Sound between 2 and 3 miles wide is noted for its strong tidal streams and overfalls notably the race known as Slough-na-more S of Rue point, the SE point of the island, especially between + 0100 and + 0300 HW Dover. This race can be dangerous in a W-going stream against a westerly wind or swell. Fog is not unusual.

Tide In the centre of the Sound;
W-going stream commences at HW Dover and runs for 5 hrs. As from 1 hr after HW Dover E-going eddies develop between Fair Head and Ballycastle and further W. The main W-going stream and eddies reach their strongest rates during the 2nd and 3rd hrs after HW Dover.

E-going stream commences –0530 HW Dover. A W-going eddy develops between Ballycastle and Fair Head as from –0400 HW Dover continuing until –0100 Dover.

Caution Due to inshore rocks and groundswell the coast between Fair Head and Ballycastle should be given an offing of at least 2 cables.

Lights

Altacarry Head (Rathlin East)	Fl (4) 20s 74m 26M	Wh Twr, black band, Racon (G)
Rue Point	Fl (2) 5s 16m 14M	Wh octagonal Twr, black bands
Rathlin West	Fl R 5s 62m 22M	Wh Twr
Detection light in fog VQW		

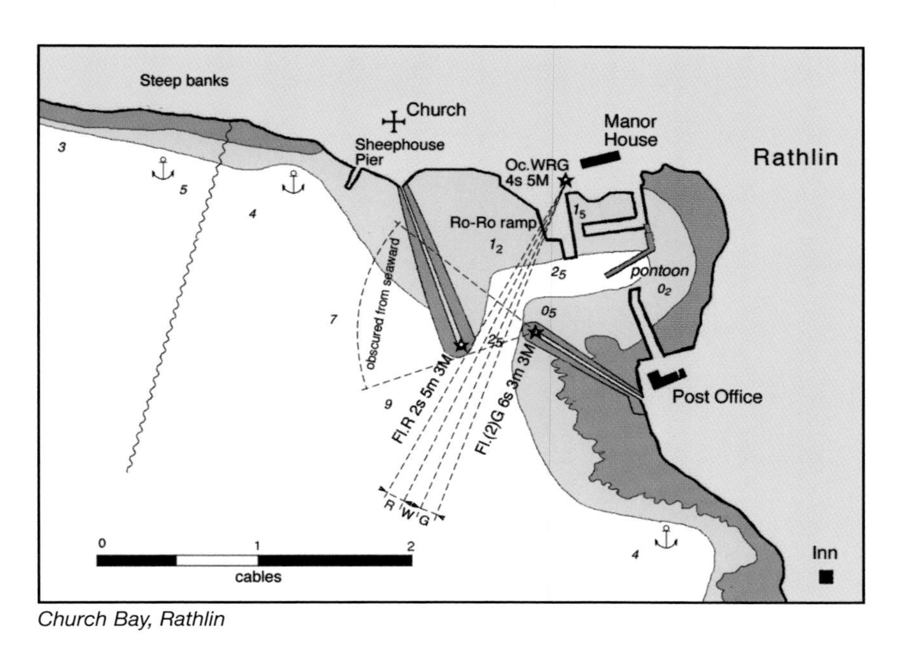

Church Bay, Rathlin

Rathlin Island, Church Bay

Chart (i) 2798—Lough Foyle to Sanda Island including Rathlin Island

General In the event that a yacht bound N round the Mull of Kintyre is faced with a freshening NW wind making progress difficult, shelter can be found at Church Bay 12M W of the Mull of Kintyre. The bay is sheltered from winds between NW through N to SSE.

Tide Const. –0445 Dover at Sp. –0200 Dover at Np. Rise Sp 1.2m Np 0.7m

Anchorage The best anchorages outside the harbour are W of Sheephouse Pier where the holding ground is reported as good but take care to avoid the underwater electricity cable shown on Chart 2798 and approximately on the plan above.

Harbour The depths and lights are as shown on the plan. The entrance to the inner harbour and depths alongside the outer quay wall are 1.5m LWS. There is a pontoon for yachts in the position shown on the plan. Water and electricity available on the pontoon. Harbour dues are payable.

Facilities Shops, PO, pub, water on quay. No fuel. Ro-Ro ferry to Ballycastle.

Interest Sea bird viewing sites.

Ballycastle

Chart (i) 2798—Loch Fyne to Sanda Island including Rathlin Island

General Situated on the North Antrim Coast 3 miles W of Fair Head, 33M from Campbeltown and 33M from Gigha, Ballycastle provides an attractive and secure harbour with marina before proceeding further W with the aid of the *Irish Cruising Club Sailing Directions.* Alternatively as a deviation during a passage round the Mull of Kintyre (distant 20M) before proceeding to or from Gigha, a visit to Ballycastle may be favoured, and similarly a long weekend visit from the Firth of Clyde is a possibility.

Tide The tidal conditions in the North Channel (see p.71) and in Rathlin Sound (see p.73) must be taken into account. Const. HW Sp –0445 HW Dover HW Np –0200 Dover Rise 1m average

Harbour Protected from the N and W by a substantial breakwater with quay for the ferry service to Rathlin Island. Within the inner harbour a marina has been positioned inside the S breakwater providing shelter from the E.

Ferry pier
Ramp
Terminal Building
Visitors berths
Car park
Ballycastle
Fl.(3)G 6s 6m 6M
Fl.(2)R 4s 5m 1M
3
3
3
2.1

Ballycastle Marina

Lights

N Breakwater	Fl (3) G 6s 6m 6M	Tubular pole
S Breakwater	Fl (2) R 4s 5m 1M	Tubular pole

Approach After making into Ballycastle Bay the approach is straightforward on a NW'ly heading. The harbour entrance between the breakwaters is open to the SE. The ferry quay on the N breakwater lies directly ahead in the approach from the SE. Turn to port off the end of the S breakwater giving the ballast at the end a fair berth before turning hard-a-port to enter the inner harbour where the marina is situated. It has been reported (2009) that depths in the harbour entrance can be up to 4m less than charted. Before approaching contact should be made with the HM.

Marina There are 74 pontoon berths including 16-20 for visitors with depths of 3m and 2m on the inner berths. Contact Marina ch 80 or telephone 02820 768525 (mobile 07803 505084).

Facilities Water and electricity on pontoons. Toilets, showers and laundry adjacent to marina. Repair facilities, engineering and electrical. Shops, pubs and restaurants.

Ballycastle Marina *Mike Balmforth*

Glenarm Marina (looking North) *Barrie Waugh*

Glenarm

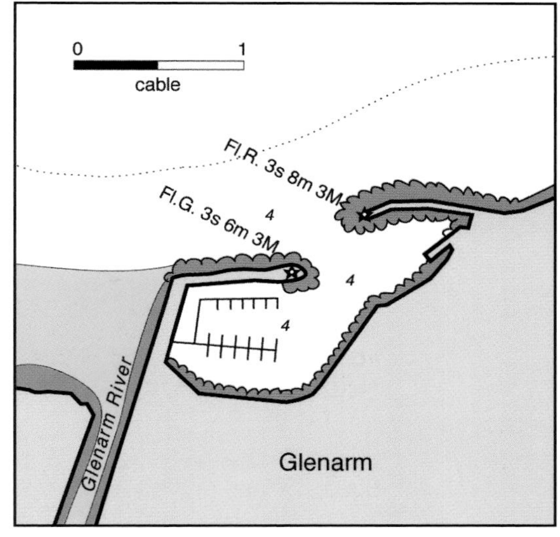

Glenarm Marina

Charts (i) 2724—North Channel to the Firth of Lorne
(i) 2199—North Channel, Northern Part

General The provision of a marina has made Glenarm a welcome safe haven for yachts making passage from and to the Firth of Clyde, and also provides a convenient jumping off or arrival point for direct passage to or from the Sound of Jura and the Firth of Lorne.

Tide Const. +0032 HW Belfast (+0020 HW Dover)
There are no tidal constraints as harbour depths are LWS 4m, HWS 6m.

Lights

W Breakwater	Fl R 3s 8m 3M
E Breakwater	Fl G 3s 6m 3M

Approach Although the harbour entrance is exposed to the N the harbour is accessible in a N'ly wind up to force 6. Apart from the large fish farm offshore the approach is straightforward by day and by night. There is good manoeuvring space within the harbour before turning to starboard to the pontoons. Pontoon lengths 11m. Depth 4m. Berths (with rafting) for 30 visiting yachts. Some swell in strong N'lies. There is no VHF communication. Contact HM on mobile 07703 606763.

Facilities Water and electricity on pontoons. Showers and toilets. Small shops and two pubs. Hotel and restaurant at Carnlough (1.5M). Tourist information, tel 02828 272677.

Fair Head to Belfast Lough

Charts (i) 2199—North Channel, Northern Part
(i) 2198—North Channel, Southern Part

General Between Fair Head and Belfast Lough all the anchorages are only tenable in offshore winds but, not withstanding this, they are often useful as stopping off points while waiting for a favourable tide in the North Channel, for a break during the passage in interesting surroundings or for shelter in strengthening offshore winds.

Anchorage **Cushenden Bay** Temporary anchorage in depth of 4-10m. Anchor off hotel (conspic.) in the S of the bay and not N of the centre of the bay which is encumbered by rocks and an unmarked wreck. **Facilities** - Hotel and shops.

Red Bay Good anchorage in 5m can be had in offshore winds from SE to NW close in at the village of Waterfoot. Subject to heavy squalls if wind is SW. Holding is reported as good. In the approach from the S keep 2-3 cables off Garron Point and clear of the two ruined piers. Adjacent to the Cushendal S&BC and the RNLI station there are five (10 tonne) yellow **visitors' moorings** provided by the Club. Payment, £10 per night, should be made to Red Bay Boats whose premises are nearby. The Boat club welcomes visitors.

Brown's Bay This bay is 7 cables E of the entrance to Larne Harbour (see p.77).

The Inner Harbour, Carnlough *Northern Ireland Tourist Board*

Carnlough

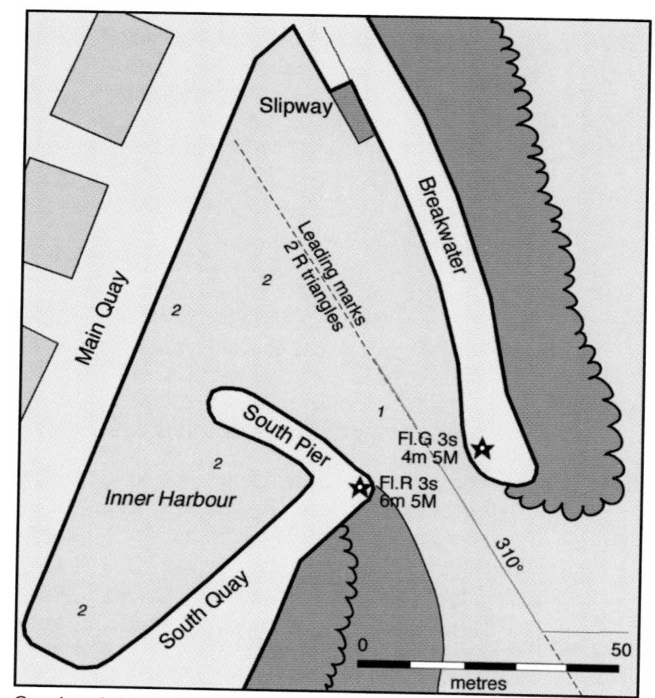

Carnlough Harbour

Chart (i) 2199—North Channel, Northern Part

General Prior to the completion of the Marina at Glenarm, Carnlough provided the only sheltered harbour between Larne and Ballycastle. Formerly a port from which limestone was shipped it is now used by local boats and visiting yachts. Carnlough provides a good base from which to explore the Antrim Glens.

Tide Const. +0032 HW Belfast (+0200 HW Dover), Rise 1.8m Sp 1.5m Np

Lights

S Pier	FR 4m 5M Wh concrete column, black bands.
N Pier	FG 4m 5M Wh concrete column, black bands.

Approach Approach the harbour on a course of 270°, heading for the South Quay, until the entrance opens and the leading marks - red triangles with a white vertical line - are in line bearing 310°. Alter course to starboard to follow this line into the outer harbour. Depth in the approach channel can be limited as silting takes place but it is reported that there is 1.7m in the channel when the ledge on the port hand wall is covered. Avoid entering with a fresh to strong onshore wind. NB: the rear leading mark is lower than the front one making identification difficult. The rear one is situated on the side of the shop store room.

Berthing & anchorage The space in the harbour, as will be seen from the plan, is very limited and usually congested. Berth in the inner harbour on the port hand or alternatively on the outer half of the N pier. Contact HM tel.02828 272677. Harbour dues payable. Good anchorage can be had in offshore winds in 4m, sand, anywhere off the head of Carnlough Bay.

Facilities Water on quay. Fuel and gas close by. PO, hotel and shops. Tourist information tel. 02828 260088.

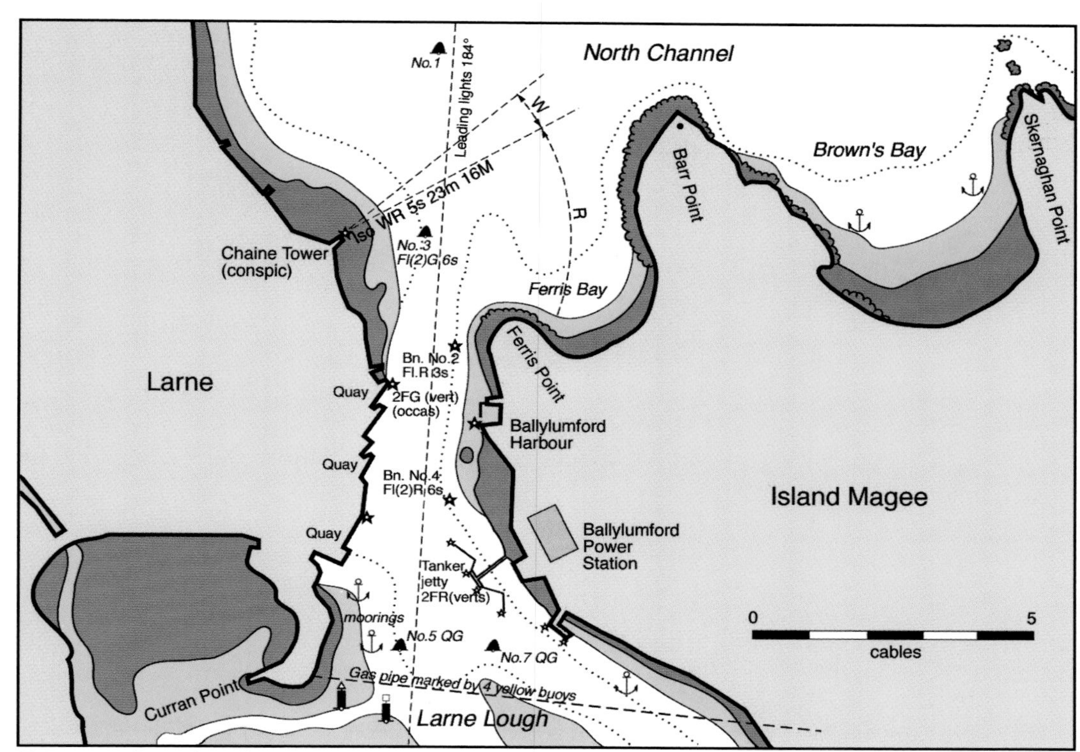

Entrance to Larne Lough

Larne Harbour

Charts (i) 2198—North Channel, Southern Part
(ii) 1237—Larne Lough and Approaches

General This very busy commercial port lying at the entrance to Larne Lough is not a harbour of first choice but can be useful if adverse weather is encountered. Glenarm is much to be preferred and consider Brown's Bay (see below).

Tides Const. + 0112 HW Belfast (+ 0100 HW Dover) Rise 2.8m Sp 2.5m Np
Offshore between Barr's Point and Hunter Rock (Q.Fl) the tide reaches 3kn particularly in the vicinity of Hunter Rock. **Note the magnetic anomaly of up to plus or minus 4° in this area.** The tidal stream in the entrance channel does not exceed 1.5kn.

Lights

Chaine Tower	Iso WR 5s 23m 16M	Grey Twr
Leading Lts (for entry to harbour) bearing 184°		
Front Lt	Oc W 4s 6m 12M	Wh diamond with red stripe on a red pile structure
Rear Lt	Oc W 4s 14m 12M	Wh diamond with red stripe on round aluminium twr
Harbour lights, beacons and buoys as shown on Chart 1237		

Approach Larne Harbour can be entered safely by night although, due to the profusion of shore lights, a daylight approach is to be preferred. From the N keep well offshore and pass to seaward of the green buoy positioned E of Chaine Tower before altering towards the harbour entrance. From the S give Skeraghan Point and Barr Point each a berth of 2 cables. Ferris Point (on E shore of the harbour entrance) should be given a clearance of 1 cable.

Call 'Larne Port Control' ch 14 (tel 02828 872179) to obtain clearance to enter harbour and to learn of ferry movements to and from the terminals on the W side of the harbour and other commercial traffic. By night, with preferably Chart 1237, continue on leading lights (184°) until abeam of the inner ferry berth on starboard hand and in the vicinity of moored yachts before seeking space to anchor in depths between 2 and 5m.

After passing the ferry terminals it is permitted to anchor on the W side of the harbour but space is much restricted by moored yachts. By contacting the East Antrim Boat Club (tel. 02828 277204) on ch 16 or M the use of a spare mooring may be arranged. There is convenient landing at the Boat Club slip. Alternatively hold to the E shore and pass the jetties opposite the Ballylumford Power Station before anchoring. Good holding in mud can be found due S of the only pylon situated right on the shore.

Facilities All stores and fuel. East Antrim Boat Club welcomes visitors. Showers and bar.

Anchorage **Brown's Bay** This bay 7 cables E of the entrance to Larne Harbour provides excellent shelter in offshore winds out of the tide and may be particularly useful when awaiting a favourable tide for passage S or N. (See tidal notes (d) and (e) on p.71). Avoid going too far in as the bay is shoal. A significant feature in the approach is the white building on Barr's Point, the W point of the bay.

Carrickfergus

Charts (i) 2198—North Channel, Southern Part
(ii) 1753—Belfast Lough

General Situated on the N side of Belfast Lough the facilities for yachts at Carrickfergus were substantially extended in 1985 by the construction of a major marina immediately to the W and separate from the original harbour. Commercial trading from the harbour ceased in 1998. There are pontoon berths for over 300 yachts in the marina and harbour both of which are administered by Carrickfergus Waterfront ch 37 (tel. 02893 366666, e-mail waterfront@carrickfergus.org). Visitors are welcome in the marina. The pontoons in the harbour are reserved.

Tide Const. + 0012 HW Belfast (HW Dover) Rise 2.9m Sp 1.8m Np

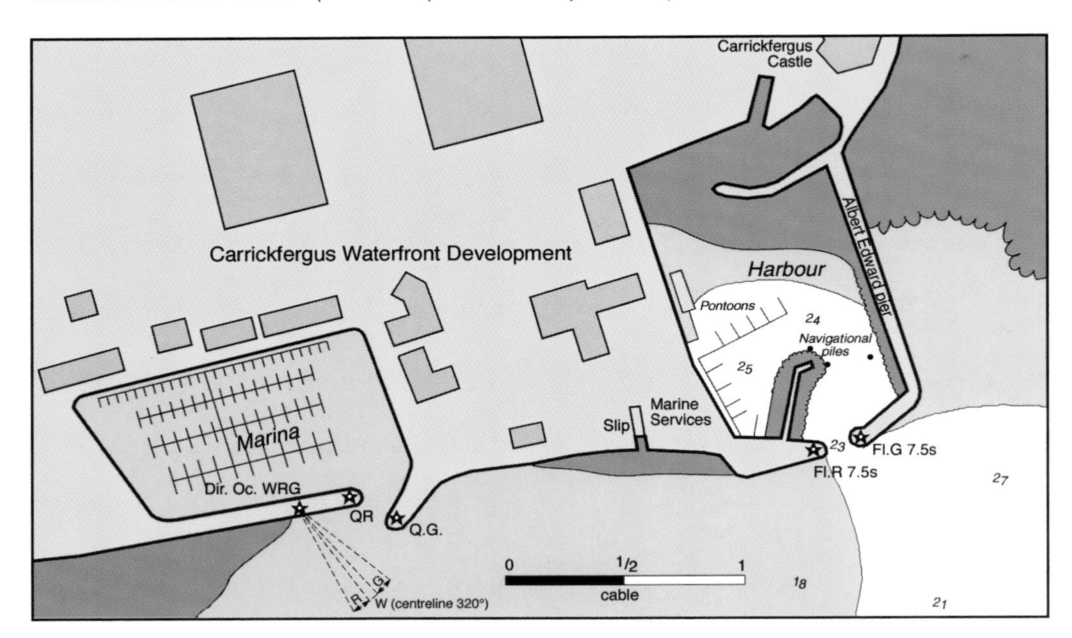

Approach The entrance to the Marina lies 300m W of the entrance to the old harbour above which stands the impressive Norman Castle (conspic!). With the aid of Chart 2198 or Chart 1753 the daylight approach from the S to the Marina is straightforward as there are no off-lying dangers but do not stray to the SW of the marina entrance. Call 'Carrickfergus Waterfront' ch 37, 80 or M or tel. 02893 366666 before entering to obtain berthing instructions.

Lights By night the Directional occulting light WRG on the W breakwater is approximately 30m W of the red navigation beacon on the end of the breakwater.
The sector widths of the light are R 9.5°, W 5°,G 9.5°. Approach with the centre of the W sector bearing 320°. See plan above for the R and G lights exhibited on breakwater beacons.

Berthing The Marina basin is sheltered by a rubble stone breakwater and is dredged to give depths up to 2.3m (7' 6") at MLWS on the outer pontoons (see plan). As the basin is subject to siltation it is advisable to check the depth at the pontoon allocated when berthing.

Facilities Visitor pontoon berths, water and electricity. Toilets, showers, sauna, laundrette. Fully equipped marine services area situated at the old harbour (see below). Diesel, petrol and Calor Gas. The Carrickfergus Waterfront in addition to providing substantial marina facilities is part of a major millennium land based leisure development – restaurants, tourism, etc. For 'repairs' see under HARBOUR below.

Carrickfergus Harbour

General Situated immediately below the 12th Century Norman Castle the Harbour consists of an outer area and an inner harbour with slipway and berths for small local boats only.

Approach The entrance is between two piers marked with red and green beacons which exhibit Fl R 7.5s 5m 4M and Fl G 7.5s 5m 4M respectively. Within the harbour pass between the perches, marking the toe of the breakwater to port and the edge of the revetment to starboard. Turn to port leaving the second breakwater perch to port before approaching the pontoons. The inner harbour and the NE section of the main harbour dries and it is inadvisable to proceed there.

Carrickfergus Harbour (continued)

Berthing The pontoons situated in the SW corner of the harbour are reserved primarily for yachts requiring repairs. These are undertaken by Carrick Marine Projects Ltd. (tel 02893 355884). There are no berths for ordinary visitors.

Facilities Fuel berth (diesel only). Marine engine and electrical repairs. Chandlery. Sail repairs. 45 ton Boat hoist and hard standing. Surveys.

Bangor Marina and Harbour

Charts
(i) 2198—North Channel, Southern Part
(ii) 1753—Belfast Lough

Tides Const. +0006 HW Belfast (+ 0004 HW Dover)

General Bangor, situated on the S side of Belfast Lough, has been developed as a major maritime leisure resort of which the marina providing berths for 550 yachts is a central feature. Visiting yachts are welcome. The substantial breakwaters ensure that there is excellent shelter from N'ly winds. The outer harbour is still used for commercial traffic which berths on the NE side of the Central Pier and on the inner North Pier.

Lights
Bangor, N Breakwater ISO R 12s 9m 9M Red concrete column
Harbour and Marina Lts - see plan.

Signals Red lights are exhibited at the end of the N breakwater and the N end of the Central Pier and when these are lit vessels are required to contact the duty berthing officer on ch 11 before proceeding.

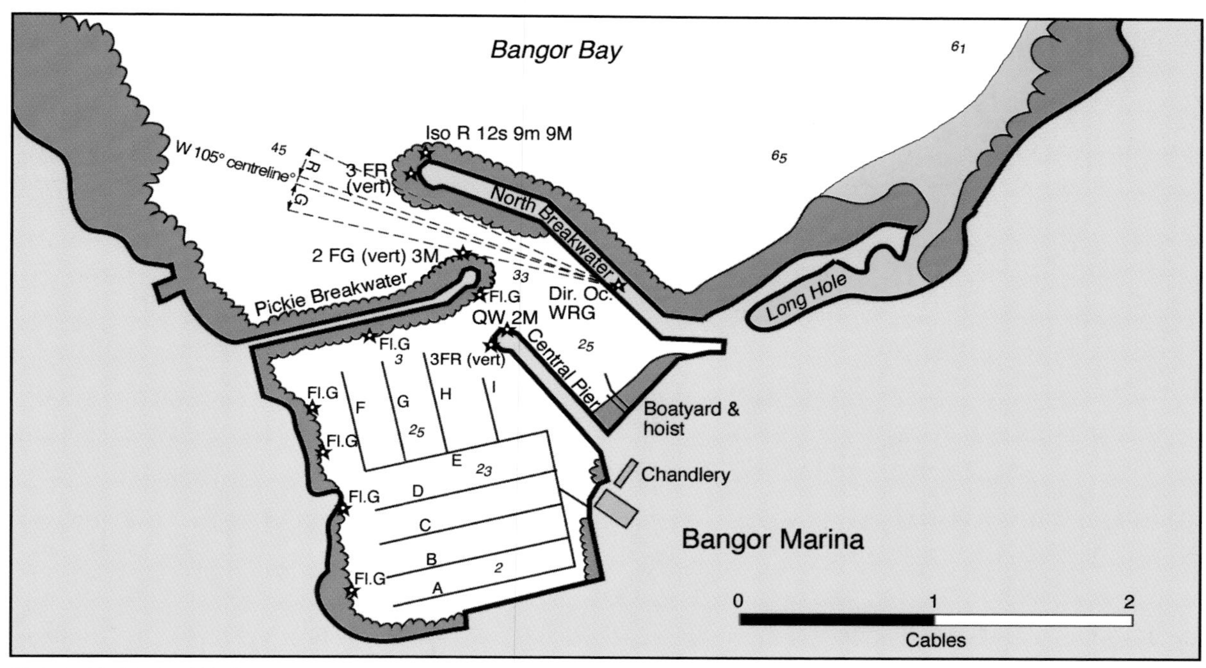

Bangor Marina and Harbour

Approach The entrance between the breakwaters faces NW and except in strong N'ly winds access is straightforward as there are no off-lying dangers. All vessels are required to call either the Harbour Master ch11 or the Marina ch 80 before entering or leaving harbour. (The Marina administration and the HM use the same office).The depth in the outer harbour is 3.3m and in the approach to and alongside the N'most pontoons is 3.0m. The inner pontoons have a minimum depth of 2m.

Berthing Visitors' pontoon berths are allocated by the Marina Office ch 80 (tel. 02891 453297; mobile 07764 313383). Access to the pontoons from the shore requires a PIN number or card issued by the Marina Office.

Facilities Water and electricity in pontoons. Fuel berth on inner side of Central Pier. Toilets, showers and laundry. Hull, engine, electrical and rigging repairs and servicing available from those contractors registered with the Marina. Shopping Centre close to the Marina. Also hotels and restaurants. Bangor is the Headquarters of the Royal Ulster Yacht Club, Coastguard MRSC (Belfast CG) and RNLI Inshore Lifeboat.

Corsewall Point to Mull of Galloway

Charts

(i) 1411—Irish Sea, Western Part OS 82
(ii) 2198—North Channel, Southern Part

General

The Rhinns of Galloway extend about 28 miles from Corsewall Point in the north to the Mull of Galloway in the south. The coast is steep-to and has no natural harbours. Between Corsewall Point and Craig Laggan (marked by a green cage beacon) a series of dangerous rocks, including the Oust Rocks, extends 2 or 3 cables off shore. From Craig Laggan to the Mull giving the shore a reasonable berth clears all but tidal race hazards. These can be cleared by keeping close inshore or else by passing several miles south of the Mull. Arrival at the Mull should be timed for slack water. The light on the Mull is often obscured by low cloud and this should be borne in mind when navigating in this area.

Caution

a) The passage round the Mull of Galloway can be hazardous particularly in the out-going tide and SW winds above force 4. In such conditions it should not be attempted.

b) When heading N remember the rounded hill, Knockdollan, 2 miles NE of Ballantrae has an outline very similar to Ailsa Craig and is sometimes mistaken for it in conditions of poor visibility, especially in the early morning when fog is often low on the sea. Knockdollan is commonly called the "False Craig"

Constant

Portpatrick const. +0020 HW Liverpool (+0035 Dover) Rise 3.5m Sp. 2.1m Np
Mull of Galloway const. –0100 HW Greenock (+0015 HW Dover)

Tides

Between Corsewall Point and Craig Laggan the stream reaches 4 knots springs in either direction. Off Black Head it reaches 5 knots springs. These inshore streams follow the coast between Corsewall Point and the Mull of Galloway as follows:

Direction	Time
S going stream begins (incoming)	+0310 Greenock (+0425 Dover)
N going stream begins (outgoing)	–0250 Greenock (–0135 Dover)

Further off shore the streams run as follows:

S going stream begins (incoming)	+0440 Greenock (+0555 Dover)
N going stream begins (outgoing)	–0120 Greenock (–0005 Dover)

Tidal races There are no tidal races between Corsewall Point and Portpatrick. However S of Portpatrick there are tidal races off Morroch Bay, off Money Head, off Mull of Logan and SE of Crammag Head. Keeping a mile or two offshore clears them. The race at the Mull of Galloway extends well offshore both S and NE of it and may be unavoidable at certain states of the tide unless the course is several miles off shore.

Lights & marks

Corsewall Point Lt	Fl.(5) 30s 34m 22M	Wh. Twr. Vis 027°– 257° (230°)
Crammag Head Lt	Fl.10s 35m 18M	Wh. Twr.
Mull of Galloway Lt	Fl. 20s 99m 28M	Wh. Twr. (often obscured by low cloud)
Portpatrick Leading Lts.	Front FG, Rear FG	Bearing 050°30
Craig Laggan	Unlit	Green iron cage beacon

4 Radio masts with red obstruction lights are situated about 3 miles N of Black Head.

Anchorage

Portmullin Temporary anchorage in settled weather about 1/2 mile E of the Corsewall Point in 9m 1 cable off a shore which is rocky and steep to. St Columba's Well and Corsewall Castle are of interest.

Dounan Bay About 2 miles SW of Corsewall Point, the most E'ly of the bays whose W end is marked by the Craig Laggan beacon which lies on an outlying rock. Anchor in 4m, sandy bottom. A convenient anchorage in off shore winds. Exposed from S to W winds.

Portpatrick Harbour *Barrie Waugh*

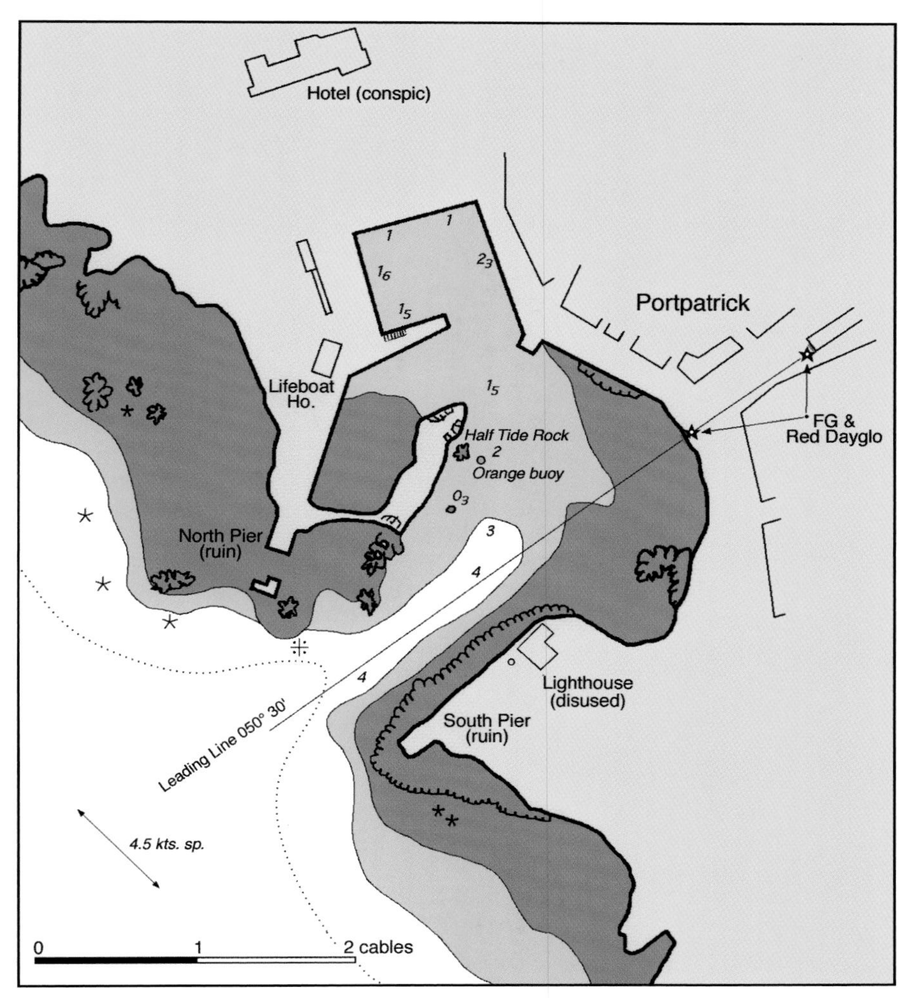

Portpatrick Harbour

Portpatrick

Chart (ii) 2198—North Channel, Southern Part

General About 2 miles SE of Black Head, a small natural indentation with a harbour within. There is a conspicuous TV mast behind Portpatrick. Approaching from the N the harbour is hidden until close-by when its red day-glo and (when shown) fixed green leading lights are suddenly visible. From the S the hotel above the harbour is conspicuous and at night its lights are clearly seen.

Tides Const. +0020 Liverpool (+0035 Dover) MHWS 3.8, MHWN 3.0, MTL 2.0, MLWN 0.9, MLWS 0.3.

Approach The entrance is narrow, between the N pier and the S pier which is marked by a disused lighthouse. Tidal streams set across the entrance strongly and entry should not be attempted in fresh to strong winds from the SW. In doubtful conditions for entering the harbour the Lifeboat Station (tel; 01776 810 251) or the Lifeboat Coxswain (tel; 01776 810 542) will be pleased to advise.

Enter on the leading line until abeam the disused lighthouse, then alter course to leave the orange buoy marking Half Tide Rock 4.5m to port. For deepest water pass close, 6m or so, to the arms which extend eastwards to protect the outer and inner harbours. Bottom clean sand. The entrance is reported as having a dredged depth of 2.4m but the depth is less in the approach to the Inner Harbour. Tie up in the inner harbour. Do not affix warps to the scaling ladders or to the harbour railings.

Facilities Shops, PO, tel, hotels, shower at public toilets Calor gas, petrol. Water at harbour. Limited boat repairs. Bus connections to Stranraer. EC Thursday. Lifeboat. **Interest:** Old church and graveyard behind Crown Hotel. Dunskey Castle.

Anchorage **Port Logan** About 4 miles N of Crammag Head. Temporary anchorage in 6m off the breakwater. Exposed from W to S winds. Although the breakwater has many rocks and boulders strewn around it and the inside dries out at LW, bilge keel boats can find shelter and dry out on level, firm sand behind the mole.

Interest The Botanical Gardens and Saltwater fish pond.

The Solway Firth

Charts

(i) 1826—Irish Sea Eastern Part.
(i) 2094—Kirkcudbright to Mull of Galloway & Isle of Man
(i) 1346—Solway Firth and Approaches
(iii) 1344—Kirkcudbright Bay

General

The Solway Firth from the Mull of Galloway to the Estuary of the Urr, a distance of 40 miles, provides in suitable conditions, interesting and safe sailing particularly for vessels which can take the ground. All the harbours on the Scottish shore dry out at LW. However with careful use of the tides and the comparatively short distances between anchorages, it is possible to avoid the hazards associated with running aground especially in a strong swell. Though some shelter from strong S'ly winds can usually be found, the coast in general is exposed to the S.

Constant

Portpatrick	+0020 HW Liverpool (+0035 HW Dover)	Rise: 3.5m Sp. 2.1m Np
Mull of Galloway	0000 HW Liverpool (+0015 HW Dover)	
Drummore	+0025 HW Liverpool (+0040 HW Dover)	Rise: 5.2m Sp. 2.9m Np
Port William	–0005 HW Liverpool (+0010 HW Dover)	Rise: 5.5m Sp. 3.1m Np
Isle of Whithorn	+0020 HW Liverpool (+0035 HW Dover)	Rise: 6.4m Sp. 3.4m Np
Kirkcudbright	+0015 HW Liverpool (+0030 HW Dover)	Rise: 6.7m Sp. 3.5m Np
Hestan Island	+0025 HW Liverpool (+0040 HW Dover)	Rise: 7.4m Sp 3.9m Np

Tides

Off the Mull of Galloway:
E-going stream begins at –0545 Dover
W-going stream begins at +0020 Dover
During the E-going stream the race at the Mull of Galloway extends NNE towards the head of Luce Bay; during the W going stream it extends SW and W for 3 miles off the Mull.
Also during the E going stream an eddy runs W towards Calliness Point then S along the coast to the Mull of Galloway.
On the E side of Luce Bay the streams follow the coast in both directions from Burrow Head to Point of Lag.

Caution

The race at the Mull of Galloway is violent and extends well off shore both S and NE of it and may well be unavoidable at certain states of the tide. Arrival at the Mull should be timed for slack water.
The passage round the Mull can be hazardous particularly in the outgoing tide and SW winds above force 4. In such conditions it should **not** be attempted.
1.5 miles NE of the Mull there is a 10m patch with very disturbed water over it. This should be avoided.

Lights

Mull of Galloway Lt.	Fl. 20s 99m 28M	Wh. Twr. (often obscured by low cloud)
Isle of Whithorn	Fl.WR 3s 20m 6/4M	
Little Ross Lt House	Fl. 5s 50m 12M	Wh. Twr. (obsc. in Wigtown Bay when bearing more than 103°)
Kirkcudbright Lifeboat Hse.	Fl. 3s 7m 3M	
Hestan Island	Fl.(2) 10s 42m 9M	Wh. metal framework Twr.

Approach

On passage for Drummore, once round the Mull of Galloway head N to clear the race and avoid the 10m patch of very disturbed water 1.5 miles NE. Give Cailliness Point a wide berth. Off Drummore the tidal stream runs NW: SE at 3 knots Sps and 1.5 knots Nps near the yellow can buoy DZ 11 Fl Y 2s.

On passage towards Burrow Head it should be noted that the tide runs E and W at 4 knots Sps and 2 knots Nps both to the west and east of **The Scares,** an extensive unlit group of rocks in the middle of Luce Bay. As the stream may set a vessel towards them, give The Scares a good offing. There is a yellow spherical Lt buoy (Fl Y 10s) situated 1.5 miles SE of Big Scare.

Luce Bay

General

A large open bay giving little shelter and offering little to interest the cruising yachtsman. Apart from The Scares, (see above) it contains few hazards but only three anchorages or harbours. (See below and p.83).

The MOD Establishment at West Freugh (tel. 01776 888741) has extended its range danger area to cover almost the whole of Luce Bay south to Big Scare, except for strips up the west and east shores to allow access to Drummore and Port William. If firing is taking place vessels may be intercepted by the Range Safety Boat: ch.16. Consequently yachts should normally take a course S of The Scares. At night keep the Mull of Galloway light bearing N of W until open of the Little Ross light.

Anchorage

East Tarbert Bay A small isolated bay in the S corner of Luce Bay about 1 mile round from the Mull of Galloway Lighthouse offering good shelter. Protected from winds from N through W to S it is well placed as a passage anchorage if awaiting the tide around the Mull of Galloway. Good anchorage in sand in 4 to 8m about 1 cable off shore from an old stone quay and house. Exposed from NE to SE winds.

Drummore

General On a westerly passage, this is the nearest port to the Mull of Galloway and is the most convenient place to await the tide or suitable weather conditions for rounding the Mull. A harbour, 4 miles N of the Mull which, though sheltered from all winds, dries out completely. Entry should be possible from half tide. Enter the channel between the NE pier and the rock causeway on a bearing of 140° from seaward. The level of silt is varied and no vessel of draft greater than 1.0m should attempt entry.

Anchorage Awaiting entry, temporary anchorage in 4 to 6m may be had in the bay in line with the main street and outside the line where the Mull Lighthouse bears over a prominent farm on a ridge 1/2 mile south of the village. Exposed from S through E to N.

Facilities Shops, PO, tel, hotel, Calor gas, petrol, water at quay. EC Wednesday. Slip for launching small craft.

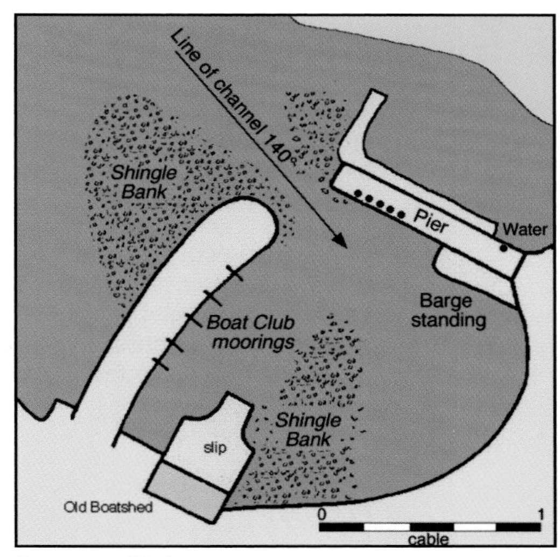

Drummore Harbour

Port William

General This very small harbour, 11 miles from Isle of Whithorn is the only one in Luce Bay between Drummore and Burrow Head. Despite the narrow entrance it offers little or no protection from strong N or NW winds. Yachts can tie up against the inner pier. Further along the inner quay wall a small pocket of shelter may be found for two yachts to tie up. This harbour is packed tight with small craft all summer. The harbour dries out and may only be entered after half tide. Approach harbour from the 'Danger Zone' yellow can buoy (DZ 6Fl Y 6s). There are no moorings but anchorage can be had in the bay in stones and mud. The bay is exposed from S through W to NW.

Lights S. Pierhead Leading Lts. bearing 105°, Front Fl.G 3s 7m 3M, Rear (130m from front) FG 10m 2M

Anchorage There is a temporary anchorage in 5m in the middle of **Monreith Bay** 2 miles SE of Port William. Good shelter from N and E winds. Completely exposed from S to NW.

Facilities Shops, PO, tel, hotel, Calor gas, limited engine repairs, petrol, water at pier. Doctor. EC Thursday

Interest Remains of 10th Century Chapel, 5 miles to the N of Port William. Gavin Maxwell Memorial on a headland at Front Bay with Kirkmaiden nearby. St. Ninian's Cave at Port Castle Bay.

Burrow Head

Tides a) There is a heavy race off Burrow Head when the W-going stream is opposed by a strong W wind. This should be avoided by holding well inshore or well out into the Firth.

b) Due to an eddy the tidal stream at the entrance to the Isle of Whithorn and for some distance off sets in springs W from 1.5 hours after LW until 2 hours before the next LW (9 hours approx.) reaching a rate of 3 to 4 knots. From 2 hours before LW until 1.5 hours after LW it sets NE and is not strong.

c) Half way across Wigtown Bay the stream reaches 4 knots springs in either direction
Tide sets E at –0600 Liverpool (–0545 Dover)
Tide sets W at HW Liverpool (+0015 Dover)

Close inshore off Burrow Head the streams begin nearly 2 hours before these times.These streams are local and are affected by eddies. The in-going tide sets ENE into Wigtown Bay before turning E. The outgoing tide sets W across the bay and then SW.

d) When making passage westward from the Isle of Whithorn against the incoming (E going) tide it is advisable to follow the shore for 4 miles round Burrow Head to take advantage of an eddy setting into Luce Bay then head for the Mull passing S of the Scares.

Isle of Whithorn

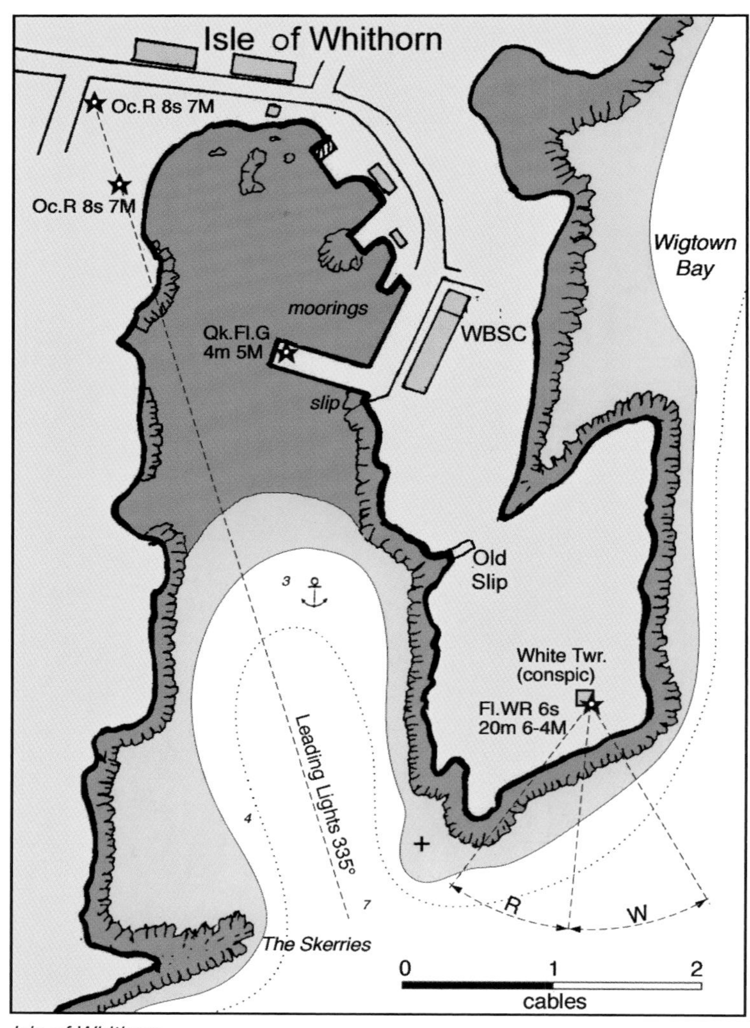

Isle of Whithorn

Charts (i) 2094—Kirkcudbright to the Mull of Galloway and Isle of Man.

General Isle of Whithorn is 18 miles from the Mull of Galloway and is the nearest port on the Solway coast to the Isle of Man, a distance of 17 miles. The harbour dries out to 10m S of the pier but yachts can enter soon after half tide.

Tides +0020 HW Liverpool (+0035 HW Dover)
Rise: 6.4m Sps 3.4m Nps

Lights Isle of Whithorn E Pier: Qk Fl G 4m 5M
Leading Lts. and day marks bearing 335°:
Front Oc R 8s 7m 7M Red disc
Rear Oc R 8s 9m 7M Red disc

Caution When entering the bay at Isle of Whithorn, allowance must be made for tidal stream setting towards the Skerries (the Screen Rocks), particularly on the ebb.

Approach The entrance, is difficult to distinguish from seaward but is marked on its E side by a low square white tower on a knoll (small peninsula). The bay has a fast tide across the mouth. A reef, The Skerries or Screen Rocks runs out from the W shore. The E shore must be given a fair berth to avoid a rock. These dangers make it advisable to enter only with a favourable wind or under power and to keep to the middle third of the apparent channel following the line of the leading lights or marks bearing 335°.

Once inside there are no outlying dangers giving both shores a fair berth. Enter the harbour and tie up against the inner quayside. Contact the Harbour Master, Channel M (37) Call sign 'Isle of Whithorn', 1000 to 1800 hours. The pier is used by fishing boats. The harbour is completely sheltered.

Anchorage Good anchorage in the bay in 2 to 6m off the old slip but SE to SW winds bring in a heavy swell which is dangerous. Avoid anchoring N of the old slip as a boat may take the ground and pound heavily. Make landing at the LW Jetty just N of the old slip. Pathway to village. **In S winds seek shelter** in Portyerrock Bay (see p.85) 1 mile to the N or alternatively if Isle of Whithorn is not available because of tide or S'ly winds, run to Little Ross (see p.88).

Isle of Whithorn Ian Michie

Facilities Shops, PO, tel, hotels diesel, petrol, limited chandlery, yacht and engine repairs. Water at quay. EC Thursday. Wigtown Bay Sailing Club. Slip for launching small boats and yachts.

Interest St Ninian's Kirk, ruined 13th C. chapel.

Wigtown Bay

General

While the southerly part of Wigtown Bay gives good sailing in the lee of the Machars peninsula, the northerly part at the mouths of the Cree and Bladnoch rivers has many mud banks and is exposed to E and to S. This produces a dangerous breaking sea. Nevertheless, the area can be explored in good weather particularly with a bilge keeler.

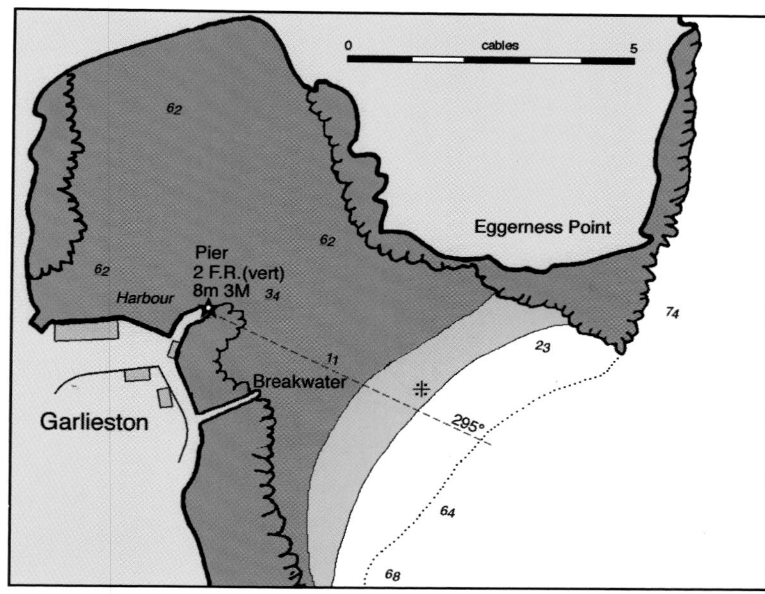

Garlieston Harbour

Anchorage

Portyerrock Bay 1.5miles N of Isle of Whithorn. Good anchorage. The use of a tripping line is recommended because of the presence of old hawser coils. Sheltered from S through W to N. Exposed NE to SE.

Garlieston Harbour 6 miles N from Isle of Whithorn. Garlieston Bay dries out but there is sufficient depth to enter the harbour soon after half tide. A rocky ledge extends 3 cables SE from Eggerson Point at the N end of the bay. A rock with 0.8m over it lies in the middle of the bay 0.5 cable seaward of the LW line and a rocky patch lies 0.5 cable off the seaward end of the pier.

All these dangers may be avoided by approaching the harbour entrance bearing 295° from some way out. When near the pier pass it at least 1 cable off its seaward end to avoid the rocky patch previously mentioned. Keep to the harbour wall side of the channel to avoid the mud bank on the other. Tie up alongside. Vessels up to 700 tons use this harbour. **Facilities:** Shops, PO, tel, hotel, Calor gas, petrol. Water at quayside. EC Wednesday. Slipway for launching small craft. **Anchorage** with fair to moderate holding ground lies 1 mile SE of Garlieston harbour entrance. Exposed to the SE

Brighouse Bay This small bay In the SE of Wigtown Bay is much used by small boats in the summer. It is dangerously exposed to winds from the S when the waves pile up in shallow water. The bay dries half way out. Enter towards the E side as Dunrod Point runs out some way from the W side. The best anchorage is reported to be where Rockvale and Brighouse farm steadings are in transit. Near the head of the bay on the E side there is a small pier.

Isles of Fleet

Anchorage

Murray's Isles 9 miles NE from Isle of Whithorn. An attractive anchorage with good holding ground off the E shore at a bay below a ruined cottage. Exposed to S. There is an isolated rock, Horse Mark, NW of Murray's Isles.

Ardwall Island Good holding ground in 4m at LW off the W shore of Ardwall Island SW of the Old Man of Fleet reef. Exposed from S to W. There is a soft mud berth off the N end of the island for yachts that can take the ground. It is completely sheltered by the island and the Old Man of Fleet reef.

Another anchorage lies off the SE shore of the island. Look for a small inlet formed by quarrying SE of a house which shows up prominently on the island. Exposed to S.

The Fleet estuary is ideal for small craft. Dinghies can be launched from nearby caravan sites. The estuary is exposed to S'ly winds. Give a wide berth to stake nets.

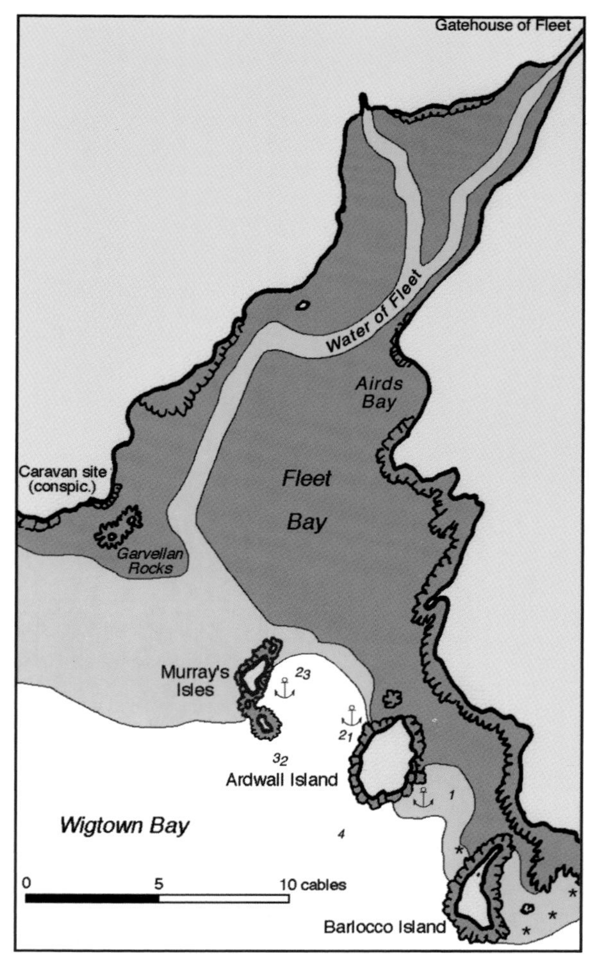

Fleet Estuary & Isles of Fleet

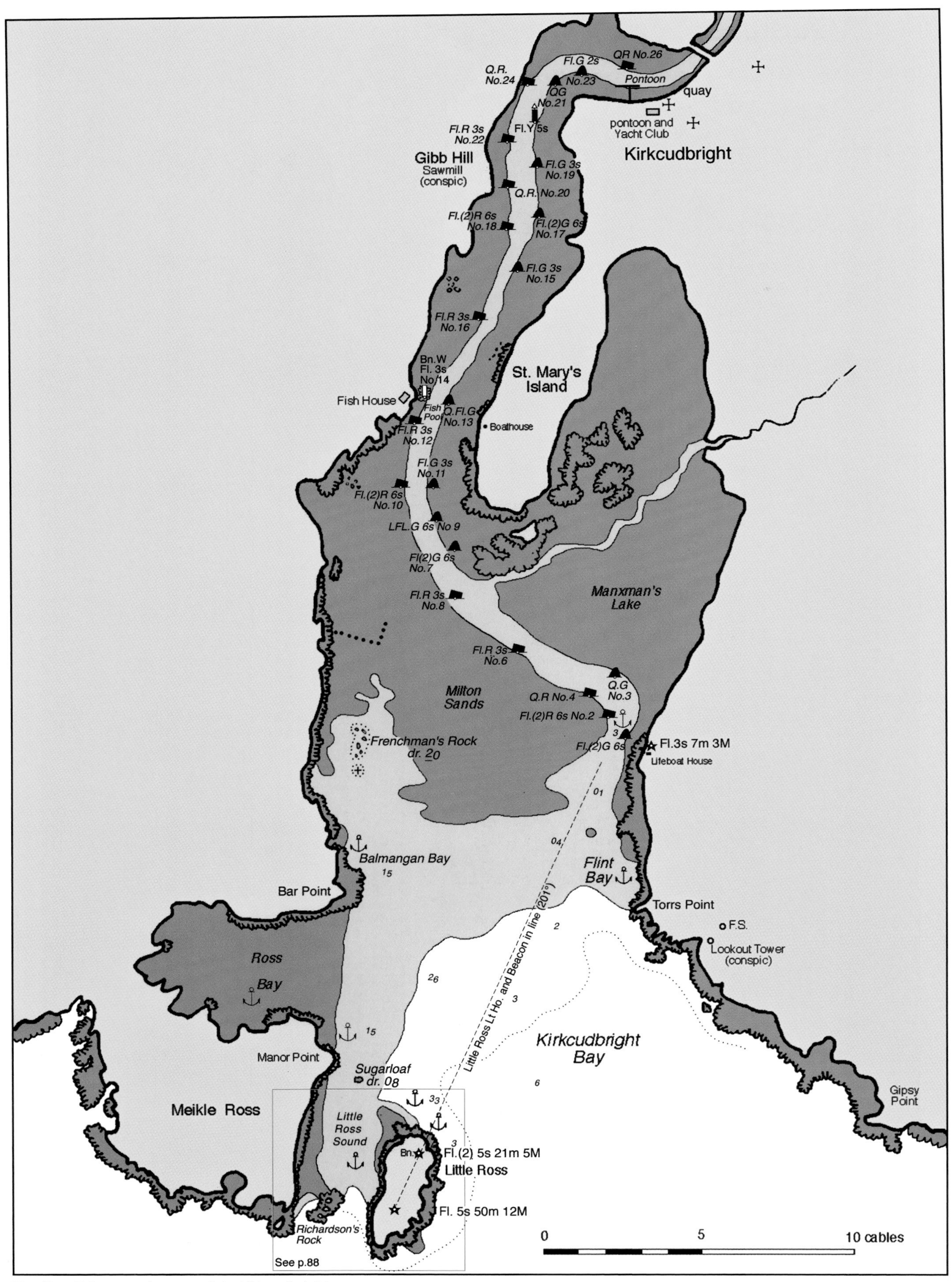

The Dee Estuary and approach to Kirkcudbright

Kirkcudbright

Charts

(i) 2094—Kirkcudbright to the Mull of Galloway and Isle of Man
(i) 1346—Solway Firth and Approaches
(iii) 1344—Kirkcudbright Bay

General

The estuary dries out and the river is not navigable at LW though coasters drawing 5m can use Kirkcudbright at HW. Yachts should not cross the bar and go up river earlier than 2.5 hours before HW making allowance for draft and weather conditions.

Constant

+0015 HW Liverpool (+0030 Dover) Rise 6.7m Sp 3.5m Np.

Tides

Off Kirkcudbright Bay and in the entrance to the River Dee the streams reach 4 knots springs in each direction.

Interval from HW	Direction
–0600 Liverpool (–0545 Dover)	E-going (In-going in River Dee entrance)
HW Liverpool (+0015 Dover)	W-going (Out-going in River Dee entrance)

Lights

Little Ross Island Light House	Fl. 5s 50m 12M	Wh. Twr.
Little Ross Island Beacon	Fl (2) 5s 21m 5M	Stone beacon
Kirkcudbright Bay Lifeboat Hse No. 1 .	Fl. 3s 7m 3M	

Channel buoys and beacons are shown on the plan opposite

Approach

Enter with white beacon and Little Ross Lighthouse in transit bearing 201° astern (Track 021°). There is a conspicuous notch in the skyline dead ahead. Maintain this heading until 3 or 4 cables before the Lifeboat Station then alter course to enter the channel leading between No.2 port hand buoy, Fl.(2)R 6s, and the starboard hand buoy, Fl.(2)G 6s, NW of the lifeboat station. Take care to avoid the uncharted Mussel Rock (dr 0.6m) which projects 20m into the channel from the E shore near the lifeboat veering buoy off the N side of the jetty. From here alter course NW to pass the reefs at the S end of St. Mary's Isle. The channel is well marked with port and starboard light buoys and perches. Off the point of St. Mary's Isle the channel is shallow and the tide runs strongly. Near Fish House on the W shore the channel is narrow and runs N'ly. In front of Fish House is Fish Pool which has a depth of 2m at LW. A beacon on the rocky beach just N of Fish Pool marks the point to turn NE.

Off Gibbhill Sawmill on the W shore, the channel is narrow and a line of old fishing stakes projects from the E shore. The channel makes a sharp turn eastwards just below the town and more fishing stakes run out from the NW bank.

Berthing

The mooring poles in midstream at the harbour have been used to secure 300 metres of pontoon berthing with electricity, water and shore access. Visiting yachts should berth on the north side of the pontoons. Numbered from seaward the least depth at LWOS between poles is as follows :– between poles 1 and 7 depth 1m, increasing to 3.6m between poles 9 and 12, with lesser depths beyond. For berthing instructions contact the Harbour Master on Ch16/12, or mobile 07709479663 or at Harbour Office (tel. 01557 331135). Upstream the channel dries out in patches and depths depend partly on the water coming down the river, especially when sluices higher up river are opened.

There is a quay on the SE side of the channel in the middle of the town, upstream from the high warehouse (block of flats). It is used by coasters and fishing boats but yachts can tie up against it, taking the ground on very soft mud. Motor boats can pass up river and anchor beyond the bridge. There is a good hard and slip just below the town quay. The slip at Gibbhill Sawmill is private but is usually available.

Facilities

Shops, PO, tel, hotels, cafes, calor gas, petrol, limited engine repairs and chandlery, cranes. Water at shops or houses. EC Thursday. Slips for launching small craft. The Kirkcudbright Sailing Club (tel. 01557 330963) can offer showers.

Interest

McLellan's Castle built in 16th century.

Caution

Firing Range There is a Ministry of Defence tank firing range on the shore extending Eastwards from the Dee Estuary to Abbeyburnfoot near Abbey Head with a danger area extending 14 miles South. When firing is in progress vessels should keep clear. A vessel on passage and unable to avoid the area should cross it with all speed at the Northern end about half a mile offshore after contacting the Range Safety Boat.

Information on firing programmes can be obtained from Range control by phoning 01557 500271, ext. 8552. Alternatively call 'Kirkcudbright Range control' on ch16 and 73.

When firing is taking place the Range Safety Boat will be on duty listening out on Channel 16. A Range Firing Programme will normally be displayed on the notice board outside Kippford Slipway Ltd.

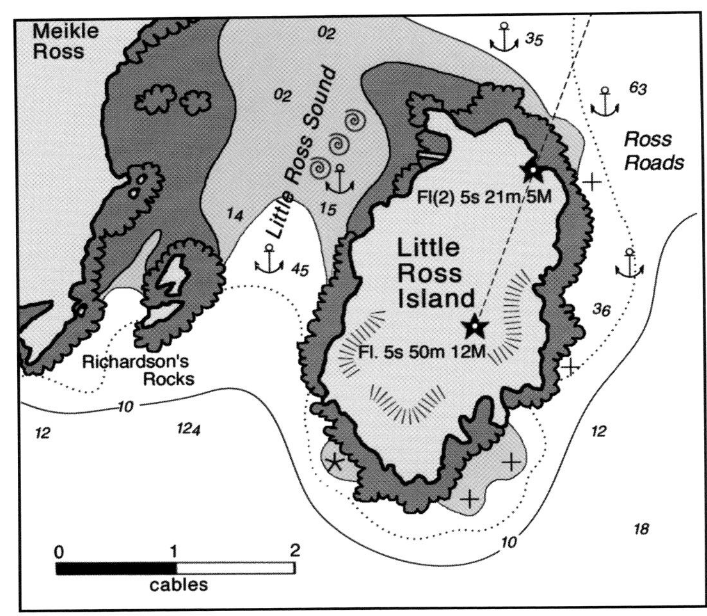

Little Ross Island, Dee Estuary

Little Ross Island

Chart (iii) 1344—Kirkcudbright Bay

Lights

Little Ross Island Lt. Ho.	Fl. 5s 50m 12M	Wh. Twr (obscured in Wigtown Bay when bearing more than103°)
Little Ross Island Beacon	Fl (2) 5s 21m 5M	Stone beacon

Tides See p 87

Anchorage **Little Ross Sound** At the SW entrance to the Dee Estuary 11 miles from Isle of Whithorn. The sound can be entered from the S at all states of the tide avoiding Richardson's Rock, some of which is always above water. Anchorage in 4 to 6m may be had between Little Ross and Richardson's Rock. The out-going tide runs strongly so beware of swinging on shore. The north entrance to the Sound is closed by a spit running out from the NW of Little Ross and a bar barely covered at LW. Enter after half tide from the NE avoiding Sugarloaf Rock (dr 0.8m) lying 2.5c NNW of the N point of Little Ross and 1.2c due W of the shore S of Manor Point. When past the spit turn SE and anchor SW of the quay where soundings permit. It is sometimes better to anchor here in the eddy caused by the north west spit, but keep an eye on the depth.

Both anchorages in Little Ross Sound are exposed from S to SW and from N.

Ross Roads Although exposed from N to SE it provides the best anchorage in the area giving some protection against SW to S winds. In bad weather seek shelter in Kirkcudbright, tide permitting. Anchor off the E, NE or N shore of Little Ross whichever gives best shelter and far enough out not to swing in shore in the tidal swirls. Watch out round Little Ross for poorly marked lobster creels.

The Dee Estuary

Anchorage **Lifeboat Station** Temporary anchorage in 3 to 4m at LW. The bar with a datum of 0.3m is 1/2 mile downstream from this but it is a convenient place to await the tide when bound up-river to the port of Kirkcudbright. Do not anchor opposite the Lifeboat slip. Find one of the holes 0.5 cable downstream or 1 cable upstream. These are sheltered by banks until the tide rises high enough to allow passage up river.

Manor Hole Anchor N of Manor Point at the entrance to Ross Bay. Good holding ground, beware of drying out at LW springs.

Ross Bay Suitable yachts can comfortably take the ground in the S side of Ross Bay on soft mud, opposite Ross Bay cottages. It is reckoned to be safe even if it blows up from SE to E.

Balmangan Bay Anchor N of Ross Bay off the southern part of Senwick Wood. An attractive little bay with sand at LW but rocky to the N and S. Good holding ground and sheltered from W winds. Exposed to SE but a very good anchorage in the usual prevailing winds.

Flint Bay Anchor N of Torrs Point at the E side of the entrance to the Dee Estuary. Sheltered from E'lies. Enter from the SW as there are half tide rocks N and S of the bay. Exposed from S to SW.

Barlocco Bay This is a temporary anchorage half way between Abbey Head and the Urr Estuary. Exposed from E through S to SW. This anchorage is off Barlocco Cave. This sea cave can be entered by dinghy in good weather at most states of the tide.

Kirkcudbright *Dumfries & Galloway Tourist Board*

Kippford *Dumfries & Galloway Tourist Board*

Kippford

General

The Urr Estuary affords the most easterly anchorages in this part of the Firth which are unobstructed by shifting sandbanks. Like Auchencairn Bay to the W the Estuary dries out completely at LW except for the bed of the river which is not navigable within 2 hours each side of LW. At HW the banks are well covered and yachts should keep to the channel.

If arriving anywhere near LW, anchor to await the tide either in the lee of Balcary Point, 1 cable off the old lifeboat slip, or well in on the W or E side of Hestan Island. Even in strong S'lies some shelter may be had very close in on the E side beyond the light tower. Anchor in 1.5 to 2m as the cottage comes into view.

Lights

Hestan Island Light Tower Fl. (2) 10s 38m 7M

Constant

+0025 HW Liverpool (+0040 HW Dover) Rise 7.4m Sp 3.9m Np

Tides

Between Abbey Head and Hestan Island and the streams at a spring rate of about 3 knots in each direction. They begin as follows:

Liverpool	Dover	
–0545	–0530	In-going
+0015	+0030	Out-going

Caution

E of the Urr Estuary in the upper part of the Solway Firth the rate and range of the tidal stream is considerable and the rise from LW very rapid especially near springs. The shifting sandbanks are extensive and navigation without local knowledge is not recommended.

Approach

The Urr's river bed is not navigable within 2 hours either side of LW. Approaching from the S or SE to clear the Craig Roan Rocks, a dangerous half tide reef extending S just E of Castle Point, keep the coast to the westward 'open' outside Hestan Island and keep Rough island 'open' of Castle Point.

Once in the channel head NW towards the steep wooded rocky shore at Gibb's Hole where the channel deepens and runs very close to the shore. Keep at least a cable off the point at Horse Isles Bay. From Gibb's Hole to Glen Isle the channel is buoyed with a series of red can buoys all of which should be left 5 to 10m on the port hand. These should not be confused with nearby orange spherical buoys which are racing marks. The channel varies from year to year. However, within 2 hours of HW there is more than 1.5m over the mud flats.

When you can see straight up the channel to Kippford village turn N and pass midway between the two perches of the Solway YC's starting line. Do not pass close to these marks as they are positioned well beyond the limits of the navigable channel. Thereafter keep between the lines of moored yachts to Kippford.

Mooring

Kippford is the main yachting centre on the Solway and is very full of yachts. As all moorings dry out all yachts must be suitable for taking the ground. Anchor temporarily off the village and enquire at Kippford Slipway, with floating pontoon nearby, for a mooring or recommended berth. The tide runs strongly in the channel off Kippford.

Palnackie 1.5 miles upriver from Kippford. The channel is not buoyed. 'Seafield Dry Harbour' has visitors' moorings and repair berths alongside staging. Facilities: Shops, PO, tel, hotels, chandlery, repair facilities.

Facilities

Shops, PO, tel, hotels, Calor gas, petrol and diesel, chandlers, yacht and engine repairs Kippford Slipway. Water at pump or club pier. Bus to Dumfries. Slip for launching small craft. Solway YC clubhouse near pier at N end of village welcomes visitors. Showers.

The Urr Estuary and Hestan Island *Dumfries & Galloway Tourist Board*

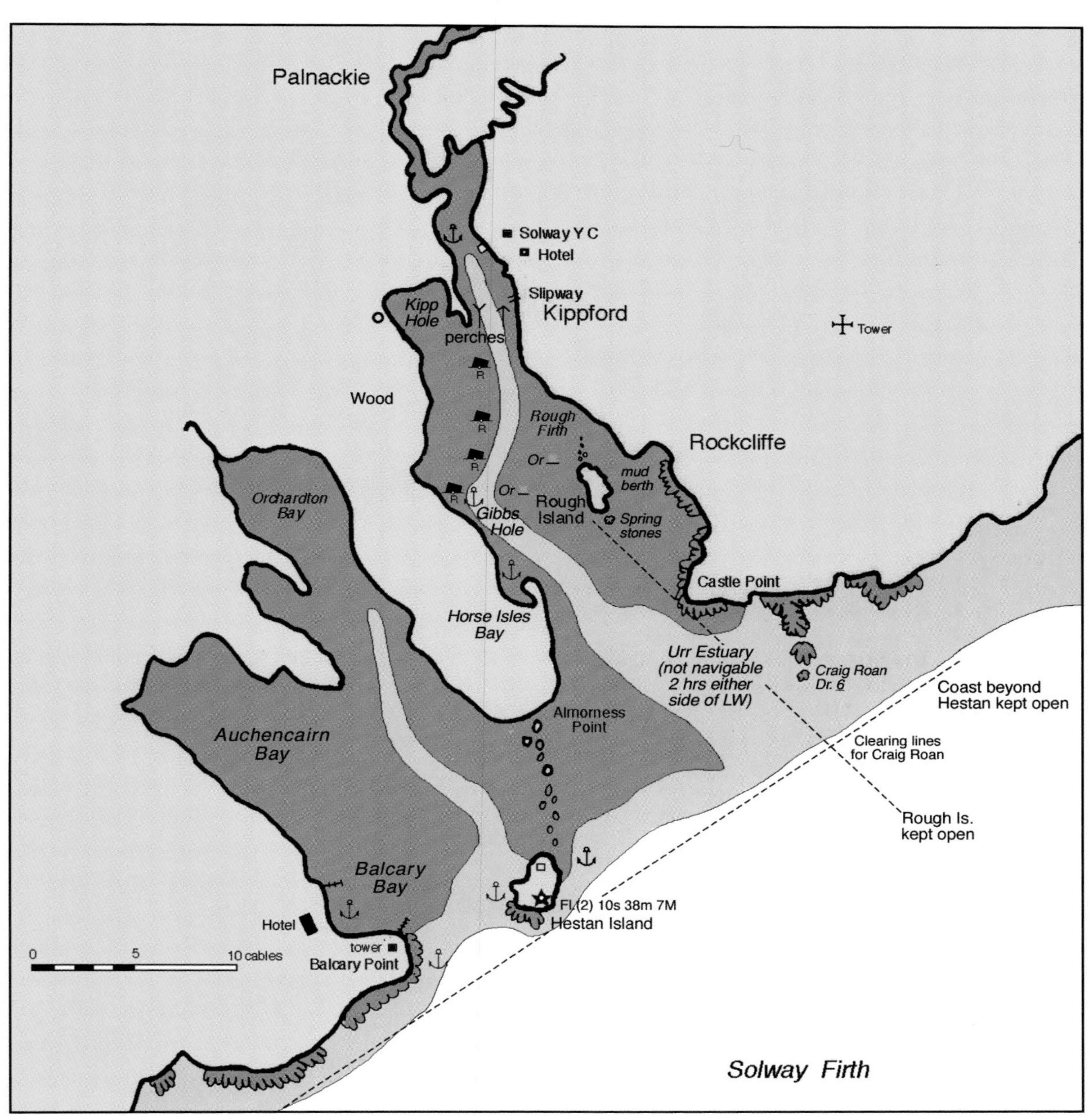

The Urr Estuary and approaches to Kippford

The Urr Estuary

Anchorage

Balcary Point and Hestan Island Temporary anchorage when awaiting the tide to enter the Urr Estuary, or for the ebb to travel westwards. In W'ly winds anchor in 2m, 1 cable out from the old lifeboat slip on Balcary Pt SE of the square tower on the shore. Exposed from E to S. In E'ly winds anchor in 2m, 1 cable out from the W shore of Hestan Island. Exposed from S to SW.

Hestan Island The best offshore anchorage in this part of the Solway E of Ross Roads. Anchor NE of a cottage at the N end of the island, in the best shelter that will still give adequate depth at LW. A spit runs from the NE end of the island to Almorness Point, well covered at HW. Exposed from E to S.

Balcary Bay Dries out at LW N of the square tower but is well sheltered and available after half tide. A suitable yacht can take the ground off the hotel, inshore of but clear of moorings. Beware of nearby stake nets which cover at HW.

Horse Isles Bay Suitable yachts can take the firm mud inside the N end of Horse Isles peninsula. Enter 2 hours either side of HW. Well sheltered though there is some swell in strong S'ly winds.

Gibb's Hole Anchor in this deep part of the approach channel off a bulge of smoother rock on the rocky wooded shore. At LW springs a spot to float a boat of draft 1.3m should be found. A convenient place to await the tide. Exposed to SE but protected by sandbanks until after half tide.

Rockcliffe Mud berth behind Rough Island. Dries out after half tide. A spit known as the Rack between Rough Island and the shore across the W entrance of Rockcliffe Bay covers only near HW.

Maryport to St. Bees Head

Charts (i) 1346—Solway Firth & Approaches
(ii) 2013—St. Bees Head to Silloth

General N of a line between Workington and Hestan Island the Solway Firth is encumbered with drying and shifting sandbanks interspersed by channels and it should not be navigated without local knowledge unless using the buoyed channel known as the English Channel. This runs parallel with the Cumbrian coast at a distance off between 2M to 3M and should be followed if making for Workington or Maryport from the SW. Approaching from the W or NW three shoals should be noted; **Two Feet Bank** which lies 6M W of Maryport marked by a W Cardinal Lt. buoy, Q(9)15s, at its W extremity which should be passed to the S, **Three Fathoms Bank** which lies 3.5M WNW of Workington and the **Workington Bank** lying 2M W of Workington and marked by a N cardinal mark, Q.Fl and a S cardinal mark, VQ(6)+L.Fl.10s. All three shoals can raise a heavy sea in strong W or SW winds. S of the Workington Bank the Firth is clear to St Bees Head which is marked by a lighthouse, Fl(2) 20s.102m18M.

Tides

Liverpool	(Dover)	Direction
–0515	(–0500)	In-going
+0045	(+0100)	Out-going

Streams run mainly in the direction of the coast and attain a spring rate of approximately 3 knots.

Maryport

General Maryport is now used mainly by fishing boats and yachts, which can lie in complete shelter in the Senhouse Dock, now developed as a marina. The lock gate to the marina is open for a minimum of 2.5 hours each side of HW.

Tides +0020 Liverpool (+0030 Dover)
Rise 7.7 Sp. 6.6 Np.

Lights Pierhead Fl.5s.10m 6M

Approach The plan shows the leading line to be followed until the Senhouse Dock lock gate is abeam. Take care not to cut the corner. **Caution** In strong W to SW winds there are overfalls at the outer entrance on the ebb. See above for off-lying shoals.

Berthing Visitor's berths are available and yachts should contact the Marina, VHF ch 12 (16), for berthing instructions.

Facilities Water and electricity to all pontoons. Toilets and showers. Slipway. Boatyard with 45t. boat hoist. Boat and engine repairs, chandlery. Marine diesel.

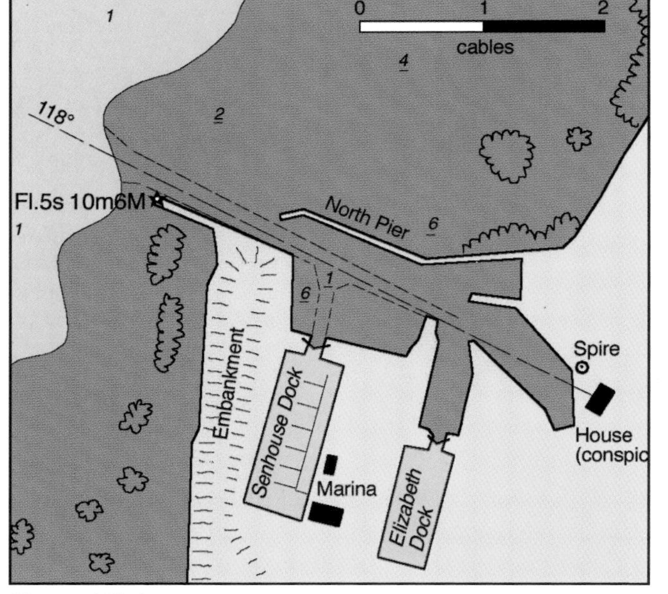

Maryport Harbour

Interest Maryport is a 19C town and the harbour was built for the coal trade. Roman camp and museum.

Workington

General Workington is a commercial port with a 1.8m dredged channel allowing access at virtually all states of tide. Good shelter is available in the Prince of Wales Dock which is also dredged to 1.8m

Tides Constant +0015 Liverpool (+0025 Dover)
Rise 7.0 Sp. 5.6 Np.

Approach The dredged channel is identified by leading marks, FR lights on white triangular towers, bearing 132°. These may be moved as the channel varies.

Berthing Berth where possible in the dock or contact the HM (VHF ch 14/16 or 01900 602301) for directions. If the dock gates are closed (HW+1.5 to HW–2) anchor in the turning basin outside the gates.

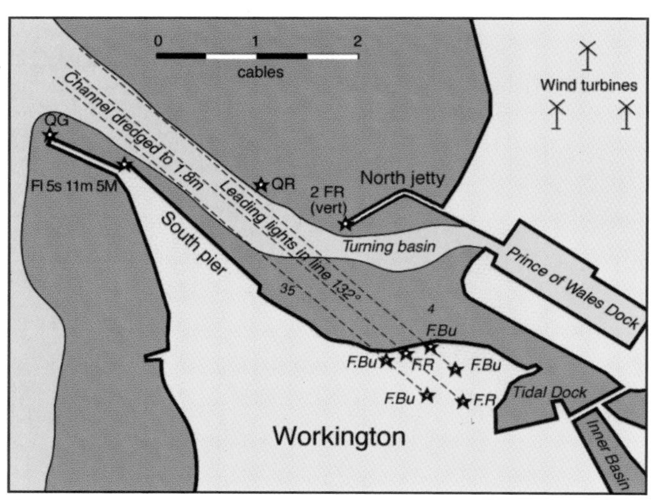

Workington Harbour

Whitehaven

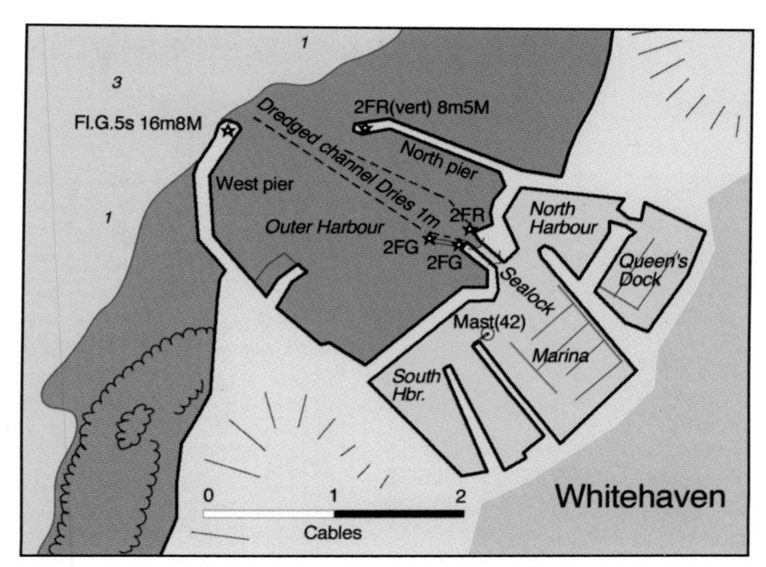

Whitehaven Harbour

Charts (i) 1346, (ii) 2013 (titles as opposite)

General Formerly a busy commercial port, Whitehaven has recently been transformed into an attractive harbour with excellent facilities for yachts in the newly formed marina and a growing fishing fleet. The installation of a sealock has impounded a large area of water allowing access for up to 4.5 hours each side of HW.

Tides Constant +0005 Liverpool (+0015 Dover) Rise 7.0 Sp. 5.6Np.

Lights West pierhead: Fl.G.5s 16m8M North pierhead: 2FR(vert) 8m5M. Others as shown on plan.

Approach There are no off-lying dangers in the approaches to Whitehaven. The Outer Harbour is approachable in most weathers with the exception of NW to N'ly gales. Entering the harbour hold towards the North Pier head until lined up on the axis of the sealock, to avoid a bar off the West Pier, but allow for a strong E-going stream on the flood. The sealock is manned 24 hours a day and should **always** be contacted on VHF ch 12(16) before entering or leaving. For a limited period each side of HW both outer and inner sealock gates will be open simultaneously permitting uninterrupted passage through the sealock. At other times make fast to the pontoon in the sealock. The outer gate cill is at Chart Datum.

Berthing Over 200 berths have been created in the main marina and the adjacent Queen's Dock. It is most likely that visitors will be allocated a berth in the Queen's Dock but yachts should initially contact the HM (tel. 01946 692435) or Sealock control for instructions. In suitable conditions anchorage can be found in 10 metres to the W of the West Pier. Good holding in mud. Do not anchor in the Outer Harbour.

Facilities Water and electricity to all pontoons. Toilets, showers and laundry. Slipway. Boatyard with 45t. boat hoist. Boat and engine repairs, chandlery. Marine diesel. Supermarket near harbour and all usual facilities in town.

Interest Whitehaven is an early example of Georgian planning and contains many interesting buildings within a short walk of the harbour. It has a long maritime history which is interpreted in 'The Beacon' which adjoins the South Harbour.

Whitehaven, Local yachts moored in the South Harbour *Edward Mason*

Mull of Galloway to Point of Ayre

Charts

(i) 2094—Kirkcudbright to Mull of Galloway & 1826—Irish Sea Eastern Part
(iii) 2696—Plans In the Isle of Man
Isle of Man OS 95 Imray C62
Note: The above charts apply to all the Isle of Man directions and are not listed in each section.

General

The Point of Ayre is the most N'ly point on the Isle of Man and lies 21 miles SE of the Mull of Galloway and 17 miles due S of the Isle of Whithorn. It is advisable to leave the Mull of Galloway at about LW to gain from the incoming tide. If heading for Ramsey, the Strunakill Bank should be left on the starboard hand before an inshore course is set down the east coast of the island. The streams run nearly continuously eastwards across this bank and breaking seas may be encountered on it.

Lights

Point of Ayre:	Fl (4) 20s 32m 19M	Wh. Twr. 2 red bands, Racon (M)
Maughold Head	Fl(3) 30s 65m 21M	Wh. Twr.
Douglas Head	Fl 10s 32m 24M	Wh Twr. and buildings
Langness, Dreswick Pt.	Fl (2) 30s 23m 21M	Wh. Twr.
Chicken Rock Lt Ho.	Fl 5s 38m 13M Horn (1) 60s	Granite Twr.
Calf of Man Lt Ho.	Fl I5s 93m 26M Horn(1) 45s	Wh. oct. Twr. on granite building

These are the major lights around the island. Other lights, e.g. harbour lights, are referred to in the relevant text.

Constant

Pt of Ayre const. 0000 Dover Rise 5.4m Sps 2.4m Nps.

Tides

Streams between the Mull of Galloway and the Point of Ayre are strong. The main incoming tide from the North Channel divides, part going into the Solway Firth and the other part going south to the Isle of Man. The Solway branch divides further to form a branch into Luce Bay. At the Point of Ayre rates up to 5kn are attained. The tidal diamonds on Chart 2094 indicate rates and direction offshore.

Point of Ayre to Douglas Head

General

Leaving Mull of Galloway on the flood, the point of Ayre should be passed close to in order to reach a position to avoid the Whitestone Bank and the Bahama Bank which run from about 3/4 mile off shore south-easterly for about 4 miles. The banks are marked at the NW end by a W cardinal pillar buoy (YBY) Qk Fl (9)15s. The inshore passage is about 3/4 mile wide and is used by commercial traffic. The Bahama Bank stretches SE, its end being marked by the Bahama Buoy, S cardinal pillar buoy (YB) Q(6) + L.Fl 15s

The coast from the Point of Ayre southwards to Douglas Head is free from dangers, although a tide of 2 to 3 knots may be experienced along the coast.

Tides

The N going stream runs for 9 hours and the S going stream for 3 hours as follows:

Liverpool	(Dover)	Direction
–0345	(–0330)	NW-N
+0515	(+0530)	SE-S

For detailed tidal Information and general Sailing Directions see 'Sailing Directions, Tidal Streams and Anchorages of Isle of Man' by the Manx Sailing and Cruising Club, The Lookout, Queen's Promenade, Ramsey. IM8 1BG

Port St. Mary, Inner Harbour *Peter Killey*

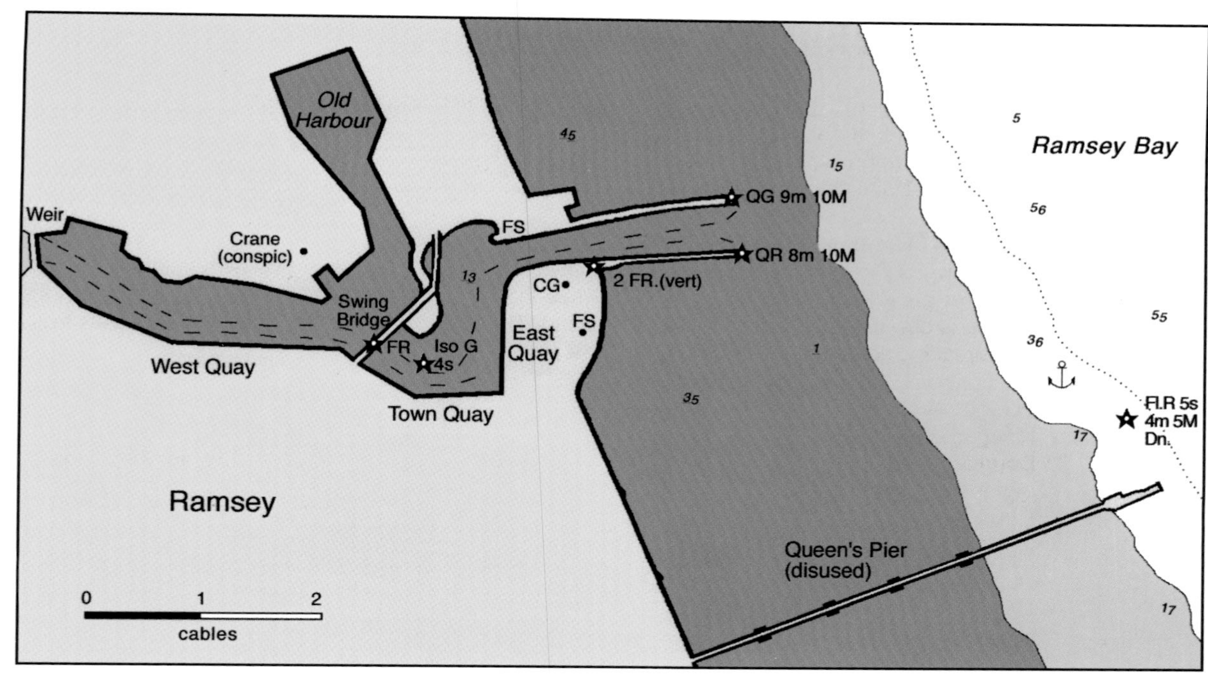

Ramsey Harbour

Ramsey

General Ramsey is a tidal harbour 6M S of the Point of Ayre and is used by commercial and fishing traffic. Shelter is very good except in strong NE winds. The harbour can only be entered 2 hours either side of HW as it dries. Approach is made between two piers. The entrance is 43m wide and the tide sets across it. For berthing directions contact HM on VHF ch.12 or tel. 01624 812245 during working hours. Outside these hours contact Douglas Harbour Control on VHF ch.12. Yachts normally tie up to the Town Quay as near the swing bridge as possible.

Constant –0004 Liverpool (+0011 Dover) Rise Sp. 6.3m, Np. 5.3m

Lights

N Pier Head	Occ.G 5s 9m 5M	Wh Twr. Black base
S Pier Head	Occ.R 5s 8m 4M	Wh. Twr. Red band, Black base

Anchorage Anchor 0.5 cable NNW of the dolphin N of Queen's Pier in 4m sand. 2 orange visitors moorings may be available. **Note;** Landing at Queen's Pier is prohibited.

Facilities The Manx Sailing and Cruising Club is very welcoming. All facilities including diesel and electronic engineers. Shops, Hospital and RNLI lifeboat. Public toilets. Swimming pool.

Laxey

General Lying approximately halfway between Ramsey and Douglas. A small boat harbour which dries. Entry is confined to 2 hours either side of HW. The harbour is full of small craft but alongside berthing at the pier is possible.

Constant 0000 HW Liverpool (+0015 Dover)

Lights

Pier Head	Oc.R 3s	Wh. Twr. Red band
Breakwater Head	Oc.G 3s	Wh. Twr. Green band

Anchorage In settled weather anchor 3c off Laxey Beach in 3m. Good holding in sand. Visitor's mooring in the area of Garwick Bay during summer months.

Facilities Shops. Electric train to Douglas and Mountain Railway. to summit of Snaefell.

Interest The Laxey Water Wheel. Snaefell Motorcycle Museum.

Point of Ayre Lighthouse *Peter Killey*

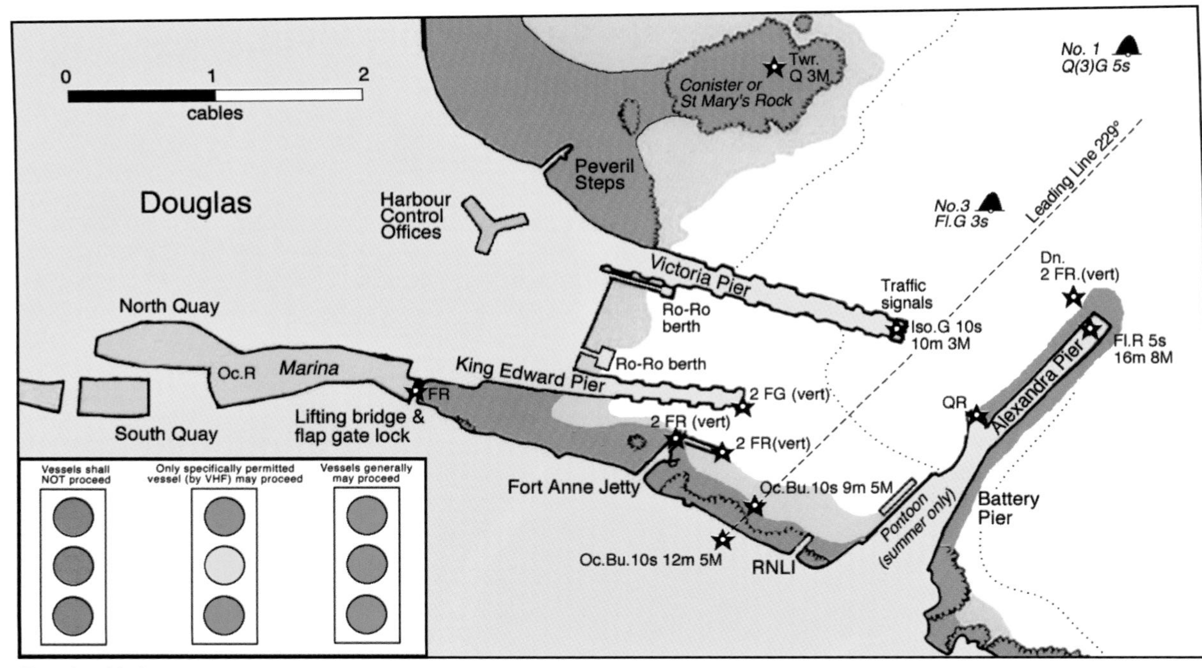

Douglas Harbour

Douglas

General Douglas, the best harbour on the island, lies in the SW corner of Douglas Bay which is bounded by Onchan Head in the N and Douglas Head to the S. Douglas Head is very prominent and is identified by a light Fl 10s 32m 24M. The area is busy with commercial traffic, there being a Ro-Ro Terminal and several ferry services. The HM should be called on VHF ch.16,12 or tel. 01624 686628 when approaching harbour. By day or night traffic movements may be controlled by light signals exhibited from the signal mast at the outer end of the Victoria Pier (see diagram) Supplementary lights below the above signals may be shown: A red cross - 'Do not proceed'; A white arrow - 'Proceed in the direction indicated'.

Constant –0004 Liverpool (+0011 Dover.) Rise Sp. 6.8m Np. 5.3m

Lights

Douglas Head Lt. Ho.	Fl.(6) 10s 32m 24M	W. Twr.
Harbour Lights	See plan above.	

Approach This is made from the NE. Pick up No.1 channel marker buoy (Q(3)G 5s) then, after obtaining HM permission and when approaching the outer end of the breakwater, pick up leading line, bearing 229° both Occ 10s 9/12m 5M, front and rear red triangles on white posts. This course will lead past channel marker buoy No.3 (Fl G 3s) to starboard. Yachts entering will normally be contacted by HM launch with specific instructions.

Berthing During the summer months there is a pontoon at the inner end of the Battery pier, but availability of this is subject to tanker movements. Also 3 large communal visitors moorings between Fort Anne jetty and RNLI slip. At the inner end of the harbour a marina has been established. This is approached through a lifting bridge and flap gate which operate for 2 hours before and after HW and access must be arranged with the HM. Yachts up to a max. draft of 2m and max. length of 14m can be accommodated.

Facilities All facilities. inc. Lifeboat, Marine diesel; Douglas Bay Yacht Club, with showers, situated on The Tongue near the marina.

Douglas Head to Spanish Head

General From Douglas Head to Langness (Dreswick Point) the shore is rocky, the only danger being Baltic Rock which lies 0.5 cable off the S of Santan Head. Langness Peninsula should be given a good offing as a ledge, the Skerranes, extends 1 cable SW of Langness Point. Langness Lt House (Fl (2) 30s 23m 21M Horn (2) 80s) is situated at Dreswick Point at the SE end of the peninsula. Tidal streams run strongly off Langness reaching a maximum of 5 knots springs. Eddies form on both sides of the peninsula especially in Castletown Bay where a nearly continuous S-going stream occurs along the SE shore of the bay. From Langness to Spanish Head the only danger is The Carrick, a drying rock in the centre of Bay ny Carrickey, which has a light on a black and red conical tower Q (2) 5s 6m 3M.

Anchorage **Derby Haven** Lies on the NE side of Langness peninsula and is sheltered from all winds except NE. The head of the bay dries and a detached breakwater has been constructed on a drying rocky ledge. A light (Iso G 2s 5m 5M) is at the S end of this breakwater. The Haven itself is used by small boats but dries out beyond the breakwater. Anchorage may be had off the jetty on St Michael's Island in 2 to 3m clear of moorings.

Douglas Head to Spanish Head (continued)

Castletown Bay The bay dries out all round for about 2 cables from the shore. The W side of the bay is bordered by the Lheeat-rio Rocks marked on the E side by a red can light buoy (Fl R 3s) with bell. Temporary anchorage can be had N of a line between Castletown Harbour and Boe Norris (dr 0.1m) which is unmarked, in 3 to 5m at a distance of 3 cables offshore. The plan on chart 2696 must be referred to.

Castletown Harbour The harbour and approaches which dry can only be entered 2 hours either side of HW. It is marked by a light on the outer breakwater (Occ R 15s 8m 5M) and red and green entrance lights. Before making approach call the Harbour Master (VHF ch 16, 12) and if no response call Douglas HM. Keep NE of the breakwater as a landing hard for small craft which can take the ground projects from it for 0.75 cable. Tie alongside the Irish Quay in the Inner harbour and contact the Harbour Master. The harbour is used by small coasters. The outer harbour is subject to swell from the S and SE. but can be used in settled weather.

Facilities Shops, PO, tel, hotels, EC Thursday. Calor gas. Water at quay. Lifeboat. Nautical Museum.

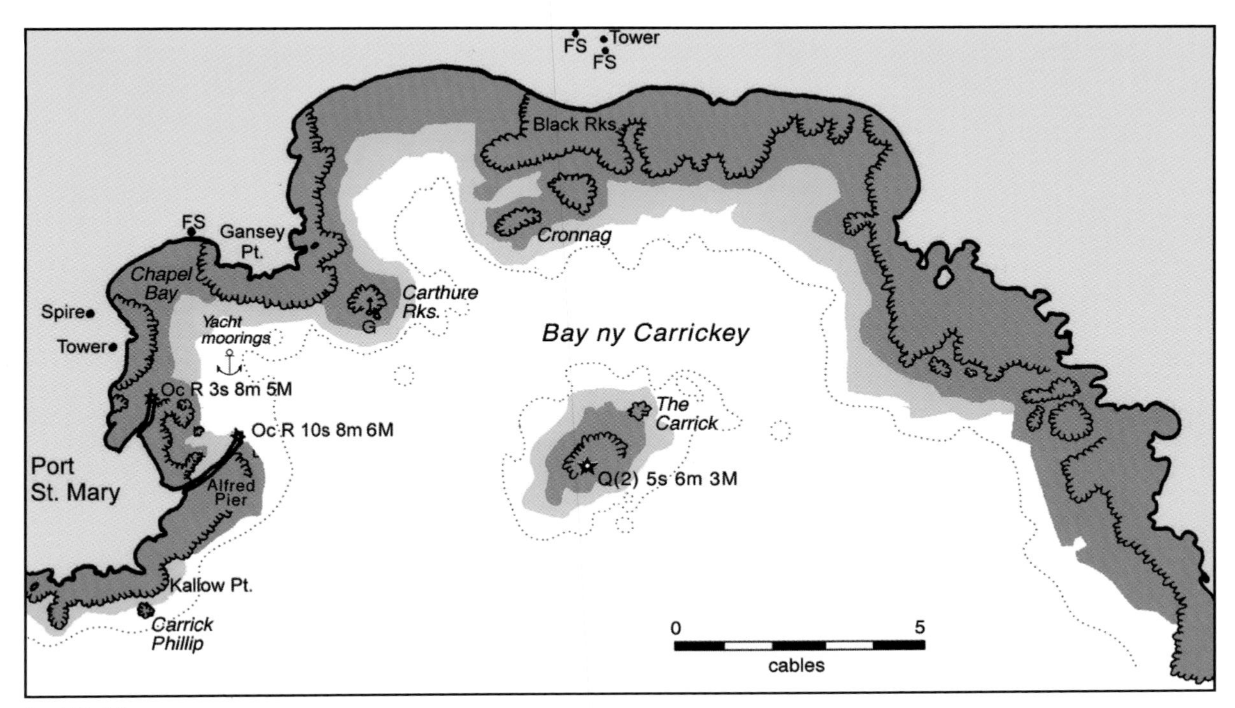

Port St. Mary

Port St. Mary

Constant –0004 HW Liverpool (+0011 Dover). Rise Sp. 6.8m Np. 5.3m

General An attractive small harbour 5 miles W of Langness Point, Port St. Mary lies in the SW corner of Bay ny Carrickey and offers good shelter in most conditions.

Lights For details see plan and text below.

Approach From the E round Scarlett Point, keeping the light at the head of Alfred Pier in line with the E Pier light of the Inner Harbour (bearing 301°) leads S of The Carrick which is a rocky patch lying in the centre of the bay. It is marked by a light on a black and red conical tower Q (2) 5s. From the W give Kallow Point a berth of 2 cables and, keeping the same offing, turn to port where the E pier head (of the Inner Harbour) is open N of Alfred Pier (Oc R 10s 8m 6M Wh. Twr. Red Band). The E pier shows a light (Oc R 3s 8m 5M Wh. Twr. Red band).

Anchorage Fishing boats use the outer end of Alfred Pier but it is possible to tie up inshore of them. If the wind is in the E a large swell can be experienced here. The Inner harbour can be entered 3 hrs. each side of HW but it dries at its head and is very busy. Report to Harbour Master on arrival or call Harbour Master on VHF Ch 16,12 before entry.

Anchorage may be had, or perhaps a visitor mooring, in the centre of Chapel Bay, S of Gansey Point and the Carthure Rocks, marked by a green post with a cone top mark.

Facilities Shops, PO, tel, hotels. Water at pier. Isle of Man Yacht Club, showers. Marine engineer, Sailmaker, EC Thursday. Lifeboat.

Point of Ayre to Calf of Man

General From the Point of Ayre to Jurby Head the coast is low lying. The only danger is a sand spit off Jurby Head ending in Jurby Rock with depths of 2.7m over it. Jurby Rock is 4 cables W of Jurby Head. From Jurby Head to Peel the coastline is rocky and a course 1/2 mile off shore avoids all dangers. S of Contrary Head the coast is steep-to and with the exception of Niarbyl Island, where a rocky ledge extends 3 cables WSW of Dalby Point, there are no dangers outside 1 cable off shore.

Tides The SE going and NW going streams of the North Channel divide and meet off Contrary Head and run as follows:

6 mlles N of Contrary Head

Liverpool	(Dover)	Direction	Mean Sp Rate
+0610	(–0600)	NE by E	1kn
HW	(+0015)	WSW	1.25kn

5 miles W of Contrary Head

+0610	(–0600)	SSE	1.25kn
HW	(+0015)	NW by W	1.25kn

From Contrary Head N to the Point of Ayre the stream runs parallel to the coast and increases to 3 knots springs at the Point of Ayre. Similarly the stream between Contrary Head and the Calf of Man runs in the direction of the coast and increases in strength towards the S. Between Dalby Point and Bradda Head the stream is almost continuously N going due to an eddy which runs N during the S going stream.

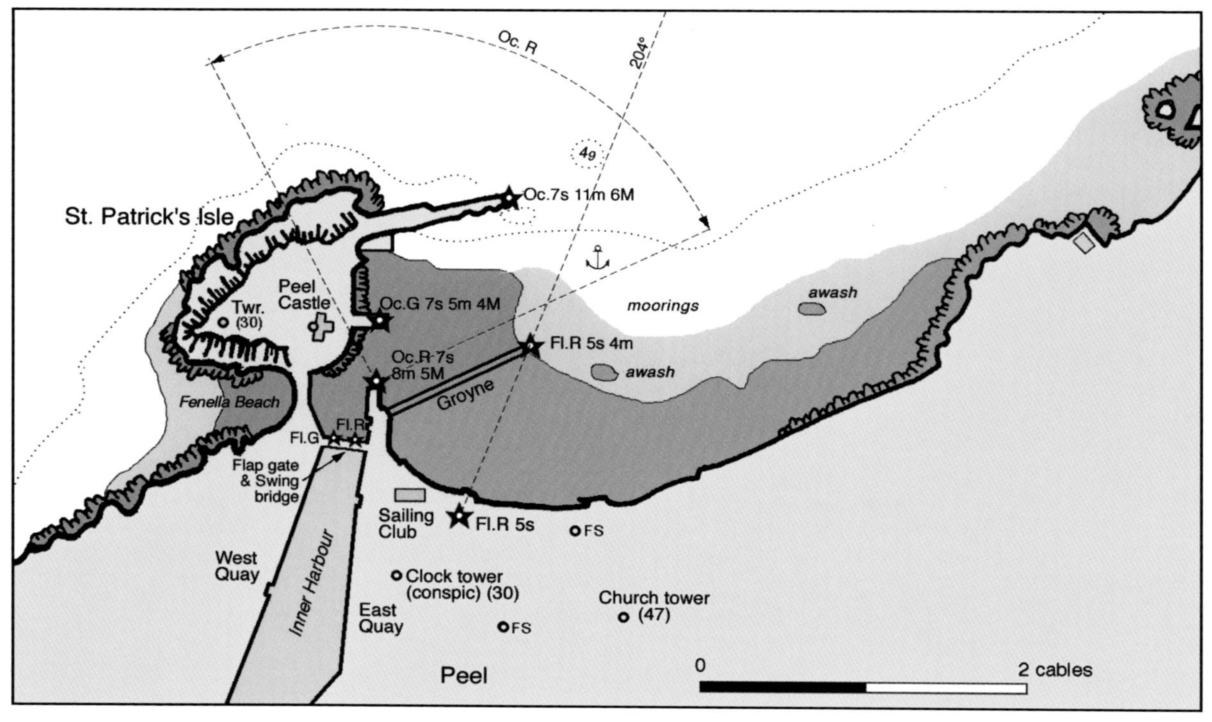

Peel Harbour

Peel

General From the N the breakwater light (Oc 7s 11m 6M) exhibited from a white tower is easily visible. From the S Peel Castle on St. Patrick's Isle is conspicuous. The harbour and breakwater are on the NE side of the island. There are depths of 4 to 6m along the S side of the breakwater and yachts may be able to tie up alongside although local trawlers use this facility. Anchoring is possible within 0.5 cable of the breakwater on its S side in 3m. Sheltered from NW through S to E but a swell may set in from the NW. The groyne shown on the plan may cover near HW. It is marked by a black and white striped light beacon (Fl.R.5s 4m) at its outer end. There is access to the inner harbour two hours either side of HW over a Flap Gate with 2.5m over the sill. Contact the HM on ch.12 or tel 01624 842338 or mob 07624 495036. There is a pedestrian bridge which must be opened. The HM will give directions for berthing. There is 2.5m depth on W and E quays for a distance of 100m from the bridge.

Constant +0008 Dover. Rise Sp. 5.6m Np. 4.3m. The tidal gauge on the S side of the breakwater shows a depth of one metre greater than is available over the sill of the Flap Gate.

Facilities Shops, PO, tel, hotels, petrol, diesel, boat and engine repairs. Bus connection to Douglas. RNLI lifeboat. Coastguard Station. EC Thursday. Sailing Club.

Anchorage **Fleshwick Bay** 3 miles S of Niarbyl Island. Temporary anchorage may be had in off shore winds in 6 to 8m.

Port Erin

General Port Erin lies 1M SE of Bradda Head which is 7 M S of Contrary Head. Milner's Tower on Bradda Head is conspicuous from the W. The Sker Rock and a shallow patch (1.5m) are the only dangers on the N side of the bay.

Approach A ruined breakwater extending from the S side of the bay is marked by an unlit green conical buoy which must be left to starboard when entering the bay from the S. There are leading lights (bearing 099°) into the bay.

Anchorage Anchor in line with the Lifeboat House due S of the leading line in 5 to 7m. Bottom sand and gravel. There are two yellow visitors mooring buoys near this position. The bay is exposed to W winds. Raglan Pier dries out.

Facilities Water at pierhead. Shop, PO, tel, hotels, petrol, limited yacht repairs. Lifeboat (inshore).

Interest Marine Biological Station. Steam railway to Douglas.

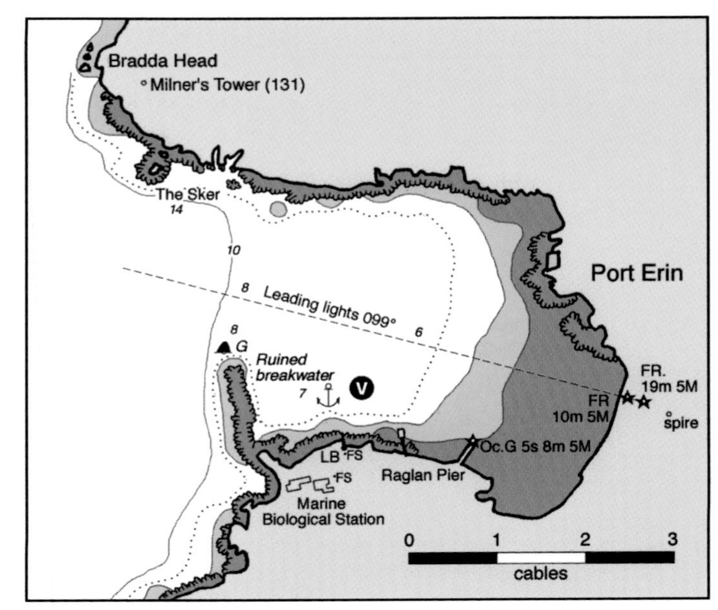

Port Erin

Calf of Man & Calf Sound

Lights Chicken Rock Light House Fl.5s 38m 21M Granite Twr.
Thousla Rock Fl R 3s 9m 4M. Wh. pillar.

Approach **The Calf of Man** is the island at the S end of the Isle of Man separated from it by Calf Sound. Care should be taken if rounding the Calf since tidal streams run strongly and overfalls extend E'wards from Chicken Rock, during the E going stream, and N'wards on the W going stream. Although there is little stream close in to the W and S sides of the Calf, a spring rate of 4 knots is found off Chicken Rock. It is therefore advisable to plan one's passage to arrive off Chicken Rock at slack LW. Passage between the Rock and the Calf of Man may be attempted in fine weather.

Calf Sound The passage is less than a cable wide and lies between Thousla Rock marked by a concrete beacon to the W and the island of Kitterland to the E.

Tides The tide runs at 3.5 knots springs through the Sound. The N going stream begins at –0145 Liverpool (–0330 Dover) and the S-going stream at + 0345 Liverpool (+0400 Dover).

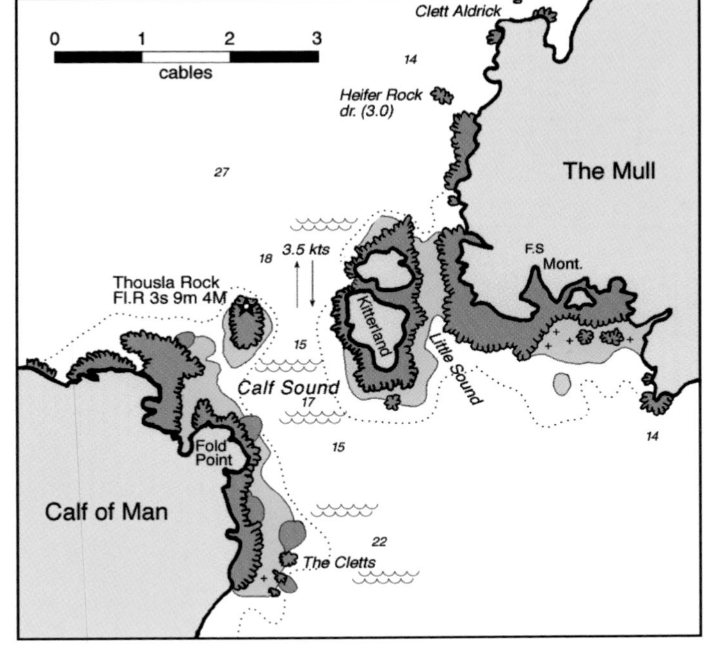

Calf Sound

British Waterways
Boat Safety Scheme

Introduction
British Waterways welcome visitors to our canals. To make sure that this and future visits are as safe as possible, we have introduced the Boat Safety Scheme.
The Boat Safety Scheme is designed to minimise the risks to people and property of fire and explosion on board boats. British Waterways have also introduced a requirement that all boats should have at least third party insurance.

General Requirements
From 1 January 1998 owners wishing to get a licence to use our canals for short periods (for example trail boats arriving by land and launched into our waterways) will have to:

- show us a Boat Safety Certificate showing that their boat meets the Boat Safety Scheme standards: and
- show us evidence that their boat has cover for third party liabilities in Great Britain of at least £1 million.

Passage Waterways
Owners will have to show us evidence that their boat has cover for third party liabilities in Great Britain of at least £1 million. However, they will not have to produce a Boat Safety Certificate for licences of upto 28 days where the boat enters the British Waterways' system by water for passage to and from waters not managed by British Waterways. In this case we will expect the boat to pass a free "dangerous boat" spot check carried out by a person authorised by British Waterways. The boat will be checked to see there is no:

- Leaking fuel ;
- leaking gas ;
- damage to electrical cables; and
- no imminent danger of capsize or sinking.

Owners can have upto 56 days of short term licences in any 12 month period under this arrangement. We will require a Boat Safety Certificate to be produced for further licences.

Haven
We will offer a haven in a quarantined area when there is inclement weather for boats that do not have a Boat Safety Certificate or fail the "dangerous boat" check. We also allow boats that fail the dangerous boat check up to 48 hours in the quarantined area to allow work to be done to meet the check or to make ready for departure.

Long term users
Will have to show that they have a Boat Safety Certificate and third party insurance.

Further information please contact a local Canal Office

Crinan Canal Office
Pier Square
Ardrishaig
Argyll PA30 8DZ
Tel: 01546 603210
Fax: 01546 603941

Forth and Clyde Canal
Rosebank House
Camelon
Falkirk FK1 4DS
Tel: 01324 671217
Fax: 01324 671225

Caledonian Canal Office
Seaport Marina
Muitown Wharf
Inverness IV3 5LS
Tel: 01463 233140
Fax: 01463 710942

Submarine Exercise Areas

Keep the echo sounder running if passing through an exercise area when submarines are operating. Warnings of areas allocated for exercises are given by Clyde, Liverpool and Belfast Coastguards along with the weather forecasts at the times given in the Introduction on p.3

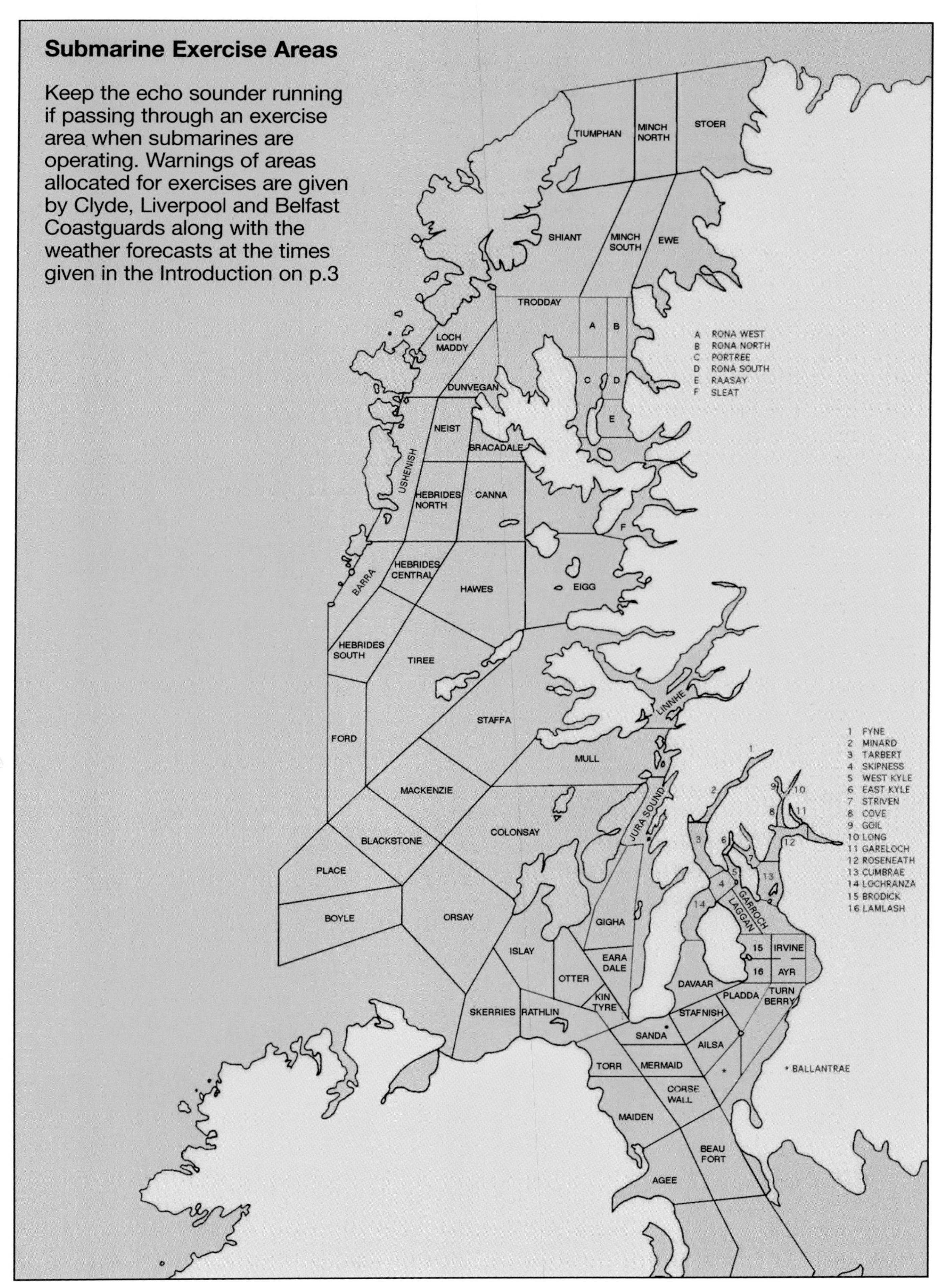

Index

A

Ailsa Craig, 67
Allens Rock (nr The Maidens), 71
Ardbeg Point, Rothesay Sound, 29
Ardbeg Pt, Loch Striven, 29
Ardentinny, 18
Ardgarten, Loch Long, 20
Ardlamont Point, 35
Ardmaleish Point, 29
Ardmarnock Bay, 37
Ardmore Head, 14
Ardnadam, 21
Ardnahein Bay (Swine's Hole), 19
Ardrishaig, 41
Ardrossan - Marina, 59
Ardrossan Harbour Signals, 59
Ardwall Island (Fleet Bay), 85
Arran, East Coast, 55
Arran, West Coast, 54
Arrochar, 20
Asgog Bay, 35
Ashton, 13
Auchalick Bay, 37
Auchgoyle Bay,(Loch Fyne), 46
Ayr, 63
Ayr Harbour Signals, 63
Ayre, Point of, 94

B

Bagh Buic (Buck Bay), 37
Bahama Bank, East of Pt of Ayre, 94
Ballantrae, 67
Ballochmartin Bay (Balloch Bay), 25
Ballycastle, 74
Bangor, 79
Bangor Marina and Harbour, 79
Barmore Island, 39
Baron's Point, 13
Bennane Head, 64
Black Harbour (Loch Fyne), 37
Black Head (Belfast Lough), 71
Blackfarland Bay, 33
Blackwaterfoot, 54
Blairmore, 18
Blindman's Bay, 33
Bowling, 11
Brighouse Bay (Wigton Bay), 85
Brodick Bay, 55
Brown's Bay, 75, 77
Buck Bay (Bagh Buic), 37
Burnt Isles,The, 31
Burrow Head (Tides), 83
Buttock of Bute, 31

C

Caladh Harbour, 32
Calf of Man, 99
Calf Sound, 99
Callum's Hole, 23
Calrndow, 47
Campbeltown, 50
Camsail Bay, 17
Carnlough, 76
Carradale, 49
Carradale Bay, 49
Carrick Castle, 19
Carrickfergus, 78
Carrickfergus Harbour, 78
Carrickfergus Marina, 78
Carrow Bay, Loch Goil, 19
Carry Rock buoy, 33
Castletown Harbour(I of M), 97
Catacol Bay, 54
Chart Agents, 8
Chart Index, 6
Church Bay, Rathlin, 73
Cloch Point, 12,22
Cloch Point to Helensburgh, 12
Cloch Point to Little Cumbrae, 22
Clydeport, 8
Clynder, 17
Coastguards, 4
Colintraive, 31
Copeland Sound, 71
Cordon (Lamlash Bay), 57
Corrie, 55
Corsewall Pt to Mull of Galloway, 80
Coulport, Prohibited Area, 18
Cove, 18
Crinan, 42
Crinan Canal, 41
Crinan Canal (passage plan), 42
Crinan Canal ,(regulations), 42,100
Culwatty Bay, 15
Culzean Bay, 64
Cumbrae Islands, 24
Cushenden Bay, 75

D

Davaar Island, 50
Dee Estuary - Anchorages, 88
Derby Haven, Isle of Man, 96
Deuchlands, The, 39
Donaghadee Sound, 71
Douglas Hd to Spanish Hd, 96
Douglas Pier, Loch Goil, 20
Douglas, Isle of Man, 96
Dounan Bay (nr. Corsewall Pt), 80
Drummore, 83
Dumbarton, 11
Dunagoil Bay, 34
Dunoon, 22
Dunure, 64

E

East Coast of Arran, 55
East Kyle, 31
East Loch Tarbert (Loch Fyne), 39
East Tarbert Bay (Luce Bay), 82
EMERGENCIES, 4
Ettrick Bay, 33

F

Fair Head, 71
Fair Head to Belfast Lough, 75
Fairlie, 25
Fairlie Quay, 25
Farland Point (Great Cumbrae), 24
Farland Point to Heads of Ayr, 59
Faslane, Prohibited Area, 17
Fast cross-channel ferries, 69, 71
Fearnoch Bay, 32
Finnarts Bay (Loch Ryan), 69
Finnart Oil Terminal, 20
Fintry Bay, Great Cumbrae, 23
Firth of Clyde, 3
Fleet Estuary, 85
Fleshwick Bay (nr Peel), 98
Forth and Clyde Canal, 11

G

Gantocks, The, 22
Gareloch Approach, 15
Gareloch Naval Dockyard Port, 15
Gareloch, The, 17
Garelochhead, 17
Garlieston Harbour, 85
Garroch Head, 22
Gibb's Hole, Urr Estuary, 91
Gibb's Point, Holy Loch, 21
Girvan, 66
Girvan Harbour Signals, 66
Glac Mhor (Loch Fyne) , 44
Glen Mallan jetty, Restrictions , 20
Glenan Bay, 37
Glenarm, 75
Glencallum Bay (Callum's Hole), 23
Gourock, 13
Great Cumbrae, 25
Greenock, 10
Grogport, 48

H

Heads of Ayr to Loch Ryan, 64
Heads of Ayr, The, 63, 64
Helensburgh, 12, 14
Hestan Island, 91
Highland Rock (at The Maidens), 71

Index

Holy Island, 57
Holy Loch, 21
Holy Loch Marina, 21
Horse Isle, 59
Hunter Rock (nr The Maidens), 71,77
Hunter Rock, Magnetic anomaly, 77
Hunter's Quay, 21

I
Inchmarnock, 34
Inchmarnock Sound, 34
Innellan, 22
Inveraray, 47
Inverchaolain, Loch Striven, 29
Inverkip Marina, 23
Inverkip Bay, 23
Irish C C Sailing Directions, 72
Iron Rock Ledges, 54, 57
Irvine, 60
Irvine Harbour bridge, 61
Isle of Muck, Antrim Coast, 71
Isle of Whithorn, 84
Isles of Fleet, 8515

K
Kames, 33
Kerry Kyle, (West Kyle), 33
Kilbrannan Sound, 48
Kilbride Bay, 35
Kilchattan Bay, 23
Kilcreggan, 15
Kildalloig Bay, 50
Kildonald Bay, 48
Kilfinan Bay, 37
Kilmun, 21
Kingscross, Lamlash Bay, 57
Kip Marina, 23
Kippford, 90
KIrkcudbright, 87
KIrkcudbright MOD Range, 87
Kirn, 22
Knap Bay, 18
Knockdollan (The False Craig), 69
Kyles of Bute, 30–33
Kyles of Bute, N channel, 31
Kyles of Bute, S channel, 31

L
Lachlan Bay (Upper Loch Fyne), 46
Lady Bay (Loch Ryan), 69
Lady Isle, 62
Lamlash , 56
Langness Peninsula, 96
Largimore,(Otter Narrows), 44
Largs, 25
Largs Channel & Fairlie Roads, 24
Largs Yacht Haven, 25
Larne , 77
Laxey, 95
Little Cumbrae, 27
Little Ross Island, 88
Little Ross Sound, 88
Loch Fyne, 35–47
  Lower Loch Fyne, 35–39
  Upper Loch Fyne, 44–47
Loch Gair, 45
Loch Gilp, 41
Loch Goil, 19
Loch Long, 18, 20
Loch Ranza, 54
Loch Riddon, 32
Loch Ryan, 69
Loch Ryan Sailing Club, 69
Loch Striven, 29
Lochgilphead, 41
Lochgoilhead, 20
Lochhead, Loch Striven, 29
Luce Bay, 82
Lunderston Bay, 23

M
Machrie Bay, 54
Magnetic anomaly (nr Larne), 77
Maidens Harbour, 65
Maidens, The, 71
Marinas
  Ardrossan, 59
  Ballycastle, 74
  Bangor, 79
  Carrickfergus, 78
  Douglas (Isle of Man), 96
  Glenarm, 75
  Holy Loch, 21
  Inverkip (Kip), 23
  Largs, 25
  Rhu, 17
  Maryport, 92
  Troon, 62
  Whitehaven, 93
Maryport, 92
Maryport to St. Bees Head, 92
McAlister's Yard, Dumbarton, 11
Measured distance, Arran, 55
Measured distance, Skelmorlie, 22
Meikleross Bay, 15
Mew Island, 71
Millport, 27
Minard Bay, 46
Minard Narrows, 46
MOD Firing Range Dee Estuary, 87
MOD Firing Range, Luce Bay, 82
Monreith Bay, 83
Moorings, for Visitors
  Ardentinny, 18
  Barmore Island, North, 39
  Brodick, 55
  Cairndow (Opposite), 47
  Dunoon, 22
  Campbeltown, 50
  Kames, 33
  Lamlash Bay, 57
  Laxey, 95
  Millport, 27
  Rothesay, 28
  Tighnabruaich, 33
Mull of Galloway, 82
Mull of Galloway to the Pt of Ayre, 94
Mull of Kintyre, 52
Mull of Kintyre, tidal atlas, 53
Mull of Kintyre, tidal streams, 52
Murray's Isles (Fleet Bay), 85

N
Naval Dockyard Ports, 9
Newton Bay, Loch Fyne, 47
North Channel, 71–79
North Channel-Passage Planning, 72
North Sannox, 55

O
One Tree Island, Loch Riddon, 32
Ormidale, 32
Otter Narrows, 44
Otterard Rock, 50

P
Palnackie, 90
Paterson's Rock, 51
Peel, 98
Pladda, 57
Point of Ayre to Calf of Man, 98
Point of Ayre to Douglas Head, 94
Pontoons, for Visitors
  Campbeltown, 50
  Girvan, 66
  Irvine, 60
  Portavadie, 36
  Rothesay, 28
  Tarbert., 39
Port a Mhadaidh (Portavadie), 36
Port Ann, 44
Port Bannatyne, 29
Port Crannaich (Carradale Hbr), 49
Port Erin, 99
Port Glasgow, 10
Port Logan, 81
Port St. Mary, 97

Index

Port William, 83
Portavadie (Port a Mhadaidh), 36
Portincaple, 18
Portkil Bay, 15
Portmullin (nr Corsewall Pt), 80
Portpatrick, 81
Portyerrock Bay (Wigton Bay), 85
Publications, 8

R

Ramsey, 95
Rathlin Island, 73
Rathlin Sound, 73
Red Bay, Antrim Coast, 75
Rhu Bay, 15
Rhinns of Galloway, 80
Rhu Marina, 17
Rhu Narrows, Restrictions, 13
River Clyde, 10
RNLI Lifeboats, 5
Rosneath Bay, 17
Rosneath Patch, 15
Ross Roads, 88
Rothesay, 28
Rothesay Sound, 28
Royal Northern and Clyde Yacht Club, 17
Russels Rock (nr The Maidens), 71

S

Saddell Bay, 48
Sail repairs, 79
Sailmaker, 17, 25, 39
Saltcoats Harbour, 61
Sanda, 51
Sanda Sound, tides, 52
Sandbank, 21
Sannox Bay, 55
Scalpsie Bay, 34
Scares, The (Luce Bay), 82
Scart Rock, Lady Isle,Troon, 62
Scottish Maritime Museum, 61
Scottish National Water Sports Training Centre, 25
Sgat Mor (Skate Island), 35
Shandon, 17
Shearwater Rock, 34
Shepherd's Point,Loch Long, 18
Shipping channels, 8
Silver's Yard, Rosneath, 17
Skate Hole, 35
Skate island (Sgat Mor), 35
Skipness Bay, 48
Skipness Point, 48
Solway Firth, 82
St Bees Head, 92
St Catherine's, Loch Fyne, 47
St Ninian's Bay, Bute, 34
Strachur Bay, 47
Stranraer, 70
Strone, 21
Stroul Bay, 17
Strunakill Bank, 94
Submarine Exercise Areas, 101
Swine's Hole, Loch Goil, 19

T

Tarbert (Loch Fyne), 39
The Maidens, 71
The Wig, 69
Tighnabruaich, 33
Toll a Bhuic, Loch long, 18
Toll nam Muc, Loch Long, 19
Tomont End (Great Cumbrae), 25
Torrisdale Bay, 49
Toward Bank (Barnhilt buoy), 23
Toward Bay, 23
Toward Point buoy, 23
Troon, 62
Troon Marina, 39

U

Upper Loch Fyne, 44
Upper Loch Long, 20
Urr Estuary, Anchorages, 91

V

Visitors Moorings & Pontoons, See Moorings/Pontoons above

W

WEATHER FORECASTS, 3
Wemyss Bay, 23
West Coast of Arran, 54
West Kyle, The, 33
Whitefarland Bay, 54
Whitehaven, 93
Whitestone Bank, E of Pt of Ayre, 94
Whiting Bay, 57
Wig, The, 69
Wigtown Bay, 85
Wood Farm Rock, 31
Workington, 92
Wreck Bay, 31

The Clyde Cruising Club was formed in 1909 with the object of encouraging cruising, cruising races, and fostering the social side of sailing. These activities are still the mainstay of the Club with cruising musters and cruises in company being held at various venues on the West Coast and further afield. Additionally the Club organises a full programme of offshore and inshore races throughout the season including the well known Tobermory race and the Scottish Series on Loch Fyne which has developed into one of the biggest yachting events in Britain.

An important part of the Club's present activities is the training and encouragement of young sailors, including especially children and young adults who are disabled, at the Club's new premises on Bardowie Loch.

The Club is also represented on many national and local organisations and is regularly consulted on matters of concern to all cruising yachtsmen: moorings, fish farms, buoyage, weather forecasts and similar topics. Anyone interested in joining the Club, taking part in any of the above activities and lending their support to the voice of the Club is warmly invited to email or write to the Secretary at the address below.

An incidental but worthwhile benefit of membership is entitlement to a very generous discount on the purchase of Sailing Directions !

Sailing Directions for Scottish Waters have been produced by the Club for more than ninety years and over this time they have become widely recognised as valuable and authoritative pilotage guides. They are published in six volumes which are regularly updated with the latest information on approximately an annual basis. The books currently published by CCC Publications are listed below and can be obtained from any good chandler or direct from the Club office.

1. **The Firth of Clyde**
   (inc. the North Channel, the Solway Firth and Isle of Man)
2. **Kintyre to Ardnamurchan**
3. **Ardnamurchan to Cape Wrath**
4. **Outer Hebrides**
5. **North & North East Scotland and Orkney Islands**
6. **Shetland Islands**

Clyde Cruising Club
Suite 101, The Pentagon Centre
35 Washington Street
Glasgow G3 8AZ Scotland
Tel: 0141 221 2774 email: hazel@clyde.org, www.clyde.org